FRENCH DRAMA OF THE REVOLUTIONARY YEARS

GRAHAM E. RODMELL

ROUTLEDGE
London and New York

First published in 1990 by Routledge
11 New Fetter Lane, London EC4P 4EE

Simultaneously published in the USA and Canada by Routledge
a division of Routledge, Chapman and Hall, Inc.
29 West 35th Street, New York, NY 10001

Data converted by Columns of Reading

Printed in Great Britain by
TJ Press (Padstow) Ltd Padstow, Cornwall

British Library Cataloguing in Publication Data
Rodmell, Graham E.
French theatre of the revolutionary years.
1. France. Theatre, 1789–1804
I. Title
792′.0944

ISBN 0–415–00808–5

Library of Congress Cataloging in Publication Data
Rodmell, Graham E., 1934–
French drama of the revolutionary years / Graham E. Rodmell.
p. cm.
Bibliography: p.
Includes index.
ISBN 0–415–00808–5
1. French drama – 18th century – History and criticism.
2. France – History – Revolution, 1789–1799 – Literature
and the revolution.
3. Paris (France) – Popular culture – History – 19th century.
4. Theater – Political aspects – France – Paris – History – 18th century.
5. Theater and society – France – Paris – History – 18th century.
6. Revolutionary literature, French – History and criticism.
I. Title.
PQ538.R6   1990
842′.6358–dc20   89–10425

CONTENTS

INTRODUCTION

The social history of a revolution is . . . essentially different from that of a society in peaceful evolution, since political action becomes more closely involved in the process of accelerated social change.

Norman Hampson, *A Social History of the French Revolution*

Two hundred years after the beginning of the Revolution it seems appropriate to consider what was happening in Paris in the world of the theatre, that most public of arts, for, as Marvin Carlson puts it, the theatre 'was affected tremendously by the social turbulence of the decade of the French Revolution. It was a period of frantic dramatic activity – new drama numbered in the thousands and new theatres in the hundreds – and the disorder of the time was clearly reflected in the careers of dramatic artists and in the productions of theatrical companies in Paris'.[1] It is proper to concentrate on the Paris theatres because, although it is true that important Revolutionary events took place in the French provinces, it was in Paris that the heart of the Revolution was to be found, and it was in Paris that theatre was above all significant, becoming directly involved in the political action of the time.

The Paris theatres and those who performed in them found it quite impossible to remain anonymous during these tumultuous years. Indeed, it is the very essence of the life of an actor or a playwright that he is in the public eye. Obscurity means oblivion for the theatrical profession. Small wonder, then, that in Revolutionary Paris the theatres were to be found adapting themselves, in varying degrees, to the views of a succession of dominant political groups in government or in the street. This is perhaps particularly

1

true of the three 'establishment' (in *Ancien Régime* terms) theatres, the Comédie-Française, the Comédie-Italienne/Opéra-Comique and the Opéra. In broad terms (although, as we shall see, the picture is less simple than this) the so-called popular theatres of the boulevards, which one might superficially have imagined to be likely to be closer to popular, revolutionary attitudes than their more august counterparts, did not play an especially important part in spreading radical social or political attitudes during the Revolutionary years. As Michèle Root-Bernstein puts it,

> Though it was part of the literary underworld, the boulevard did not rise in the years 1789-94, in tandem with the political ascendance of a Marat or a Fabre d'Eglantine. Very few of the minor authors who served the boulevard stage under the old regime became involved in revolutionary politics; not many more are known to have participated in radical theater. . . . The ideological direction of the cultural revolution in theater did not come from the minor stage. . . . The enduring repertory of the popular stage only stood in the way of the radical theatrical politics revealed in the year II. In order to consummate a republican theater, the revolutionaries of 1793-1794 had to neutralize and repress what they could of traditional dramatic culture. Far from celebrating the popular dramatic idiom of the boulevard, such as it had developed over many decades of the eighteenth century, the Revolution moved to destroy it.[2]

It is proposed in the following chapters to attempt what can only be an outline of the somewhat complicated history of Paris theatres during the Revolutionary years and then to consider seven sample plays from various stages of the Revolution, attempting to link them to their historical context and to suggest something of their significance in terms of the social history of the French Revolution. These plays differ quite considerably in terms of their political force and implication, but can be seen as offering an interesting glimpse into the ever-moving, complicated, and all too frequently ephemeral theatrical life of Revolutionary Paris.

The problem, as Louis Moland found over a hundred years ago when publishing the text of a number of plays which had made an impact during the Revolutionary years, was the matter of choice:

Parmi la grande quantité de pièces de théâtre qui se produisirent dans cet espace d'une dizaine d'années, le lecteur pourra nous dire: Pourquoi n'avoir ajouté celle-ci, préféré celle-là?[3]

Amongst the vast quantity of plays produced during this ten-year period, the reader will be entitled to ask, why did you not include this one, or prefer that one?

One could no doubt have justified quite a different set of plays from the ones which are examined in this volume. For that matter, it would have been tempting to write yet another very general book giving a survey of many more plays than are examined here but with the inevitable consequence (as Carlson's book amongst others demonstrates) that one does not then have the space available to suggest anything like the real flavour of any of the plays mentioned. One is moved to wonder whether there might be room for a series of critical editions of plays from the Revolutionary period.

The justification for choosing the seven plays to which some fairly detailed attention is given here is essentially a practical one. In the hope of encouraging the reader to go to the texts themselves it seemed appropriate to try to choose plays which were readily available in modern editions. This immediately limited the choice considerably, but the advantage of the reader being able without too much difficulty actually to refer to the texts under consideration seemed to be a major one. Thus, six of the plays examined are all to be found in one place, namely the second volume of Jacques Truchet's two-volume collection of plays under the title *Théâtre du XVIIIe siècle*. These plays are M.-J. Chénier's *Charles IX* (first performed in November 1789), the Marquis de Sade's *Oxtiern* (October 1791), Collin d'Harleville's *Le Vieux Célibataire* (February 1792), Jean-Louis Laya's *L'Ami des lois* (January 1793), Sylvain Maréchal's *Le Jugement dernier des rois* (October 1793) and Pigault-Lebrun's *Les Rivaux d'eux-mêmes* (August 1798).[4] The seventh play considered will be Ducancel's *L'Intérieur des comités révolutionnaires* (April 1795). It was felt worthwhile to include some reference to this play because, although the other six can be said to represent in one sense or another interesting and important moments in the development of the French Revolution, Ducancel's play fills a gap by illustrating the Thermidorean reaction after the Reign of Terror: in this respect it makes a particularly poignant contrast with Maréchal's play, which is very much a product of the Terror.

The text of Ducancel's play can be found in Moland's collection to which reference has already been made. It might well be an appropriate text with which to begin a series of modern critical editions of plays from the Revolutionary period such as is suggested above.

PART ONE

THE PARIS THEATRES IN THE REVOLUTIONARY YEARS

1

AFTER FIGARO: THE LAST YEARS OF THE MONARCHY

The history of the Parisian theatres in the Revolutionary years is a complicated one, and it would be quite impossible to give a full and detailed account of it in a book such as this.[1] It is nevertheless hoped that, by outlining the principal events in those years and by taking a somewhat closer look in subsequent chapters at seven sample plays, it will be possible to convey something of the flavour of the theatrical life of Paris in terms of the way in which it reflected some of the social and political preoccupations of the time.

If one is to understand the significance of certain developments in these years, for instance the fact that 'new drama numbered in the thousands and new theatres in the hundreds',[2] then it is important that one be aware of the situation which held good in the world of theatre under the *Ancien Régime*. Although Paris was slower than London in seeing the establishment of a permanent theatrical company, by the end of the seventeenth century there were in Paris three permanent theatres of high prestige enjoying royal support. The Académie Royale de Musique (the Opéra) was established in 1669 as the national theatre for operatic productions. After Molière's death in 1673 his company merged with that of the Marais theatre to form the Théâtre Guénégaud, this merger being followed by a second one, with the Hôtel de Bourgogne (where Racine's tragedies had been performed), which in 1680 created the Comédie-Française, with monopoly rights over all performances of plays written in French. In 1697 the third theatrical troupe in question, the Théâtre Italien, the Italian actors then occupying the Hôtel de Bourgogne, was expelled from France by the ageing Louis XIV: until the Italians were recalled by the Regent in 1716 the

Comédie-Française had a total monopoly of dramatic performances in Paris and although the *théâtres de la foire* and the boulevard theatres (about which more later) attempted to make inroads into this monopoly, the fact remains that, as John Lough puts it, 'during the eighteenth century the Comédie-Française was responsible for the production of almost all new plays of any importance'[3] (the brilliant comedies of Marivaux in the first half of the century, almost all of which were performed by the Théâtre Italien, being the most obvious exceptions to this).

The strength of the position of the Comédie-Française lay in the fact that not only did it possess a monopoly of plays from the golden years of the seventeenth century but also in the fact that the overwhelming majority of playwrights in the eighteenth century eagerly sought to gain the prestige which derived from having their plays included in the Comédie's repertory. In 1689 the company had moved into premises in what is now the Rue de l'Ancienne Comédie, moving into the Tuileries in 1770 and remaining there until moving in 1782 into their new theatre on the site of the present Salle Luxembourg, Odéon or (post 1959) Théâtre de France (the changing of theatre names according to political circumstances is one of the characteristics both of the history of the Revolutionary period and of more recent times in France). It was in this new theatre that the Comédie-Française was to be found at the outbreak of the Revolution.

The Théâtre Italien had a somewhat more complicated history during the pre-Revolutionary part of the eighteenth century. After their recall to Paris in 1716 under the regency of the Duc d'Orléans the Italians began gradually to introduce French elements into their Italian performances and finally to perform plays entirely in French, very often parodying the productions of the Comédie-Française. They also performed musical productions, particularly ballet. In 1762 they were merged with the Opéra-Comique, which had been developed in the Paris fairgrounds and had first taken the name Opéra-Comique in the 1720s whilst under the direction of Honoré and Picard. The Opéra showed itself more pliable than the Comédie-Française in the face of competition in the eighteenth century and on occasion leased permission to perform opera to booth theatres in the fairs.[4] So popular was the comic opera side of the enterprise's activity that in 1769 the company stopped performing plays in French. In 1780 they changed policy, reintroducing plays in French and dropping plays in Italian, partly in response to a growing feeling that Paris needed a second theatre which could compete with the Comédie-Française. In 1783 the company moved out of the Hôtel de Bourgogne, where the Italians had performed ever since the foundation of the Comédie-Française in 1680, and established itself in a new theatre which gave its name to the Boulevard des Italiens.[5]

In addition to these established theatres, there were the *théâtres de la foire*, which were given new strength with the expulsion of the Italians in 1697 but which were to be vigorously attacked both by the Comédie-Française and by the Théâtre Italien after the return of the Italian actors in 1716. Michèle Root-Bernstein observes that these two companies in concert managed a complete suppression of the fair theatres in 1718-19, but were 'unable to prevent a vigorous resurgence of these spectacles in the coming year'.[6] A running war continued throughout the eighteenth century as the two established theatres sought to maintain their monopoly position. The fair theatres did not have an easy existence, but they undoubtedly enjoyed considerable popularity of a sort. There were two principal fairs in Paris, the winter fair of Saint-Germain and the Saint-Laurent fair from June to October.

The theatrical staple offered by the *théâtres de la foire* was popular in the broadest sense of the word, but it would be a mistake to suppose that only the lower orders frequented them or that here were the seeds from which a radical theatre would be born to mould the future of the new politics after 1789. Members of the aristocracy (ladies and gentlemen alike) were known to frequent them, and Bachaumont remarked in 1769 of one of the chief of these theatres, Audinot's, that 'la modicité des places, dont les plus chères sont à 24 sous, met tout le monde à portée de se régaler de cette foire, en sorte que la duchesse et le savoyard s'y coudoient sans distinction'[7] ('The cheapness of the seats, the most expensive of which cost 24 sous, means that everybody is in a position to treat himself to this example of the fun of the fair, so that duchesses and savoyards rub shoulders without distinction'). Lough maintains, no doubt rightly in strict terms, that 'despite their popularity it cannot be maintained that these little theatres contributed anything of importance to the drama of the century'.[8]

There resulted from the *théâtres de la foire* the establishment by about 1760 of a number of small, permanent theatres, and by 1789 the Boulevard du Temple had half a dozen such theatres. In the late seventeenth century part of the fortifications of Paris had been levelled and turned into a fashionable promenade, originally known as the Promenade des Remparts. This promenade gradually saw a burgeoning of cafés, sideshows and the like. During the 1770s the promenade had come to be known as the Boulevard du Temple (it was close to the site of the former fortress of the Knights Templar). The first theatres on the Boulevard were similar to the booths at the fairs but well before the end of the century there had appeared what John McCormick quite properly calls 'handsome buildings of some architectural pretension'.[9] These new, permanent theatres seem to have been looked upon with a fairly benevolent blind eye by the authorities for much of the time during the latter part of the eighteenth century, as a means of keeping the populace out of more serious mischief.

Some writers, however, were inclined to take a less indulgent view as to the value of these theatres. Louis-Sébastien Mercier argued in his treatise *Du Théâtre*, in which he preached the need for a new type of drama suited to the values and aspirations of the masses, that the dramatic fare served up in the theatres of the fairs and of the boulevard was noxious to the 'petit peuple': 'on empoisonne son âme de ces sales turpitudes'[10] ('the soul of the common people is poisoned by these filthy depravities'). Mercier had a very serious – not to say solemn – view of the function of the theatre: for the people, the theatre should be 'un objet d'instruction, un honnête délassement, un plaisir utile, et non une distraction, ou un moyen politique pour l'étourdir et pour l'amuser, loin de toute réflexion sérieuse et patriotique'[11] ('a means of education, of honest relaxation, a utilitarian pleasure and not a distraction, not a political tool to beguile them and amuse them, far removed from any serious, patriotic consideration'). The development of a sense of national – as opposed to class – identity is one of the threads running through the history of eighteenth-century France and by the time of the Revolution it becomes a major thread, with Chénier claiming to have written the first national tragedy in the French language. Writing, it seems, in the early part of 1795 the young Pixerécourt argued that the *Ancien Régime* had tolerated only two sorts of theatre: 'Ceux dont l'éclat ne permet la fréquentation qu'aux riches sont consacrés à perpétuer la flatterie; ceux que l'on abandonne au peuple ne creusent pour lui que le précipice de la débauche'[12] ('Those the brilliance of which meant that only the rich could frequent them were devoted to the perpetuation of flattery; those which were left for the people merely opened up for them the precipitous drop into debauchery'). It may be that Pixerécourt is oversimplifying the truth concerning the social structure of the audiences at the more 'popular' theatres, but there is no mistaking his view as to the worth of the theatres in the fairs and on the Boulevard: 'Quel cloaque de saletés! quelle boue d'impures inepties' ('What a cesspit of dirtiness! what a filthy mess of impure nonsense!'). When he goes on, in what seems to have been a report for the police under the Convention, to argue that it took the Revolution for the nation to realize, apart from a few intellectuals (such as Diderot, no doubt, who had realized this some time earlier) the positive influence which theatres could have on public opinion, there is more than a grain of truth in what he says, but the fact of the matter is that most of the significant opinion-forming by means of dramatic production seems to have taken place at the major, erstwhile privileged theatres rather than in the fairs or on the Boulevard,[13] although it is of course true that a number of the minor theatres did present works intended to celebrate civic anniversaries or military victories or support a particular faction in the ever-moving kaleidoscope of Revolutionary politics. This kind of play, which was a departure from the traditional offering either of the fairs or of the Boulevard, a sort of play of circumstance and often extremely ephemeral, also invaded the major theatres during the Revolutionary years. Michèle Root-Bernstein makes an important point when she concludes that the boulevard theatres did not rise in importance in tandem with the political rise of Marat (a journalist) or Fabre d'Eglantine (a playwright).[14]

The publisher's 'blurb' on the cover of Daniel Hamiche's book, *Le Théâtre et la Révolution*, accurately defines the impression which is all too easily gained by students of French drama: 'L'histoire du théâtre en France semble s'assoupir au *Mariage de Figaro* pour se réveiller dans le tumulte d'*Hernani*. Rien ne semble s'être passé entretemps. . .' ('The history of the theatre in France seems to drop off to sleep with *Le Mariage de Figaro*, to wake up again with the uproar surrounding *Hernani*. Nothing seems to have happened in between . . .'). In fact a good deal did happen in the French theatre between Beaumarchais's last comic masterpiece and Victor Hugo's first great dramatic success – rather more, in fact, than is represented by the two plays on which Hamiche concentrates in his book, Chénier's *Charles IX* and Maréchal's *Le Jugement dernier des rois*. It may well be that not much of the drama produced in France in these years was of the very first flight in aesthetic terms, but much of it is of considerable interest as a reflection of what was going on politically in France – and, of course, what was going on was something rather more complex than a straightforward progression from 'l'idéologie bourgeoise . . . en lutte . . . contre l'idéologie aristocratique qui n'a pas disparu'[15] ('Bourgeois ideology . . . at war . . . with the aristocratic ideology which has not disappeared'), as represented by Chénier's play, to what is for Hamiche, viewing life from his particular Marxist standpoint, 'une pièce révolutionnaire modèle',[16] namely Maréchal's play.

It is true that *Le Mariage de Figaro*, in purely dramatic terms, considerably overshadows anything produced on the Paris stage during the Revolutionary years. Beaumarchais's play, however, although the difficulties which the playwright experienced in securing a first public performance for it are undoubtedly one indication of the nervousness of insecure absolute monarchy in decline, is perhaps rather less 'revolutionary' in content and implication than it has sometimes been represented as being. No doubt for Daniel Hamiche, who said of Beaumarchais that after his letter to the actors after the opening of *Charles IX* there was hardly any difference between him and Suard, the royal censor,[17] *Le Mariage de Figaro* represents bourgeois ideology too. It is certainly a good deal cosier, a good deal less incendiary than many works that were to appear on the various stages in Paris in the years following 1789.

The story of the struggle to have *Le Mariage* performed publicly is a well-known one, and it is not appropriate to repeat it here, although it is interesting to note the comparison between the campaign of readings and polemic indulged in by Beaumarchais (whose play was written in 1778 and accepted in that year by the Comédie-Française but did not open until April 1784 after it had been considered by no fewer than half a dozen censors) and the similar campaign waged by Chénier in the case of *Charles IX*.[18] There can be little doubt that the difficulties experienced with the authorities added to the success of both plays – a not uncommon phenomenon. Both Beaumarchais and Chénier submitted their plays to the Comédie-Française because not only was this the outstanding theatre for serious playwrights of the time but, as has already been pointed out, it enjoyed a virtual monopoly of serious dramatic productions. It was not the only theatre in Paris, however, and it will be worthwhile to try, before going on to look at our sample plays from the period under review, to give an outline of the history of Paris theatres in the eighteenth century and more particularly during the Revolutionary years.

If in the last years of the *Ancien Régime* Paris had three powerful theatres enjoying royal patronage and support, increasingly these three theatres were beginning to have to face competition from smaller theatres often with limited licences but very often determined to indulge in one subterfuge or another to present plays (as opposed to juggling acts, puppet shows, etc.). In 1759 Jean-Baptiste Nicolet was given permission to move out of his fair-booth theatre into permanent premises on the Boulevard du Temple. It is not precisely certain what sort of licence he had but he clearly produced tight-rope and acrobatic shows as well as plays and it is known that he added musicians and actors to his troupe. Speech was suppressed on the minor stages in 1764.[19] In 1769 Nicolas-Médard Audinot set up his marionette theatre, Les Comédiens de Bois, next to the Théâtre de Nicolet on the Boulevard. The clown Nicolas Vienne in partnership with the harlequin Louis-Gabriel Sallé established a third important theatre, the Théâtre des Associés, on the Boulevard in 1774. In 1784 no less than two puppet theatres opened in the Duc d'Orléans's Palais-Royal, Delomel's Beaujolais, and Gaillard and Dorfeuille's Variétés Amusantes. Delomel used child actors miming on stage whilst adults spoke the lines in the wings. Throughout the period the Comédie-Française sought to have such rival ventures penalized for impinging on that theatre's monopolistic position.

Early in 1789, under the protection of Monsieur, the King's brother, Léonard Autié was authorized to open a new theatre, the Théâtre de Monsieur. Autié took into partnership Mlle Montansier, the directress of the royal theatre at Versailles. Apart from Italian operas, the new theatre was confined, at the instigation of the Comédie-Française, to one- and two-act comedies. On 12 July the theatres closed in consequence of riots in protest at the dismissal of Necker. By the time they reopened their doors, on 21 July, the Bastille had fallen and France was, whether she was aware of it or not, at the beginning of a new era.

In the spring of 1790 Gaillard and Dorfeuille, the directors of the Variétés Amusantes, moved to a new theatre in the rue de Richelieu in which the Duc d'Orléans had originally hoped to establish the Opéra. The two directors aspired to nothing less than to turn their new theatre into a second Comédie-Française: the need for such a theatre had long been felt by public and playwrights alike, and the time seemed ripe for reform of the world of the Paris theatre.[20]. Some of the minor houses seized the opportunity when the theatres reopened on 21 July to present occasional pieces celebrating recent events. We need to be careful here, however: it would be mistaken to suppose that the events of July 1789 immediately effected a radical transformation in either the organization of the Parisian theatre world or the nature of plays performed on its stages. This is as true of the popular stage as of the privileged theatres. As Michèle Root-Bernstein puts it,

> Dramatic, revolutionary events in the real world – the fall of the Bastille, of absolute monarchy, and the jeopardy of the old order – took the popular stage by surprise. Much that was potentially radical in the boulevard repertory had yet to be drawn out and developed. Though written in 1782, *Blaise the Ill-Tempered* [i.e. Dorvigny's *Blaise le hargneux*], with its outspoken advocacy of social before sentimental equality, did not reach the peak of its success until 1794. But that is to anticipate five years of social and ideological upheaval. In the midst of the Revolution's second year boulevard actors still sang not of political change but of moral resolution to social conflict and a return to the stability of the traditional social order.[21]

Even the establishment-minded Comédie-Française found it politic to reopen under a new name, the Théâtre de la Nation, although the members of the company retained their title as 'Comédiens-Français ordinaires du Roi'. This gave rise to the following satirical verse:

> Les Comédiens-Français très prudemment calculent.
> En citoyens ardents ces messieurs s'intitulent
>   Théâtre de la Nation,
> Titre qui promet à leur ambition
> Une recette toujours riche;

> Et 'Comédiens du Roi' reste encore sur l'affiche
> Pour garantir la pension![22]

The Comédiens-Français work things out very prudently. As passionate citizens they take the name Théâtre de la Nation, a title which promises them receipts plentiful enough to satisfy their ambition; and yet 'King's Actors' remains on their posters to guarantee their pensions!

Even the Comédie-Française – or the Théâtre de la Nation, as we must learn to call it – felt moved to mark the new political situation by presenting patriotic plays, albeit established patriotic plays of a distinctly royalist tinge, De Belloy's *Gaston et Bayard* and Collé's *La Partie de chasse de Henri IV*. In future years much more explicit political messages were to be conveyed through the medium of the Paris stage, and this is a development which was not to be long in coming about.

On 14 August the Théâtre de Monsieur performed Joseph Audé's *Le Retour de Camille à Rome*, modelled on Lafayette who, since his return from America was as great a hero as the popular minister Necker. At about the same time, the Théâtre de la Nation saw fit to put on a play which was likely, in view of its topic, to be popular in the new climate but which did not attack the established constitutional order of things. The play in question was Jean-Gaspard de Fontanelle's *Ericie* which, under a transparent Roman disguise, mounted an attack on the conventual system, with vestal virgins representing nuns (the convent play was to become a popular genre in the Revolutionary years). Fontanelle's play had been accepted by the Comédie-Française as early as 1768 and had promptly been banned. Things were now different: in five months' time, on 13 February 1790, a decree would be passed prohibiting monastic vows. On 19 August, however, the second night of *Ericie*, there was a demonstration in the theatre. Pamphlets were distributed couched in the following terms:

Frères,
Dans le moment du triomphe de la liberté française, verrons-nous de sang-froid le génie dramatique succomber sous les derniers efforts du despotisme? *Charles IX ou la Saint-Barthélemy*, tragédie nationale, dont la réputation est déjà faite en naissant, *Charles IX* est arrêté à la représentation, ainsi que plusieurs

autres pièces. L'inquisition de la pensée règne encore sur notre théâtre: secouons enfin un joug si odieux, et réunissons nos voix pour demander, au nom de la liberté, la prompte représentation de *Charles IX*.[23]

Brothers,
In the moment of the triumph of French liberty, shall we calmly watch dramatic genius succumb to the last efforts of despotism? *Charles IX ou la Saint-Barthélemy*, a national tragedy whose reputation was made the moment it was created, *Charles IX* is banned from the stage, along with several other plays. The thought inquisition is still controlling our theatre: let us at last throw off such a hateful yoke and unite our voices to demand, in the name of liberty, the prompt performance of *Charles IX*.

Whoever wrote the text of these pamphlets, they were part of the campaign waged by Marie-Joseph Chénier after the manner of Beaumarchais to ensure the performance of his play, a campaign which was to culminate with *Charles IX* being performed for the first time at the Théâtre de la Nation on 4 November 1789. This play of Chénier's was to prove to be one of the most significant productions of the Revolutionary period. It will be examined in some detail later.[24]

In December 1789 the National Assembly debated the social status of actors. Rœderer, Clermont-Tonnerre, Robespierre and Mirabeau all spoke in favour of members of the acting profession, who heretofore had been 'not only barred . . . from a citizen's rights in life but notoriously denied Christian burial in death'[25] and actors became full citizens of France.

François-Joseph Talma, who had had a great success in the title role in *Charles IX*, his first major part, was the most prominent figure in a group of younger members of the Théâtre de la Nation who were distinctly more favourable to the new ideas abroad than were the older Comédiens. The differences between the two groups were to become more and more marked. The company began 1790 with its first play to deal directly with the Revolution. This play, *Le Réveil d'Epiménide à Paris* by Carbon de Flins des Oliviers, is a sort of Rip Van Winkle play about a man who never dies but sleeps for a hundred years at a time. He is shown awaking in contemporary Paris, having been asleep since the hey-day of the absolutist monarchy under Louis XIV. It praises the new liberalism and eulogizes the king.

January 14 saw the twenty-fifth performance of *Charles IX*, put on at scant notice as a benefit for the poor. The turn-out was low and Chénier withdrew his play from the company in order to protect his rights over it. 12 February saw another attempt to make the most of Louis XVI's period of popularity as the restorer of French liberty with the production of Charles-Philippe Ronsin's *Louis XII, père du peuple*. This play, which failed on its first night, was in some measure intended as a riposte to *Charles IX*.[26] This was followed on 22 February by Fabre d'Eglantine's sequel to Molière's great high comedy *Le Misanthrope*, entitled *Le Philinte de Molière*, a work which enjoyed considerable success. *Charles IX* returned to the stage in March, with success once again. On the 18 March the Comédie Italienne performed Georges-François Desfontaines's *Le District de village*, a characteristic play of the time, depicting the local aristocrats gladly renouncing their feudal rights in the spirit of the Assembly's decree on feudalism of August 1789.

After Easter the Théâtre de la Nation reopened with Pierre Laujon's *Le Couvent*, a play which took advantage of the new liberal spirit abroad to break new ground by depicting a Christian ecclesiastical setting unambiguously on stage. Prior to this, the convention had been for comments on matters religious to be cloaked in classical garb, as in the case of *Ericie*. Laujon's play was anodine enough, but once this break-through had taken place, the way was open for a good many further plays set in convents, some of them decidedly scurrilous in nature.

Talma, outside *Charles IX*, was still not being given leading roles by the Théâtre de la Nation company and had taken to appearing with other actors, not infrequently amateurs, in Versailles and elsewhere in Paris, thus building up his following.

Inevitably, when the first anniversary of the storming of the Bastille came along, there was a veritable flurry of patriotic productions backing up the Fête de la Fédération on the Champ de Mars. On 14 July 1790 the Théâtre de Monsieur revived *Le Souper de Henri IV*, by Bouthellier and Desprez-Valmont, the Comédie Italienne performed the anonymous *Le Chêne patriotique* and Mlle Montansier's Variétés put on Ronsin's *La Fête de la liberté ou le Dîner des patriotes*. Mirabeau had requested the Théâtre de la Nation to put on a special performance of *Charles IX* for provincial visitors to the capital for the Fête de la Fédération. The company, however, divided amongst its members by the controversy caused by Chénier's tragedy, ignored this request and instead marked the occasion with a performance of Joseph Audé's *Le Journaliste des ombres ou Momus aux Champs-Elysées*, with Talma as the shade of Rousseau. The company took the line that they would perform Chénier's play again, but only in its proper turn: they could not allow their repertory to become dominated by one or two plays, however popular. On 21 July, when the company was performing Voltaire's *Alzire* and *Le Réveil d'Epiménide*, there was a disturbance involving demands from a group including Chénier himself for a performance of *Charles IX*. The company made a statement to the effect that, in consequence of ill health affecting key members of the cast, namely Saint-Prix (who played the Cardinal de Lorraine) and Mme Vestris (Catherine de Médicis) this was impossible. Talma then took a step which he must have known, in the heated climate within the company, was bound to have serious consequences: he advanced to the front of the stage and announced that Mme Vestris, who like Talma himself was part of the 'progressive' group within the company, as proof of her patriotism, was prepared to perform in *Charles IX*, ill though she was, and that Saint-Prix's part could be read.[27] It was declared that Chénier's play would be performed the next day. Not surprisingly, it was a riotous occasion and the troops were called upon to empty the theatre. Nonetheless, the performance finally took place and the provincial deputies enjoyed the show.[28] All this did nothing for relationships within the company, and on 27 July Talma was expelled.

The monopoly enjoyed by the Comédie-Française under the *Ancien Régime* and in essence continued into the early part of the Revolutionary period caused a good deal of dissatisfaction, and a large number of playwrights made common cause with the unprivileged theatres and organized a committee of thirty to examine the question of freedom in the theatre. Most of the important dramatists of the time figured on this committee: Beaumarchais, Cailhava, Chénier, Collot d'Herbois, Ducis, Fabre d'Eglantine, La Harpe, Lemierre, Mercier, Palissot, Sedaine. La Harpe presented a petition prepared by the group to the National Assembly, stressing the potential of drama as a tool in the freeing of humanity and calling for the abolition of special privileges within the world of the Parisian theatre. They sought freedom for the establishment of an unlimited number of theatres and for all works on the classical repertory to enter the public domain, whilst seeking the right of all living authors to control their work as their own property and to be able to make their own terms with actors and directors. This was a direct threat to the monopoly rights enjoyed by the Théâtre de la Nation, the old Comédie-Française, and not surprisingly that company lodged a protest. However, the proposals put forward in the dramatists' petition were accepted almost completely in a law promulgated on 13 January 1791. This law had seven articles, which stipulated,

(Art. I) that, merely by making a declaration of intent to the municipal authorities, any citizen was free to establish a public theatre and produce any type of play in it,

(Art. II) that the work of dramatists who had been dead for five years or more fell within the public domain and could, despite traditional privileges, be performed on any stage,

(Art. III) that the work of living dramatists could not be performed on any stage within France without the formal, written permission of the author, on pain of confiscation of any revenue from illegal performances to the benefit of the author,

(Art. IV) that the provisions under Art. III applied to works already performed, despite any previous regulations, although any agreements involving living authors (or authors dead for less than five years) would be honoured,

(Art. V) that the heirs or executors of a dramatist would be proprietors of his works for the period of five years after his death,

(Art. VI) that the directors or members of the different theatre companies would, by reason of their position, be subject to inspection by the municipal authorities. They would take orders solely from the municipal authorities who would, however, be unable to stop or forbid a performance of any play except when asked to do so by the author or by the company and subject to the laws and to police regulations, and

(Art. VII) that guards should remain outside the theatre unless formally asked to enter by representatives of the municipality.[29] In the words of Marvin Carlson, 'Nothing in the course of the Revolution was to have more effect on the theatrical world than the adoption of this legislation'.[30]

The controversy over the exclusion of Talma from the Théâtre de la Nation company rumbled on. Bailly, the mayor of Paris, asked them to restore Talma to their ranks. They refused, taking the line that Bailly had no authority in the matter, and that they would submit their case for judgment to the King alone. On 25

September 1790 the *Chronique de Paris* published a critical comment on this approach, pointing out that 'si toutes les corporations du royaume méprisoient l'autorité municipale et les magistrats du peuple, si elles ne vouloient reconnoitre d'autre pouvoir que celui du roi, la *contre-révolution* seroit faite' ('If all the corporations in the kingdom held the municipal authorities and the representatives of the people in contempt, if they were unwilling to recognize any power other than that of the King, the counter-revolution would be an accomplished fact').The article went on to say that the Comédie-Française (as it still tended to be called, despite its official change of name) had taken over from the Opéra as the crucible of aristocratic reaction. On 27 September Bailly declared the Théâtre de la Nation closed: the company capitulated at once and advertised a performance of *Charles IX* with Talma in the lead for the evening of 28 September. Chénier's play was repeated two days later, after which the dramatist withdrew it from the company. This was his response to what was no doubt a deliberate ploy on the part of the company: it certainly seems that this last performance was advertised without reference to Chénier himself, and the laws of the time provided that a playwright lost all rights to his play when receipts for two or three consecutive performances fell below a given figure. Chénier announced that he was withdrawing his play pending the results of the dramatists' petition concerning their rights (which was, as we have seen, to result in the law of 13 January 1791).

The atmosphere within the company cannot have been a pleasant one: Talma was virtually ostracized by the more conservative members. On 17 November 1790 the company put on Voltaire's *Brutus* as a sign of their patriotism: this was greeted by a royalist demonstration and a republican counter-demonstration. The next performance, perhaps rather tactlessly, was Voltaire's *La Mort de César*. On 2 December the Théâtre de la Nation turned its hand to an example of what was to become a very common feature of Revolutionary theatre, the dramatization of a contemporary incident, in the shape of Desfontaines's *Le Tombeau de Desilles*, concerning a young officer of that name killed whilst helping to suppress a mutiny amongst soldiers in Nancy in August of that year.

The first year of the Revolution was a distinctly troubled one from the point of view of the basically conservative troupe at the

Théâtre de la Nation. At this stage the Comédie-Italienne and the Opéra, the other two 'establishment' theatres, were less affected. The Opéra had been handed over to the municipality by the King, although for a while it remained overwhelmingly patronized by a privileged clientèle. The Comédie-Italienne, as we have seen, marked the first anniversary of the storming of the Bastille with *Le Chêne patriotique* and on 23 August put on the anti-clerical *Les Rigueurs du cloître*, by Fiévée and Berton, very much in the spirit of the time. It closed the year with a play seeking to glorify Rousseau as one of the fathers of the Revolution: Nicolas Bouilly's *Jean-Jacques Rousseau à ses derniers moments*. Early in 1790 it began to face competition in the field of comic opera from the Théâtre de Monsieur. The Monsieur had a great success later in the year when, on 17 July, capitalizing on the spirit of the 14 July Fête de la Fédération, it produced Collot d'Herbois's *La Famille patriote ou la Fédération*, which included much singing of the Revolutionary song, the 'Ça ira'. The Théâtre de Monsieur moved out of the Saint-Germain fair early in 1791 and moved into its new premises in the rue Feydeau, ready to take advantage of the new legislation and attempt to become one of the main theatres of Paris. Indeed, a number of new theatres had opened up, many of them destined to be short-lived, during the course of 1790. The most important of these was the opening of the Variétés-Palais-Royal in spring 1790 in the new theatre in the rue de Richelieu in which the Duc d'Orléans had hoped to house the Opéra. The first half of 1790 also saw the opening of the Théâtre-Français Comique et Lyrique in the rue de Bondy and of Mlle Montansier's new theatre in the former home of the Beaujolais. Both of these theatres quickly became popular. Five other theatres, all located on or near the Boulevard du Temple, survived the first year of the Revolution: the Beaujolais, now at the end of the Boulevard, and surviving by means of a series of patriotic revues; the Délassements-Comiques, noteworthy under its director Plancher Valcour for strongly republican productions of a frequently less than subtle type; Nicolet's Grands Danseurs du Roi; Audinot's Ambigu-Comique and Sallé's Théâtre des Associés. None of them, however, offered very sophisticated material. As for the year which followed the law of 13 January 1791, it has been calculated that during that period twenty-three new theatres opened their doors to the public and that these theatres, added to those already existing, meant that at a time when the Paris population was about 65,000, no fewer than 60,000 daily theatre attendances would have been necessary for all the theatres to maintain themselves.[31] It is not surprising that many of them were very ephemeral.

On 10 January 1791 the *Chronique de Paris* announced Talma's reconciliation with the Théâtre de la Nation,[32] a reconciliation which was not to be of long duration. The same month also saw the beginnings of the consequences of the reforming law of 13 January. The established theatres sought to claim that the law was not retroactive and that therefore they were entitled to keep control of works written before 13 January. The dramatists again went to the Assembly and a further law was passed making it quite clear that that was not the intention and that no works of living authors could be performed without their written permission. The same applied to the permission of the heirs and executors of authors dead for less than five years.[33] A rash of new theatres sprang up in response to the law of 13 January, although many of these too proved to be extremely ephemeral. Another consequence of the new law was the abolition of the office of censor. This made it easy for a number of playhouses to perform very bawdy plays, often anticlerical in nature.

On 27 April the Variétés-Palais-Royal reopened after the Easter break under the new name of Théâtre Français, rue de Richelieu. It became in practical terms a second national theatre in that not only did it, in the matter of repertory, take full advantage of the liberating provisions of the law of 13 January, but it also recruited all the liberal group from the troupe of the Théâtre de la Nation: Talma, Mme Vestris, Dugazon, Mlle Desgarcins, Grandménil, Mlle Simon, Mlle Lange. Not surprisingly, in view of the relationship between this group and Chénier, the play with which they opened was his *Henri VIII*, which had been accepted by the old Comédie-Française on 14 February 1789, but censored because its cast included a prelate of the Church (it also includes thrusts at tyrants and priests). Talma played Henry, Mme Vestris was Anne Boleyn and Mlle Desgarcins Jane Seymour.[34] Having lost half its company in this way, the Théâtre de la Nation was slow in reopening after Easter. Rivalry between the Nation and the Richelieu was henceforth to be very keen indeed.

Soon there were so many theatres seeking to take advantage of the new liberalism that it was quite impossible for Paris to sustain them all. Other attractions such as the Vauxhall d'Eté also date from this period. The Comédie-Italienne survived these difficult times remarkably well with its light operas. Things were not propitious for the Nation, however, still very much seen as a reactionary troupe. In June 1791 J.-F. Boursault-Malherbe, a member of the National Assembly and an adventurous entrepreneur, opened a new theatre intended to concentrate on plays of a patriotic character. His theatre, the Théâtre-National Molière, opened with Ronsin's *La Ligue des fanatiques et des tyrans* and its subsequent productions were not infrequently rather strident in tone.

June 20-21 saw the flight of the royal family from Paris and their arrest at Varennes. Prior to this, Louis XVI had enjoyed a reasonable degree of popularity as the monarch who had given freedom to the French people, but henceforth he and the whole notion of monarchy were increasingly suspect, a process which cannot but have been furthered by the tone and contents of the proclamation which Louis left behind on his flight from Paris, a proclamation which was in effect, as D.I. Wright puts it, 'a counter-revolutionary manifesto'.[35] Plays concerning this royal betrayal were rapidly written for the boulevard theatres, for example *La Journée de Varennes ou Le Maître de poste de Sainte-Menehould* at the Ambigu-Comique and *La Journée de Varennes* at the Molière. The authorities feared that works with such potentially inflammatory titles might lead to riot in the streets and in some quarters there were thoughts of reintroducing censorship and governmental control of the theatre, although other factions in the municipal government remained rigorously opposed to censorship of the stage and tolerant of political demonstrations in and around theatres.[36]

After the King was brought back to Paris from Varennes, the members of the Théâtre de la Nation ceased describing themselves as 'Comédiens Ordinaires du Roi', the Académie Royale de Musique formally changed its name to that by which in any case it was already generally known (the Opéra), and the Théâtre de Monsieur dropped its royalist title and became the Théâtre Français et Italien de la rue Feydeau, a name commonly abbreviated to simply the Feydeau.

The only new offering at the Richelieu in the whole of July was Chénier's new play, *Calas ou l'Ecole des juges*, a subject (described by

Marvin Carlson as 'the Dreyfus affair of the eighteenth century')[37] which was by this time well worn: Laya had brought out his *Jean Calas* and Lemierre d'Argy his *Calas ou le Fanatisme* some six months earlier.[38] For its part, the Nation put on on 13 July Billardon de Sauvigny's *Washington ou la Liberté du Nouveau-Monde*, no doubt as an attempt to spike charges of aristocratic leanings. The play was not a success. In August and September the Richelieu sought to appeal to the widespread anti-royalist feeling by mounting a series of productions such as the anonymous *L'Hôtellerie de Worms*, a dull farce on the flight to Varennes (11 August), Pierre-Mathieu Parcin's *La Prise de la Bastille* (25 August) and a revival of *Charles IX* (3 September): the flight to Varennes and the proclamation left behind by Louis XVI made all the hope in Chénier's play illusory. On 5 September the Nation revived Collé's *La Partie de chasse de Henri IV* yet again, an event which occasioned clashes between monarchists and revolutionaries. The Nation went through a period of two months without presenting a new play. Neither the Richelieu nor the Nation was distinguishing itself at this time, but at least it can be said that the Richelieu was proving itself to be on a par with the Nation: in particular, under the inspiration of Talma, it was winning renown for its authenticity of costume.

On 13 September the King sent a message to the National Assembly announcing his acceptance of the Constitution and swearing to uphold it. He declared that from the very beginning of his reign he had desired the reform of abuses, that discord and anarchy were the enemies which had to be vanquished and that he was determined to demonstrate that he was the King of all the French. As an attempt to rally support to the monarchy this was a desperate, last-ditch effort. For a short while, however, there was a resurgence of benevolence towards the King. Carlson argues that 'perhaps no play presented in these weeks more clearly expressed the public spirit than Charles Demoustier's *Le Conciliateur*, offered at the Nation on September 19, in which a warm and gentle love is shown healing a family feud.[39] The royal family made a point of being seen out and about in Paris during this period. Louis XVI was applauded when he appeared at the Nation and at the Opéra. 22 October saw the first performance at the Molière of the Marquis de Sade's *Oxtiern, ou les Malheurs du libertinage*, a play which, even if it is somewhat extreme in certain respects, none the less retains a certain belief in the good will of the King. This play will be examined in a subsequent chapter.

1792 opened with France facing the threat of war but in the early part of the year the most successful plays at both the Nation and the Richelieu were not politically partisan in character. Chénier's *Caïus Gracchus*, a three-act tragedy, performed on 9 February at the Richelieu, which was very much Talma's and Chénier's theatre, portrayed Gracchus as prepared to respect legality even at the cost of his own life, a line which appealed to the royalists, although his insistence that all Romans should be equal appealed at least as strongly to the republicans. This play, which was more successful than Chénier's earlier plays, with the exception of *Charles IX*, thus performed the difficult feat of being approved by both sides of the political divide.[40] The Nation sought to keep clear from political plays as far as possible and on 24 February produced what is undoubtedly one of the best plays to appear in this Revolutionary decade or so, a period admittedly not rich in theatrical master-pieces: Collin d'Harleville's *Le Vieux Célibataire*. This play too will be considered in a subsequent chapter.

On 20 April the Assembly voted to declare war on Austria and in the difficult days that followed there was not much in the way of good drama being offered in Paris, although La Harpe's *Virginie*, which was produced at the Richelieu on 9 May, did well. On 20 June, the anniversary of the flight to Varennes, an armed mob attacked the Tuileries and threatened the royal family. On 11 July a state of emergency was declared ('La Patrie en danger'). Most theatres closed, but Delomel, having dropped the aristocratic name Louvois and replaced it by Théâtre des Amis de la Patrie, stayed open with *Les Emigrés aux terres australes ou Le Dernier Chapitre d'une grande révolution* by Gamas. On 10 August there was another march on the Tuileries, and the royal family fled to the Assembly for protection. The Assembly, in a decree issued on that day, showed its concern for legality and adherence to the Constitution in provisionally suspending Louis XVI from his functions rather than removing him altogether and at once. It also called for the election by universal male suffrage of a Convention to consider the future organization of the State. As Norman Hampson puts it,

> With the fall of the Tuileries the face of Parisian society underwent an abrupt change . . . the prisons filled with what was

25

left of the liberal nobility. . . . For the Parisian nobility it was 10 August 1792 rather than 14 July 1789 that marked the end of the ancien régime.[41]

The profound social change which was about to affect not only Paris but the whole of France inevitably had implications for the theatre too. The immediate effect, so far as the Paris theatres are concerned, was that the strife in the streets meant that closures were frequent in the period between 10 August and the declaration of the Republic by the Convention on 22 September. There were to be more long-term consequences too.

It was late in August before it proved possible for most of the theatres to reopen. A number of theatres sought to ease their circumstances by appealing for a relaxation in the law governing the rights of authors. They were rewarded with a decree of 30 August which declared that any play which had been printed and published before the decree of 13 January 1791 could henceforth be performed without payment of royalty in any theatre which had performed it before that date. It was also decreed that all plays should become public property after ten years. September was not a good month, either. It opened with *sans-culotte* gangs butchering the occupants of the prisons: up to 1,400 prisoners were killed in the September Massacres. The theatres closed again. Whilst the massacres were actually taking place, on 3 September, Boursault, the director of the Théâtre National de Molière, sought financial help from the State to escape financial ruin. Danton supported this appeal, pointing out that this particular theatre 'n'a jamais présenté au public que des pièces propres à accélérer les progrès de la Révolution'[42] ('has never presented to the public anything other than plays calculated to accelerate the progress of the Revolution'). It is known that 25,000 livres each were awarded to both the Molière and the Richelieu.[43] The Opéra, taken over by the Commune, also gained a public subsidy to help offset the lack of box-office returns during the summer of 1792. It is clear that theatres with less clean revolutionary records than the Molière and the Richelieu were not likely to have many friends in the new government.

2

FROM THE DECLARATION
OF THE REPUBLIC

After the proclamation of the Republic by the Convention on 22 September the theatres began to reopen, many of them evincing an increased interest in national political questions. Morale was improved by a number of military victories. Mlle Montansier's theatre put on plays such as Joseph de Lavallée's *Le Départ des volontaires* and François Devienne's *La Bataille de Jemmapes*, whilst the Favart (the erstwhile Italienne) performed Joigny's *Le Siège de Lille*. On 17 October, Marat's newspaper *L'Ami du peuple* attacked Talma and other members of the Richelieu company for being too friendly with Dumouriez, the victor of Jemmapes but distrusted by the Jacobins. On 25 October the Richelieu again showed revolutionary credentials by performing the patriotic *L'Emigrant ou le Père Jacobin* by a member of the company, Dugazon, and followed this up on 12 November with Hyacinthe Dorvo's *Le Patriote du dix août*.

Towards the end of the year real-life events came to a critical point. On 3 December the Assembly decided to put Louis XVI on trial, and on 11 December the King appeared before the Assembly. 2 January 1793, with the King's trial still in full swing, saw the first performance at the Théâtre de la Nation of an important play, and one which suggests that the company had strong feelings about the current political situation and, furthermore, that it was not lacking in courage. The play in question is Jean-Louis Laya's *L'Ami des lois* a moderate, Girondist comedy which argues for freedom with order and which attacks the Jacobin extremists, more than one of whom, such as Marat and Robespierre, is readily recognizable in the play, at a time when they were growing in influence. The text of this play and its implications will be considered in a subsequent chapter.

Complaints were lodged with the Convention, but that body was engrossed in the trial of the King and the matter of Laya's play was referred to a committee. Political sensitivities were inevitably particularly pronounced at this moment, and things were further complicated three days later with the production at the Théâtre du Vaudeville of Jean-Baptiste Radet and Georges Desfontaines's *La Chaste Suzanne*, which was basically an anodine enough adaptation from the Apocrypha of the story of Suzannah and the Elders, except that in the play Azarias is made to cry out to the elders that since they were Suzannah's accusers they could not be her judges too: this was promptly seen by both republicans and monarchists as an allusion to the trial of the King at the Convention. Complaints about this play were made not to the Convention, where the protests about *L'Ami des lois* seemed to have been side-tracked, but to the Commune of Paris and the authors rapidly agreed to alter offending parts of the script. The protest about Laya's play was then also taken to the Commune, who decreed that its performance should not continue, on the grounds that it was causing 'une fermentation alarmante dans les circonstances périlleuses où nous sommes' ('alarming unrest in the perilous circumstances in which we find ourselves') – clearly an allusion to the trial of Louis XVI.[1] Laya protested to the Convention (he also dedicated his play to that body). He wrote,

Citoyens législateurs,
Un grand abus d'autorité vient d'être commis contre un citoyen dont le crime est de proclamer les loix, l'ordre et les mœurs. . . . Je me suis rallié dans cet ouvrage aux principes éternels de la raison; c'était m'identifier avec vous, et l'on vous a calomniés dans le disciple qui ne faisait que répéter vos leçons. . . . La Commune, en suspendant les représentations de mon ouvrage, argumente d'une prétendue fermentation alarmante dans les circonstances: le trouble qui se manifeste aujourd'hui n'est dû qu'à son arrêt placardé à l'heure même où le public était déjà rassemblé pour prendre les billets. C'est à la cinquième représentation, après quatre épreuves paisibles, qu'elle ose suspendre *l'Ami des loix*. . . l'ancienne police vient de ressusciter sous l'écharpe municipale . . .[2]

Citizen legislators,
A great abuse of authority has been committed against a citizen

whose crime is to have proclaimed the importance of law, order and morality. . . . In my work I have rallied to the eternal principles of reason; to do so was to identify myself with you, and you have been slandered in the pupil who did no more than repeat your lessons. . . .

The Commune, in suspending the performances of my work, justifies itself by referring to alleged alarming unrest in the present circumstances: the trouble which we are experiencing today is due solely to the Commune's decree being posted at the very moment when the public was already gathered to purchase tickets. It was at the fifth performance, after four peaceful ones, that it dared to suspend *l'Ami des lois* . . . the old [censorship] controls have been resurrected under the municipal sash of office. . .

On 12 January crowds at the theatre demanded Laya's play. The Convention decreed that no municipality had the right to ban plays and *L'Ami des lois* was immediately performed, although it was already late (about 9 p.m.) when this decision of the Convention became known. There was, however, no public unrest.

The following evening the audience at the Nation again demanded Laya's play. The company must have been aware of the inadvisability of provoking the radicals of the Commune too far, having won a moral victory the previous day. It has to be admitted, however, that there is a touch of provocative irony in the words of the actor Dazincourt, as reported by the *Chronique de Paris*: Dazincourt asked the crowd to allow the company a few days before they put on *L'Ami des lois* again, to allow time for the 'esprits prévenus' ('prejudiced minds') to familiarize themselves with the comedy in question and ensure for subsequent performances that calm on which those prejudiced minds were so insistent and which was necessary to the actors.[3] Nevertheless, Dazincourt had in the end to promise that the company would perform Laya's play the following day. The Commune responded by ordering the immediate closure of all the Paris theatres, for fear of unrest if *L'Ami des lois* were performed again. The Convention, no doubt fearing that the Commune's measure might well provoke the very violence which it purported to prevent, denounced this abuse of power by the municipal authorities and Roland, the Girondin Minister of the Interior, sent a memorandum to Santerre, the commanding officer of the Paris National Guard, informing him that the Conseil

Exécutif of the Convention had decreed that the capital's theatres were to stay open as usual, despite the decree issued by the Commune, and reminding Santerre of his responsibility for peace and good order in Paris.[4] For all that, the Nation decided to offer two plays by Molière, *Le Médecin malgré lui* and *L'Avare* rather than *L'Ami des lois* on 14 January, although they did give a reading of it when a demonstration broke out in the theatre demanding the play (they would have been in the wrong to act a play other than those advertised). To bolster their position relative to the Commune the company at once posted all over Paris a statement entitled 'Les Citoyens composant le Théâtre de la Nation à leurs concitoyens' in which they sought to demonstrate the impeccable legality of all their actions in this affair.[5]

It may well be that it was fortunate for the company that public attention now focussed on what was going on in the trial at the Convention. Voting on the verdict began on 15 January and on 20 January the Convention condemned Louis XVI to death. He was executed the following day. On 28 January Hébert demanded the banning of *La Chaste Suzanne*, which was still running in its amended form at the Vaudeville: the Convention acceded to this demand and the authors (Radet and Desfontaines) and the director of the Vaudeville (Barré) were arrested. The Nation announced a performance of *L'Ami des lois* for 5 February, with the profits to go to aid the war effort. On 4 February, however, they announced that this performance would not take place. The kind of moderation which *L'Ami des lois* sought to express was now thoroughly out of style and Laya's play was not performed again until after the fall of Robespierre when, in the words of A. Pougin, 'son retour à la scène. . . passa complètement inaperçu' ('its return to the stage . . . passed totally unnoticed').[6]

On 9 February the Richelieu performed for the first time Chénier's *Fénelon ou les Religieuses de Cambrai*. Although it is no doubt true that Chénier was growing increasingly out of sympathy with the way in which the Revolution was developing, and although the play stands as a plea for tolerance, there was nothing in it to compare with the direct references to leading Montagnards in *L'Ami des lois*.[7] The public mood was one of militarism. On 23 January the Richelieu had produced *L'Entrée de Dumouriez à Bruxelles* to appeal to this spirit. On 2 February the Convention had declared war on England and Holland. On 7 March came a declaration of war with Spain. There were food riots in Paris under Varlet and Roux, and revolt broke out in the Vendée. On 10 March the Revolutionary Tribunal was set up to judge political offenders, on 19 March the death penalty was introduced for all rebels captured under arms and on 21 March the decision was taken to set up *comités de surveillance* in all Communes and in the Sections of the bigger towns. On 3 April the Richelieu produced La Martellière's *Robert, chef de brigands*: this play had been performed earlier at the Marais, when the Jacobins had objected to it. When it was performed at the Richelieu there was no objection, perhaps because (as Carlson argues) 'Robert's actions in taking the law into his own hands were interpreted as justifications of the Revolutionary Tribunal'.[8] The Théâtre de la Nation produced a series of politically inoffensive, undistinguished plays. The traditional Easter closing of the theatres was universally ignored: this was in itself a manifestation of anticlericalism in harmony with the mood of the times (on 23 March the Departments were authorized to deport any priest denounced by six citizens from his own Canton). On 5 April General Dumouriez deserted to the enemy. On the following day the nine-man Committee of Public Safety was formed. April and May saw disturbances throughout France, including a major revolt in Lyon. On 31 May Robespierre demanded the arrest of the Girondin leaders, followed by a similar demand from the Commune of Paris on the following day. This demand was referred to the Committee of Public Safety and on 2 June the Convention agreed to place twenty-nine Girondin members under house arrest. The Terror was about to begin.

It was more than a month before either of the leading Paris theatres, the Nation or the Richelieu, produced a new play. Indeed, as Carlson points out, during the whole of this violent summer, the Nation performed only one new play, and that was a totally undistinguished one (Louis-Guillaume Vigée's comedy *La Vivacité à l'épreuve*). The Richelieu was on better terms with the authorities, but it produced nothing of note either.[9] July saw the assassination of Marat by Charlotte Corday and Robespierre's becoming a member of the Committee of Public Safety. France once again found herself being invaded by Austrians, Spaniards and Piedmontese, with the British laying siege to Dunkirk.

On 1 August, the day on which the Convention decided to put Marie-Antoinette on trial, the Théâtre de la Nation produced an apparently inoffensive play, François de Neufchâteau's *Paméla*, derived from Samuel Richardson's novel *Pamela, or Virtue Rewarded*. It was, however, banned on 29 August, after nine performances. It was a curiously old-fashioned play in one respect, in that (as had been quite common under the *Ancien Régime* with translations or adaptations from the English) a certain social upgrading of the characters had taken place. This was no doubt unwise in the changed political climate of the summer of 1793. The play was seen as hinting that it was nobility rather than virtue which was rewarded, although it seems reasonable to suppose that those newly come to power were determined on settling scores with the Théâtre de la Nation on any pretext which could be conjured up. Neufchâteau pointed out that his play had been written in 1788 and might therefore contain out-of-date elements, which he was very willing to remove. A revised version was announced for 1 September. There was further trouble, the tone and motivation of which can be judged from the note published in the Jacobin *Feuille du salut public* on 3 September by its editor, Alexandre Rousselin. Rousselin attacked Neufchâteau for having his play performed by the 'valets de l'aristocratie' in a theatre

> où les croacemens [*sic*] Prussiens et Autrichiens ont toujours prédominé, où le défunt *Veto* trouva les adorateurs les plus vils, où le poignard qui a frappé Marat a été aiguisé lors du faux *Ami des loix*.[10] Je demande, en conséquence,
>
> Que ce sérail impur soit fermé pour jamais, . . . que tous les histrions du Théâtre dit de la Nation, qui ont voulu se donner les beaux airs de l'aristocratie, dignes par leur conduite d'être regardés comme gens très suspects, soient mis en état d'arrestation dans les maisons de force . . .[11]

in which Prussian and Austrian cawing has always predominated, in which the late *Veto* [i.e. Louis XVI] found the vilest worshippers, where the dagger which struck down Marat was sharpened at the time of the false *Ami des lois*. I therefore demand,

> That this foul seraglio be closed down for ever, . . . that all the ham actors of the so-called Théâtre de la Nation, who have sought to give themselves fine aristocratic airs, and who are worthy by their conduct to be considered highly suspect, be arrested and placed in prison. . .

As early as July 1793 the Committee of Public Safety had 'suggested' to theatres that they perform more patriotic plays, and on 2 August the Convention had decreed that theatres should perform patriotic plays three times per week. The *Républicain français* on 6 September reported a debate at the Jacobin Club in which Robespierre pointed out that the same decree provided that theatres guilty of performing aristocratic plays or plays harmful to the Revolution should be closed. Robespierre put this to the Committee of Public Safety on 2 September, and the Committee resolved the closure of the Théâtre de la Nation and the arrest of the members of the company and of the author of *Paméla*. The Convention approved these steps the next day.[12] The male members of the company, along with Neufchâteau were imprisoned in the Madelonettes and the women in Sainte-Pélagie.

It has been calculated that by 1793 there were over forty theatres in Paris, some of them very small, and some of them, like the Lycée, regaling their customers with works with titles like *La Révolte des nègres*, *Les Capucins à la frontière*, and *La Guillotine d'amour*. Not everything performed was of this *engagé* kind, however: Carlson comments on the curious fact that 'a play based on the love affair of the fairy Urgande and the sorcerer Merlin [Monvel's *Urgande et Merlin*] brought crowds to the Favart on the day of Marie-Antoinette's execution, and on the afternoon when the Girondists went to their death, the Variétés Amusantes premiered a successful production of *Arlequin gardien des femmes* [anon.]'.[13]

1793 saw the Revolution change into reverse gear, certainly as far as theatrical freedom was concerned. Increasingly the tendency was for productions to become mere propaganda, a task made none the easier by the necessity to adjust to sudden changes in official policy, such as when, after a campaign of deliberate dechristianization and positive favouring of atheism in the latter part of 1793, Robespierre early in 1794 suddenly changed direction and on 8 June of that year played the leading part in the Festival of the Supreme Being. Throughout September, denunciations spread throughout French society, and the world of the theatre was in no way exempt. After the actors of the Théâtre de la Nation had been arrested, it was the turn of the Opéra to be seen as a hot-bed of counter-revolution and on 16 September its directors, Francœur and Cellerier, were arrested. The company promptly declared their loyalty to the Revolution by publicly burning all documents which pertained to their relationship with the monarchy (30 September) and by agreeing to purge all suspect works from their repertory. On 4 November it was the turn of Mlle Montansier: having just opened a new theatre, she was denounced by Hébert and Chaumette and accused of having taken money from the English and from Marie-Antoinette for this purpose. She and her assistant Neuville were imprisoned and her company sought permission to change its name to Théâtre de la Montagne, in a remarkable demonstration of sycophancy directed to the extremist section of the Convention bearing that name.

The closing of the Théâtre de la Nation left the Richelieu without question as the leading Paris theatre. It promptly sought to demonstrate its loyalty to the republican regime. As early as 1792 the company had sought to change its name from one which was so redolent of monarchical days and had called itself the Théâtre-Français de la Liberté et de l'Egalité. This wordy title lacked appeal, however, and it was after the closure of the Nation that the Richelieu, now the only remaining vestige of the old Comédie-Française, took as its official designation Théâtre de la République. Its first offering after the demise of the Nation was Saint-Aubin's panegyric to Marat, *L'Ami du peuple*. On 26 September the company sent the Convention almost 1,500 livres as a contribution to the war effort. On 5 October, during a performance of Chénier's *Timoléon*, the aim of which was, as Liéby succinctly puts it, to celebrate 'la République triomphante à la fois des tyrans du dehors et des conspirateurs du dedans'[14] ('the Republic simultaneously triumphant over external tyrants and internal conspirators'), a member of the audience, Antoine-Louis Albitte, took offence at the speeches of the tyrannical Timophane and denounced the play. The company had fresh in their memory what had happened to their colleagues of the Théâtre de la Nation on the occasion of *Paméla* and sought to take no risks. They therefore replaced *Timoléon* with Chénier's *Caïus Gracchus*, which had passed muster on earlier occasions, but now this play too was denounced by Albitte and the company dropped it in its turn.

The play with which the République sought to silence its critics and prove its Revolutionary credentials once and for all was the unmistakably republican *Le Jugement dernier des rois* by Pierre-Sylvain Maréchal. This play, or prophecy (as its author called it) was first performed at the République on 17 October 1793, the day after the execution of Marie-Antoinette and a fortnight before the execution of twenty-one leading Girondins on 1 November. It is a play which has perhaps been more written about than read, and will form the subject matter of a subsequent chapter. From a political point of view it was a considerable success.

These were days in which it was as well to give positive proof of one's loyalty: as Carlson puts it, 'the author who wrote nothing at all was as suspect as the author who openly supported Church or nobility'.[15] So it was that on 30 October the République produced Dugazon's play *Le Modéré* (the author having been thought too close to Dumouriez in the past) in which the character Modérantin is destroyed for being too moderate – or in twentieth-century English political parlance, too 'wet' – in his views. So it was too that even an old playwright such as Sedaine, now in his seventies, seems to have felt it necessary to try to adapt to the new order of things, apparently even going to the lengths of making republican amendments to the text of his *Le Philosophe sans le savoir* of 1765.[16].

Le Modéré was the last new play produced by the République in 1793. The official attitude at this time towards both the theatre and religion is demonstrated by a letter issued on 25 December 1793 by the Committee of Public Instruction:

> Il faut demander à la Convention nationale qu'elle décrète que dans toutes les villes de 4,000 habitants, il y aura une salle de spectacle où les élèves des écoles publiques et autres personnes pourront s'exercer, et ne pourront néanmoins donner que des pièces *sentimentales* et dans le sens de la Révolution. . . . Presque toutes ces villes ayant des églises vacantes, on peut éviter de bâtir. . . . Je crois que rien ne serait plus propre à instruire le peuple, à lui faire oublier les singeries des prêtres, et enfin à régénérer les mœurs.[17]

> The national Convention must be asked to decree that in all towns of 4,000 inhabitants there should be a playhouse where the pupils of state schools and other persons may perform, but only plays *of feeling* and which are in the spirit of the Revolution. . . . Since almost all these towns have vacant churches, no building will be necessary. . . . It is my belief that nothing would be more appropriate to instruct the people, to make them forget the ape-like antics of the priests, and finally to regenerate morality.

The République's first play of 1794 was very much in this kind of spirit, Hyacinthe Dorvo's *Les Contre-révolutionnaires jugés par eux-mêmes*. The same company on 3 February performed Legouvé's tragedy, *Epicharis et Néron*, dedicated to Liberty in the following terms,

> Liberté, c'est par toi que me fut inspiré
> Cet écrit où parle mon âme.
> Sur ton autel je pris la flamme
> Dont Pison fut pénétré

Liberty, this work in which my soul speaks out was inspired by you. It is from your altar that I took the flame with which Piso was imbued.

This dedication may well have diverted attention from the fact that it was by no means impossible to draw comparisons between the career of Robespierre and that of Nero in the play.[18] The Feydeau (the erstwhile Théâtre de Monsieur) was the only theatre in which the spirit of moderation more or less survived after the arrest of the Nation company: on the 8 September 1794 a police spy put in a report in which he said that this theatre should never have abandoned its royalist name and that on a visit there he had found himself surrounded by the enemies of all forms of revolution.[19]

Well before this report, representatives of all the leading theatres, including the Feydeau, were called, in January 1794, before the Committee of Public Safety and given some strong advice as to the composition of their repertories. The Feydeau's rival, the Favart (the old Comédie Italienne), despite its previous position of privilege, under the Terror took the name of Opéra-Comique National and performed during the winter of 1793-1794 a series of chauvinistic, republican pieces, although after 9 thermidor (27 July 1794) it reverted to the name, Théâtre Favart.

The directors of the Vaudeville were released in October 1793 after six weeks' imprisonment and thereafter the Vaudeville repeatedly sought to demonstrate loyalty to the republican cause. Radet and Desfontaines (the authors of the ill-fated *La Chaste Suzanne*) acted similarly with *La Fête de l'égalité*, with Desfontaines's *Les Chouans de Vitré* and Radet's *Le Canonnier convalescent*.[20]

In April 1794 the Committee of Public Safety ordered the transfer of the Opéra, in very good odour with the authorities since the arrest of its directors (although, like other theatres, it was caught out when Robespierre suddenly embraced the doctrine of religious tolerance), from its wooden theatre at the Porte St. Martin to Mlle Montansier's expensive new theatre in the rue de la Loi, near the Bibliothèque Nationale. It opened its new premises with a work in praise of the achievements of the Revolution up to date entitled *La Réunion du 10 août ou L'Inauguration de la République française* by Gabriel Bouquier, a member of the Committee of Public Safety. Both the Favart and the Molière, which was now calling itself the Théâtre des Sans-Culottes, were instructed to add the piece to their repertory.

March 24 saw the execution of the leading Hébertists, who were followed to the guillotine on 5 April by the leading Dantonists. The government of Robespierre and Saint-Just was in a position of absolute power, with the Convention and the Paris Commune both subservient to it. All power was now with the governing committees, especially the Committee of Public Safety. Controls over the world of the theatre increased sharply. In April it was decreed that all class titles should be banned from the stage and be replaced by the simple appellation 'citoyen', regardless of common sense in terms of the period in which the play was set and equally regardless of the rules of rhyme or metre. These restrictions were to some extent relaxed very quickly when the Committee of Public Safety's agent Payan reported on 8 May that he had been able to persuade Lelièvre and Faro, the police administrators who had taken the step referred to above, that it was ridiculous to hear references to, for example, Citizen Catalina or to see Jupiter decorated with a tricolore cockade and that Lelièvre and Faro were therefore writing immediately to theatre directors to inform them that they were at liberty to leave as they were tragedies written before the Revolution or whose subjects did not relate to the Revolution. As for comedies, the police administrators would leave it 'à la sagacité et au patriotisme des directeurs' to decide when styles and titles should be changed:

> En un mot, ils soumettent seulement les pièces nouvelles à se servir des mots *Citoyen* et *Citoyenne*, à moins que ceux de *Monsieur* et de *Madame* ne soient employés que comme injure ou pour désigner un ennemi de la Révolution.[21]

In short, they are insisting only that new plays use the words

Citoyen and *Citoyenne*, unless the words *Monsieur* and *Madame* are used as an insult or to indicate an enemy of the Revolution.

The Marais theatre, which was closely associated with Beaumarchais since it had had the surprising honour for such a relatively minor theatre of mounting the première of the great playwright's *La Mère coupable* (26 June 1792), closed during the Terror (Beaumarchais himself as a suspect gun-runner spent a time in prison just before the September Massacres and then went to live abroad).[22] Most of the other theatres managed to survive, although much harried by the authorities. Carlson suggests that the little Cité-Variétés theatre seems to have been the only one not to have run into trouble with the authorities during the Terror, thanks to serving up a fare consisting largely of manifestations of patriotism: 'almost nothing concerning the Revolution was too trivial for the adulation of the Cité'.[23]

Paris, however, had no theatre strictly of the type recommended for provincial towns in the Committee of Public Instruction's report of 25 December 1793, confining its activities exclusively to plays 'in the spirit of the Revolution'. The Théâtre de la Nation was, however, sitting empty and on 10 March 1794 the Committee of Public Safety issued the following decree laying down the conditions under which it was to be reopened:

Le Comité de Salut public délibérant sur les pétitions présentées par les sections réunies de Marat, de Mucius-Scævola, du Bonnet Rouge et de l'Unité, arrête:

1° Que le théâtre ci-devant Français étant un édifice national sera rouvert sans délai, qu'il sera uniquement consacré aux représentations données de par et pour le Peuple à certaines époques de chaque mois.

L'édifice sera orné au dehors de l'inscription suivante:

THEATRE DU PEUPLE.

Il sera décoré au dedans de tous les attributs de la Liberté.

2° Les sociétés d'artistes établies dans les divers théâtres de Paris seront mises tour à tour en réquisition pour les représentations qui devront être données trois fois par décade d'après l'état qui sera fait par la municipalité.

3° Nul citoyen ne pourra entrer au *Théâtre du Peuple*, s'il n'a une marque particulière, qui ne sera donnée qu'aux patriotes dont la municipalité réglera le mode de distribution [*sic*].

4° La municipalité de Paris prendra toutes les mesures nécessaires pour l'exécution du présent arrêté; elle rendra compte dans dix jours des moyens qu'elle aura pris.

5° Le répertoire des pièces à jouer sur le *Théâtre du Peuple* sera demandé à chaque théâtre de Paris et soumis à l'approbation du Comité. . .

Signé: B. BARERE, SAINT-JUST, CARNOT, C.-A. PRIEUR, COLLOT D'HERBOIS, ROBESPIERRE, BILLAUD-VARENNE.[24]

The Committee of Public Safety, after consideration of the petitions presented to it jointly by the Marat, Mucius-Scævola, Bonnet-Rouge and Unité Sections [of Paris], decrees:

1 That the former Théâtre Français, being a national building, shall be reopened without delay and that it shall be exclusively dedicated to performances given by and for the people, at prescribed times each month.

The front of the building shall bear the following inscription:

THEATRE DU PEUPLE.

The interior of the building shall be decorated with all the emblems of liberty.

2 That the companies of players established in the various Paris theatres shall be required in turn to give performances three times a décade [the ten-day week of the Revolutionary calendar adopted on 24 November 1793] according to the roster established by the municipality.

3 That no citizen shall be permitted to enter the *Théâtre du Peuple* without an identification document which shall be given only to patriots by methods to be determined by the municipal authorities.

4 That the municipality of Paris shall take all necessary steps for the execution of this decree and shall report on action taken within ten days.

5 That the repertory of plays to be performed in the *Théâtre du Peuple* shall come from each Paris theatre and shall be subject to the approval of the Committee. . .

Signed: B. BARERE, SAINT-JUST, CARNOT, C.-A. PRIEUR, COLLOT D'HERBOIS, ROBESPIERRE, BILLAUD-VARENNE.

The old Théâtre de la Nation, in other words, was to become more or less a theatre for the 'Party faithful'. The decision was taken to remove the 'aristocratic' division of the theatre into boxes, etc., and extensive remodelling was undertaken. By the time the old Théâtre de la Nation reopened on 27 June 1794 it had been decided that its new name should be not the Théâtre du Peuple but the Théâtre de l'Egalité. All boxes and balconies had been removed and what the patrons were offered was simply one vast sweep of seats from floor to ceiling. The interior had been repainted red, white, and blue, and statues of Liberty and Equality had been erected along with busts of heroes of the Revolution such as Marat.

It was on the very same day that Fouquier-Tinville, the public prosecutor, was asked by Collot d'Herbois to bring the imprisoned members of the Nation company to trial. The date of 1 July was fixed for the execution of those condemned (the law of 10 June (22 prairial) had widened the categories of suspects or 'public enemies' and henceforth the Revolutionary Tribunal recognized only one punishment: the death penalty). A mysterious series of events involving a clerk of the Committee of Public Safety named Charles-Hippolyte Labussière, an ex-actor, resulted in the appropriate dossiers being removed and destroyed, so that time was gained and the actors had still not been brought to trial when Robespierre fell from power on 9 thermidor (27 July 1794).[25] Within ten days of the execution of Robespierre (28 July) most of the 10,000 people in prison as political suspects, including many actors, had been released.

The freed members of the Nation company returned to their heavily transformed theatre and reopened it on 16 August with a politically anodine bill consisting of two comedies from the 1730s, Piron's *La Métromanie* and Marivaux's *Les Fausses Confidences*. It is not to be wondered at, after the experiences of members of the company, that such caution characterized the plays produced at the Egalité for some time. The Richelieu was a little bolder and on 10 September revived Chénier's *Timoléon* which, as we have seen, had fallen foul of Revolutionary opinion during the Terror. Chénier, however, was now himself falling out of favour: he was much and unfairly criticized for not having saved his brother, the poet André Chénier, from the guillotine and, having seen himself condemned for the moderation of his views by the Montagnards under the Terror, now found himself condemned as a rabid revolutionary by the moderates after the end of the Terror.

It was inevitable that there should be a strong reaction against extremist Jacobinism after 9 thermidor and demonstrations were not infrequent at theatres which were thought to have profited under the Terror. Thus there was a riot at the République on 24 January 1795 during a play thought to be by one of the actresses in the company, Amélie-Julie Candeille, entitled *La Bayadère*. The company from the erstwhile Nation alternated with the company from the Opéra at the Egalité until December 1794, when the Nation troupe came to an agreement with the Feydeau company to share the latter's much more favourably situated theatre. As victims of the Terror, the actors from the Nation were very popular and they put into rehearsal the two plays which had brought about their downfall under the Terror, *L'Ami des lois* and *Paméla*. The former play was put on by them at the Feydeau early in June. The République countered on 10 June with a performance of Népomucène-Louis Lemercier's *Le Tartuffe révolutionnaire* in which Molière's famous hypocrite is reincarnate as an extremist revolutionary who is finally exposed and taken away to prison, much like the original Tartuffe. On 4 August the Nation company put on *Paméla*, but like *L'Ami des lois*, this play seemed innocuous now that the circumstances which had made it controversial had passed. Both plays, however, did reasonable business.

Not surprisingly, indeed, the theatre-going public was beginning to show a marked lack of interest in plays with the kind of political themes which had been common for so long on the Paris stage. A reaction against what had gone before was inevitable and there emerged as a reaction to the *sans-culottes* the *jeunesse dorée*, for the most part the younger generation of the well-to-do middle-class, thugs who have been described by Norman Hampson as 'a considerably more civilized forerunner of the Storm Troops of a later age'.[26] Once again the theatres became the scene of demonstrations between conflicting factions. In the closing months of 1794 and during early 1795 salon life began to reappear and outrageously extravagant fashions were introduced by the affected young *incroyables* and their female counterparts, the *merveilleuses*.

Macabre *bals des victimes* were held, at which the families of those who had gone to the guillotine entertained themselves with their necks shaved as though for execution and a thin, red silk ribbon around their throats.

The Vaudeville, essentially devoted to satire but having for a long time been unable to produce much in that genre, found plenty of material in the excesses of the gilded youth (e.g. Picard's comedy *La Perruque blonde*, of 12 November 1794). The Feydeau, especially when joined by the freed actors of the Nation company, was the natural rallying point for the reactionary groups in society. It became the fashion, started by *la jeunesse dorée*, to throw political notes on to the stage for public reading. It seems to have been the case that not infrequently the actors picked upon to read these notes were those who were considered to have been too close to the Jacobins. The Jacobin Club itself was closed on 12 November 1794 but this, of course, did not mean that there were no Jacobins all of a sudden. They continued to meet in cafés and carried out attacks on the reactionary *jeunesse dorée*. There was an orgy of demonstrations in the Paris theatres. The flavour is given by a police report of 3 February 1795 which tells of the destruction of plaster busts of Revolutionary figures in various theatres, the Favart, the Feydeau, and the Théâtre des Arts: 'Au théâtre de la rue Feydeau on a jeté un papier, et lu, qui est un appel au meurtre contre les terroristes, pour venger les mânes des victimes innocentes égorgées par leur cruelle faction'[27] ('At the Théâtre de la rue Feydeau a paper was thrown on to the stage and read out: it was a call to murder against the Terrorists, to avenge the shades of the innocent victims whose throats were cut by that cruel faction').

On 12 February the Committee of Public Safety, in view of the fact that it was clear that not infrequently malicious intent governed the throwing of notes on to the stages of the Paris theatres, decreed that since it did not wish to interfere with public freedom of expression it would henceforth merely insist that the author of any such note should either read it himself from the stage or stand next to the actor who read it.[28] Napoleon Bonaparte, who was now military commander of the Paris region, was asked to keep an eye on the Feydeau, which was at the heart of disturbances caused by this practice. On 27 February the Feydeau was ordered to close. It reopened in mid-March. Shortly after it reopened, the Feydeau put on C.-J. Trouvé's five-act tragedy *Pausanias* (28

March), a play ostensibly about a Spartan general although in reality, as the author was at pains to point out, 'le sujet de cette pièce est le 9 thermidor' and 'Pausanias est Robespierre, à cette différence près que ce dernier fut un lâche et vil scélérat, tandis que Pausanias avait l'énergie du crime et mêlait de l'éclat à ses vices'[29] ('the subject of this play is the 9 thermidor' and 'Pausanias is Robespierre, with this difference: the latter was a cowardly, vile scoundrel, whilst Pausanias was positive in his crimes and showed a certain brilliance in his vices').

The reaction continued. On 28 March the public prosecutor Fouquier-Tinville was himself tried and subsequently executed. On 1 April the Convention was invaded by a considerable crowd demanding bread, the curbing of the activities of the *jeunesse dorée* and the release of those arrested since 9 thermidor. These demonstrators were ejected from the Tuileries with little difficulty and on 10 April the Convention ordered the disarming, throughout France, of all those who had played a significant role in the Terror. In the same month Collot d'Herbois, Billaud-Varenne and Barère were deported to Guiana. Peace was made with Holland, and on 20 May 1795 a last attempt was made by radicals from the Faubourg Saint-Antoine to wrest power from the new reactionaries. By 23 May the insurrection had collapsed. It was followed by many arrests and some executions: significantly it was a military commission which tried 149 supposed ringleaders and condemned 36 of them to death. As Norman Hampson points out, this attempted uprising – the *journées* of prairial – was the last popular uprising in Paris until 1848.[30] Demonstrations organized by the *jeunesse dorée* continued. A police report dated 19 July 1795 reveals that at the Feydeau a demonstration was begun by young people singing the anthem of the forces of reaction, 'Le Réveil du peuple', whilst at the Théâtre des Arts there was total disorder, outside as well as inside the theatre, including shouts that the government was being soft on known Terrorists and that the Convention itself still needed to be purged of Jacobins. This disturbance too was the work of young demonstrators.[31] Mlle Montansier was finally released from prison and promptly restored her own name to what had become the Théâtre de la Montagne and to mount plays calculated to appeal to the gilded youth. Her theatre became the focal point for the *jeunesse dorée* and subsequently for the fashionable pleasure-seekers of the Directory.

By far the most successful play of the early part of 1795 was the violently anti-Jacobin *L'Intérieur des comités révolutionnaires, ou Les Aristides modernes* which its author, Charles-Pierre Ducancel, claimed was written, accepted, learned and produced in the space of twenty-seven days.[32] It opened at the Cité-Variétés on 27 April. This play, which is set in Dijon, sets out to wreak vengeance on the members of the Revolutionary Comittees. At the end the order for the arrest of the members of the Dijon committee is given:

Gendarmes, saisissez ces misérables, et conduisez-les, affublés de leurs bonnets rouges, à la maison d'arrêt. . . . Qu'ils traversent à pied, et au milieu des justes imprécations du peuple, une commune qu'ils ont baignée de sang et couverte de brigandage, jusqu'à ce que le glaive de la loi en ait purgé la terre.

(III. viii)

Gendarmes, seize these wretches and take them, rigged out in their red bonnets, to the house of detention. . . . Make them, amidst the just curses of the people, go on foot across the town which they have bathed in blood and blanketed in villainy, until the blade of the law has purged the earth of them.

In the very last words of the play we are told that 'la postérité, en pleurant sur les cendres de tant de citoyens innocents, bénira leurs vengeurs' (III.ix) ('posterity, as it weeps over the ashes of so many innocent citizens, will bless their avengers'). Not very great drama, perhaps, but it must have been very satisfying to those in 1795 who had scores to settle, such as the elderly man who had been imprisoned throughout the Terror and who is said to have taken a box and attended every single performance of the play, weeping with joy and clapping his hands and repeating over and over again, 'Oh! comme je me venge de ces coquins-là' ('Oh, how I am avenged over those bastards!')[33]

During the early part of 1795 petitions appeared before the Convention complaining of the waste involved in allowing the Théâtre de l'Egalité (the old Nation) to stand empty, and in June Poupart Dorfeuille, the former director of the République and of the Bordeaux opera, took on the task of turning it into a new national theatre. No significant developments were to take place in this regard for a year.

On 8 June Louis XVII, a boy of nine, died. On 24 June the Comte de Provence, the elder of Louis XVI's brothers, proclaimed himself King as Louis XVIII and issued a violent manifesto of counter-revolution. In July a small force of *émigrés* with some English support was defeated at Quiberon and over seven hundred captured *émigrés* were shot. Peace was made with Spain. In August the Constitution of the An III was voted, the intention of which was to preserve a conservative republic from the monarchists on the one hand and revolutionary dictatorship on the other. The creation of the Directory, under this Constitution, it was hoped, would bring with it much-needed stability. The Convention dissolved itself on 26 October and the rule of the Directory (with five *Directeurs* and two legislative Chambers (the *Conseil des Anciens* and the *Conseil des Cinq-Cents*) began. The Directory was attacked from the left by a combination of Babeuf and jaundiced Jacobins in May of 1796, but the government survived this attack with little difficulty. Bonaparte enjoyed a series of military successes. Partial elections in April 1797 led to only eleven former deputies of the Convention out of 216 being returned, most of the new members being constitutional monarchists. This led, in September 1797 to the three Republican Directors, Reubell, La Reveillière-Lépeaux and Barras attempting a coup against their fellow Directors and against the royalist majority in the two Chambers. The army, under Bonaparte's lieutenant, Augereau, played a major part in events from this point on. On 4 September Paris found itself under military occupation. The legislative bodies were purged, press censorship was imposed and seventeen of the leading opponents of the republican triumvirate were sent to Guiana.

In October the Treaty of Campo-Formio between France and Austria was a major triumph for Bonaparte. Only Great Britain, of France's enemies, remained to be dealt with. Bonaparte, fully aware of British naval strength, advised the Directory against any thought of an attempted invasion. 1798 saw Bonaparte departing on his Egyptian campaign. In July he was victorious in the battle of the Pyramids but in August Nelson destroyed the French fleet at Aboukir Bay and cut off the French army from home. March 1799 saw the beginning of the war of the Second Coalition and the threat of invasion was hanging once again over France. In May Reubell retired from the Directory and was replaced by Sieyès who became the effective power in the land. Sieyès's political views had changed considerably since 1789, when he had published *Qu'est-ce que le Tiers Etat?* Having then stood for a sovereign legislature, he was now determined to consolidate the power of the executive of which he himself was, of course, now the leading member, and he realized that to this end he needed the support of the military. He seems to have thought that he was capable of using Napoleon as his tool. This, of course, was to prove not to be the case. On 9 November an alleged left-wing conspiracy was used as an excuse to move the legislature to St Cloud and on 9-10 November, in the *coup d'état* of the 18 brumaire Bonaparte, newly returned in triumph from Egypt, put an end to the Directory and established the Consulate, with Sieyès, Roger Ducos and Bonaparte himself as Consuls. In the words of Alfred Cobban, 'France's first essay in parliamentary government had come to an end'.[34]

From the theatrical point of view, the first two years of the Directory were remarkably peaceful. The threat of internal violence seemed much diminished and there was a large and eager public for theatrical entertainment. Political plays went completely out of fashion and the mood was one of escapism. Ballrooms opened in profusion, fashions became outrageously erotic and the emphasis was on pleasure and the pursuit of wealth. An upsurge of royalism was manifest and, as is clear from a police report of 8 December 1795, this royalism exhibited itself in the foyers of the capital's theatres. Prostitutes gathered at the theatres and, we are told in a report of 29 December, the theatres continued to be 'le rendez-vous des ennemis de la République'.[35] Bonaparte, as commander of the troops of the Paris region was ordered to keep an eye on the Feydeau in particular, but on 21 February 1796 it was found necessary to close it.

In July 1796 the Directory passed a decree authorizing Dorfeuille to proceed with his plans for a new national theatre at the Egalité, which was to be refurbished under the name of the Odéon as a theatre, drama school and centre for national celebrations and similar functions. Dorfeuille's two potential rivals, the Feydeau and the République were in the doldrums, producing hardly anything that was new and, by the end of the year, suffering from a sudden increase in the taxation burden which they faced.

Mlle Raucourt, a stalwart of the old Comédie and of the Nation, decided to attempt to unite the scattered actors to form a company which would be able to recapture the reputation and power of the

Comédie-Française, proposing that they set up in business on neutral ground at the Théâtre Louvois. Most of the old Nation actors supported the scheme, and the members of the République company might also have been prepared to accept it. The government, however, had given its blessing to Dorfeuille's Odéon project. Mlle Raucourt went ahead nevertheless and, with such actors as she had been able to muster, opened at the Louvois on 5 December 1795 with Laya's *Les Deux Sœurs*. She did quite well for a time. In effect there were now no fewer than three different companies descending from the old Comédie Française tradition functioning in Paris. The situation was chaotic. The Feydeau, République, and Louvois companies sought to poach each others' members, and standards of performance declined.

In mid-February 1797 the Egalité reopened as the Odéon with *Les Philosophes amoureux* by Destouches and *Les Apparences trompeuses* by Hauteroche. Attendance was poor; Dorfeuille found difficulties in attracting first-class actors from the other three major theatres and soon found himself in financial trouble. The Odéon closed temporarily on 17 March, with Dorfeuille stating that he could not compete with the other theatres without a government subsidy. On 19 June he withdrew altogether, handing his thirty-year lease on the theatre to his assistant Le Page and his architect, Le Clerc. The theatre reopened on 19 August, but still with a poor company. The Feydeau did not produce a single new work in the spring and summer of 1797, although on 5 May it did put on a revival of Beaumarchais's *La Mère coupable*.

In September 1797 Neufchâteau (the author of *Paméla*) became one of the Directors, as did Merlin, and once again the repertories of the theatres were expurgated in a republican sense. On 10 September the Louvois was closed, Merlin considering that he had been lampooned there in a performance of Joseph de Lafont's *Les Trois Frères rivaux* on 4 August.[36] All the old restrictions returned. In an official report of 2 November 1797 a play at the Feydeau, Leprévot d'Iray's *Alphonse et Léonore*, is castigated because in it 'un officier français [a] sans cesse le mot de *monsieur* à la bouche, parle de madame *de* Gercourt et [croit] le fils de son fermier fort heureux d'être son valet' ('a French officer continuously has the word *monsieur* on his lips, speaks of Mme *de* Gercourt and considers the son of his farmer fortunate to be his valet'), whilst a report of 23 January 1798 criticized Marsollier's *Alexis, ou l'Erreur d'un bon père* because the word *louis* was used: 'Pourquoi cette monnaie qui rappelle aux royalistes leur idole? Melcour ne peut-il pas donner tout simplement une *bourse*?' ('Why these coins which remind the royalists of their idol? Could not Melcour simply hand over a *purse*?'). A play entitled *Minuit*, which was premiered at the Louvois on 31 December, was immediately banned because 'Il ne s'agit guère dans la pièce que de sçavoir qui souhaitera le premier la *bonne année*. Il serait au moins inconvenant de reproduire sur la scène un usage aboli par le calendrier républicain' ('The play is about little other than discovering who will be the first to say "Happy New Year". It would be, to say the least of it, unsuitable for a custom which was abolished by the Revolutionary calendar to be reproduced on stage').[37]

The Opéra was handicapped by the fact that its theatre was taken over from time to time for public purposes such as to house the deliberations of the Council of the Five Hundred. Many of the minor theatres disappeared and such as remained followed the example of the major theatres and overwhelmingly eschewed political plays. However, on 19 March 1796 the newly opened Théâtre des Jeunes Artistes did put on Martainville's *Les Assemblées primaires ou Les Elections*, attacking the Directory as merely the old government in new clothes. The theatre was immediately closed.[38] Undoubtedly the most successful work of 1796 was *Madame Angot, ou la Poissarde parvenue*, a two-act comic opera by Antoine-François Eve (known as Maillot), which packed the tiny Théâtre d'Emulation night after night. The work, which is an uproarious satire on the *nouveaux-riches* of the day, depicts the rich fishwife of the title learning the folly of aspiring to nobility. It springs from a long tradition and spawned a whole family of copies.

Nevertheless, as Pougin points out, despite an isolated success such as this the minor theatres were in decline, partly because of competition from rival attractions including the newly fashionable pleasure gardens, such as the Mousseaux, the Tivoli, the Elysée-Bourbon, and a number of others.[39] It has been calculated that 'over half those houses still open as 1797 began had disappeared by the following fall'.[40]

The Treaty of Campo Formio brought peace to France for the first time in five years. The Paris theatres were quick to celebrate this event. Pougin offers a list of eleven theatres all offering entertainments directly inspired by the news of the treaty.[41] This was the last occasion during the Directory, however, that there was to be such a unanimous celebration of a political event by the capital's theatres. The tendency was away from plays with a political theme or message in the direction of escapism, with melodrama being particularly popular. By the end of 1797 there were only fifteen professional theatres still functioning in Paris.

The Opéra was in a state of near collapse after its move to the rue de la Loi (the Théâtre des Arts, as it came to be called in 1797). It did not mount a single new play for two years, although in May 1798 it did produce Rouget de Lisle's anti-British *Le Chant des vengeances*, but this kind of chauvinism was no longer in fashion, and it was a failure. The Opéra closed down for periods in 1797 and again in 1799. The Favart did well, with an experienced company. This theatre had the dubious distinction of provoking the last theatrical riot of the Revolutionary period – and indeed of the century – with its performance of the *drame lyrique* entitled *Montano et Stéphanie* in April 1799. This work, by Dejaure and Berton, as a police report of 16 April makes clear, caused offence for religious reasons, when it was seen that the setting of the second act was a church, with its high altar, crucifix, lighted candles and all the paraphernalia of Catholic worship. The authorities suspended the play until alterations had been made.[42]

On the Boulevard, the Théâtre d'Emulation reverted to its former title of Théâtre de la Gaîté (it had originally been Nicolet's Grands Danseurs du Roi, which title was abandoned in 1792) and staged one of the first important plays by Pixerécourt, the master of melodrama, on 12 May 1798: *Victor ou l'Enfant de la forêt*. It was the Ambigu-Comique, however, which particularly thrived on melodrama and produced many plays by Pixerécourt and his followers.

By February 1797 there were, as we have seen, four theatres in Paris claiming descent from the old Comédie-Française: the Feydeau, the Richelieu, the Louvois and the Odéon, although the company at the Louvois lost their theatre in September of that year. The Feydeau was clearly the leading company in Paris. The République was in a poor way and in need of an injection of new blood. A merger would obviously have been sensible, but old rivalries die hard. The Feydeau had been concentrating on comedy and comic opera and was not interested in merging with a company or companies mainly interested in serious drama. Eventually, the Louvois company joined forces with the Opéra, which reopened on 18 January 1798 with Racine's *Phèdre*, featuring the majority of the highly experienced Louvois company, most of whom had originally been at the Nation. This was not welcome competition for the République, which closed on 19 February. The Feydeau found itself in trouble over Marsollier's one-act comedy, *Trop de délicatesse*. The grounds on which it was criticized in a police report of 9 March 1798 make interesting reading. The play was set in America but the official view of the American republic is no longer the glowing picture of revolutionary achievement presented in Chénier's *Charles IX*:

> . . . nous ne faisons pas grande différence en ce moment entre les Anglais et les Anglo-Américains. Permettre la représentation de cette pièce, c'est souffrir que l'on mette des personnages anglais sur notre théâtre, où ils ne devraient paraître que pour y être au moins ridiculisés.[43]

> . . . we do not make much distinction these days between the English and the Anglo-Americans. To allow the performance of this play is to permit the portrayal of English characters on our stage, where they should only appear if they are to be held up to ridicule.

The French concept of the Anglo-Saxons has appeared. Performances of the play were suspended.

Sageret, the director of the Feydeau, set about wooing over to his theatre actors from the closed République by offering them high salaries. On 3 May, on the eve of his departure for Egypt, Bonaparte was present at the début at the Feydeau of Talma and Mme Vestris in Ducis's *Macbeth*.

During the spring of 1798 pressure increased for a reform of the Paris theatre world. Chénier, as a representative of the dramatists, submitted a report lamenting the decline in the quality of dramatic productions since 1791 and seeking major changes in the decree of January 1791 which he and his fellow playwrights had welcomed so warmly at the time, or even its repeal. The government was reluctant to tamper with the 1791 decree, although the Minister, François Lamarque, did point out that if further controls were put on the theatres this might make for improved public order, since some of the theatres were notorious for encouraging factions opposed to the government. The Council of the Five Hundred made a recommendation placing all theatres under the protection of the Directory but at the same time restricting their number to six: the Opéra, for tragedy and lyric drama; the Favart, for poetic comedy and vaudeville; the Odéon, for conventional comedy and tragedy; the République, to offer the spur of competition to the Odéon; and two new theatres to act as drama schools. This proposal was turned down by the Council of Ancients on 6 June. Five days earlier, the Odéon had closed.

9 August 1798 saw the premiere of Pigault-Lebrun's *Les Rivaux d'eux-mêmes* at the Théâtre de la Cité. A chapter will be devoted to this play later on, as an example of the theatre of the Directory, with the return from political considerations to frivolity and a certain ostentatious immoralism, at a time when the Consulate and the First Empire were, so to speak, waiting in the wings.

Now that Sageret was running the only theatre of the Comédie-Française tradition still open in Paris, the Feydeau, he sought to expand his interests. He rented the empty République, did it up completely and reopened it on 5 September with a performance of Molière's *Le Misanthrope*. He then did a deal with Le Page and Le Clerc and took out a three-year lease on the Odéon as well, installing an operatic troupe there on 16 September, leaving his comic and tragic actors at the République. This left the Feydeau empty: Sageret refurbished it and reopened it on 22 October under the name of Théâtre-Lyrique de la rue Feydeau, presenting musical productions only. He now was the owner of a very considerable theatrical empire covering all the activities carried out by the privileged theatres prior to 1789. It was not long, however, before things began to go wrong. The returns were inadequate to keep the empire going and Sageret imposed cuts in his actors' wages. Talma left for Bordeaux. Others soon left too. Sageret gave up the Odéon and the République closed on 24 January 1799 after a string of unsuccessful productions. The empire had collapsed.

A number of actors who had left Sageret reopened the Odéon in December 1798, and put on *Misanthropie et repentir*, an adaptation from the German of August von Kotzebue by the actress Mlle Molé, which was a great success, appealing to the sentimental in a way not dissimilar to the way in which the *drames* produced by the followers of Diderot (himself having much in common with the German Lessing) had appealed. However, in February 1799 the Directory revoked the thirty-year concession for the Odéon given to

Dorfeuille and took that theatre over themselves. In March the Odéon was burned down. Both Sageret and Le Page found themselves in custody for a while, suspected of complicity in the fire. There was now no theatre left representing the tradition of the Comédie-Française. In March a decree was passed opening the Opéra on non-performance days to the actors from the Odéon, as a temporary home. They also performed from time to time at the Favart: as the *Courrier des spectacles* for 24 floréal an VII (13 May 1799) put it, 'Les acteurs de l'Odéon, toujours errant et sans salle où ils puissent se fixer, jouent partout où ils peuvent'[44] ('The actors from the Odéon, still wandering without a theatre in which they can establish themselves, are performing anywhere they can').

The Minister of the Interior, the dramatist Neufchâteau, realized that reform was needed, and the rumour was soon abroad that he planned to restore the Comédie-Française, a rumour which inevitably revived old rivalries and controversies. Playwrights took the view that a return to the old Comédie-Française monopoly would mean that all they had fought for over the years in respect of their property rights over their work had been in vain. They therefore sought a second national theatre before Neufchâteau had succeeded in establishing the first. A petition to this end was organized by Beaumarchais, who had returned to France in July 1796, and signed by Laya, Collin d'Harleville, Ducis, Legouvé, Arnault, Demoustier, Picard and others. The petition did not succeed, and Neufchâteau proceeded with arrangements to have the République refurbished as a home for the reunited Comédie. The actors decided to forget old differences and the theatre reopened on 31 May 1799, with Talma in Corneille's *Le Cid* and Grandménil, Dugazon and Mlle Mars in Molière's *L'Ecole des maris*. The clock had been put back: all the surviving players from the old Comédie-Française were together again, along with a number of players who had started at the République or at the Feydeau.[45]

In June 1799 the Opéra decided to perform Hoffmann and Méhul's opera *Adrien*. This work had been banned in 1792 and it ran into trouble again in 1799. It was seen by the Directory as alluding to Bonaparte's ambitions and was banned after four performances. Three months later Bonaparte was to come to power.[46]

After the *coup d'état* of 18 brumaire an VIII (9 November 1799) which put an end to the Directory and established the Consulate, the new regime soon demonstrated that it was determined to avoid politically partisan plays of any complexion. Within a matter of days of the coup, on 24 brumaire, Fouché, the Minister of Police, was writing to the Favart in the following terms about a vaudeville by C.-A. Sewrin, *Les Mariniers de Saint-Cloud*, written in praise of the new regime:

> La révolution du 18 brumaire, citoyens, ne ressemble à aucune de celles qui l'ont précédée: elle n'aura point de réaction; c'est la résolution du gouvernement. Si les factions persécutent lorsqu'elles obtiennent l'une sur l'autre quelque léger avantage, la République, lorsqu'elle les écrase toutes, triomphe avec générosité. Une pièce intitulée *Les Mariniers de Saint-Cloud* a été jouée sur votre théâtre: l'intention en est louable sans doute, mais trop de détails rappellent amèrement d'anciens souvenirs qu'il faut effacer. . . j'augure assez bien de votre patriotisme pour croire que vous ferez, sans que je vous en donne l'ordre, le sacrifice de votre pièce, puisque la tranquillité publique vous l'impose.[47]

Citizens, the revolution of 18 brumaire is unlike any of those which preceded it: the government is determined that there shall be no reaction against it. If, every time one faction gains a slight advantage over the others it goes in for persecution, the Republic, in crushing them all, triumphs to the advantage of all.

A play entitled *Les Mariniers de Saint-Cloud* has been performed on your stage: its intention is no doubt praiseworthy, but too many of its details revive bitter old memories which must be obliterated . . . I have a sufficiently high opinion of your patriotism to believe that you will sacrifice your play without my needing to issue an order to that effect, since the preservation of public tranquillity requires it.

Napoleon Bonaparte proceeded quite quickly to move in the direction of establishing a theatre structure in Paris remarkably like that of the *Ancien Régime*. On 11 August 1800 the Comédie was officially given governmental protection and guaranteed a theatre. In September 1801 the Feydeau and the Favart came together and the combined enterprise was given a government subsidy in October, when it too was taken under government protection and given the name Théâtre National de l'Opéra-Comique. Attempts were made to revive the old tradition of the Comédie-Italienne: Mlle Montansier was given a subsidy to attempt to establish such a company in 1801. In July 1802 the Comédie was given a permanent government subsidy and in the following month, after Napoleon had been declared Consul for life, showed its gratitude by reserving a permanent seat for the First Consul. The Opéra came under the protection of the Consulate in November 1802 and was granted a permanent subsidy in its turn in January of the following year. Late in 1803 a Constitution was drafted for the Comédie: this formed the basis of the company's definitive Constitution, which dates from 1812.

Spring 1804 saw the election of Napoleon as hereditary Emperor. The Comédie changed its name to Théâtre de l'Empereur and had a subsidiary company, the Théâtre de l'Impératrice, established in the Odéon. In June 1806 it was decreed that no new theatres be established without special authorization, that all plays must be submitted to a censor, and that the repertories of the Opéra, the Comédie and the Opéra-Comique be reserved for those theatres alone. It was also decreed that it was a matter for the Minister of the Interior to decide what kind of performances should be permitted at all the other theatres. On 25 April 1807 Jean-Baptiste Champagny, the Minister of the Interior, issued a regulation clarifying the earlier decree.

The Théâtre de l'Empereur was confirmed in its supreme position as, in effect, the reincarnation of the monopolistic Comédie-Française of pre-Revolutionary days. Its subsidiary, the Théâtre de l'Impératrice was to concentrate on comedy alone and, in addition to plays written specially, was entitled to perform plays from the Comédie-Italienne repertory. The Opéra (the Académie Impériale de Musique) was to present serious opera and ballet and its repertory consisted of all such works to have appeared since its foundation in the seventeenth century. The Théâtre de l'Opéra-Comique was to draw its repertory from all works composed of a mixture of dialogue and song performed at the Opéra-Comique before and after its merger with the Comédie-Italienne.

In addition to these major theatres the Minister recognized, as secondary houses, the Théâtre du Vaudeville, which was permitted to perform only short plays with songs and parodies; the Théâtre des Variétés, in the Boulevard Montmartre, which was confined to popular short plays of the *grivois* or *poissard* type, with or without songs; the Théâtre de la Porte Saint-Martin, which was to concentrate on melodrama and spectacular plays; the Théâtre de la Gaîté, which was to stick to the tradition of pantomime, Harlequinades and farces established by its founder Nicolet, and the Théâtre des Variétés-Etrangères, which was to confine itself to plays translated from foreign languages. Other minor theatres were merely tolerated. A further decree of 29 July 1807 set the maximum number of theatres permitted in Paris at eight, including the four major ones. Of the minor ones, only the Vaudeville, the Variétés, the Gaîté and the Ambigu-Comique (to work in the areas earlier defined for the Porte Saint-Martin and the Gaîté) were to be permitted. The rest were to close by 15 August. The Porte Saint-Martin was to go, as was the Variétés-Etrangères and, by Carlson's reckoning, seven others, the Troubadours, the Jeunes-Artistes, the Marais, the Cité, the Jeunes-Elèves, the Jeunes-Comédiens and the Sans-Prétention, all that was left of the plethora of theatres which had sprung up during the Revolutionary years.[48] With the four main theatres heavily subsidized and protected by the government, and with the four minor theatres permitted by law confined to specific minor genres, the similarity between the old absolute monarchy and the new imperial order in the domain of the theatre was very striking indeed.

PART TWO

SEVEN PLAYS

3

A SCHOOL FOR KINGS

Marie-Joseph Chénier's tragedy, *Charles IX ou la Saint-Barthélemy*, was first performed at the Théâtre de la Nation, as the Comédie-Française had by then come to be called, on 4 November 1789. These were, of course, heady days: it was when the theatres re-opened on 21 July after the disturbances which had included the storming of the Bastille that the Comédie-Française had seen fit to change its name, although the members of the company (many of whom were rather more sympathetic to the old order than to the embryonic new one) continued to call themselves 'Comédiens-Français ordinaires du roi'. The company thought it politic, however, on 23 July, to stage performances of Charles Collé's *Partie de chasse de Henri IV*, dating from 1764 in its final version, and Pierre de Belloy's *Gaston et Bayard*, dating from 1777, in honour of the newly created National Guard. These two plays were amongst the nearest in the existing repertory to justifying the term 'national' or even 'nationalist' theatre. By the time of the première of Chénier's play, with which he was proudly to claim to have established 'la tragédie nationale' on the French stage,[1] dramatic events had taken place, in consequence of which French society was never to be the same again.

August 4-11 had seen the decree which, in its first Article, claimed to overthrow feudalism, although in fact, after the excitement of the night of 4 August, the Assembly managed in the final version of the decree to salvage many property rights and to insist on the principle of compensation. 27 August had seen the promulgation of the Declaration of the Rights of Man and the Citizen, which had announced amongst other things that men are born free and equal in rights (Art. I), that all sovereignty resides in the Nation and that no one may exercise authority which does not emanate directly from the Nation (Art. III). On 29 September Thouret had submitted to the Assembly a proposal which was to lead to radical reforms in French local government, many of which were to prove long-lasting, including the division of the country into Departments. 5-6 October had seen the march on Versailles by a mob, largely composed of women, which led to Louis XVI agreeing to move with the royal family to Paris. They were never to return to Versailles. On 2 November the Assembly approved a Bill for the sale of Church assets. And so, Chénier's play, which was very quickly re-entitled *Charles IX ou l'Ecole des rois* (according to Chénier himself, in consequence of a certain merchant by the name of Maumené calling out during the first performance, 'Cette pièce devrait s'appeler L'ECOLE DES ROIS'),[2] may well seem to be very much in harmony with the spirit of those days in late 1789, when there were some grounds for hoping that the Revolution might move fairly quickly to a settled constitutional monarchy of liberal inclination.

The fact of the matter is that *Charles IX* was not in essence the product of those early Revolutionary days, although Chénier did seize the opportunity to work in some last-minute topical references immediately before its first performance. In fact, the play antedates the Revolution quite comfortably. Chénier began it in 1786 and had a complete five-act play by 1788: it was unanimously accepted by the Comédiens-Français on 2 September of that year. Chénier however was no doubt right to boast, 'J'ai conçu, j'ai exécuté avant la Révolution une tragédie que la Révolution seule pouvait faire représenter' ('I conceived, I created before the Revolution a tragedy which only the Revolution could bring to the stage'). He went on,

> Les gens que cette Révolution contrarie, et qui, dans le moment où j'écris, commencent à lever la tête avec une audace qui n'est que ridicule, n'ont pas manqué de trouver atroce que la Saint-Barthélemy fût offerte aux yeux du peuple français; mais Voltaire, dont l'autorité est aussi grande que la leur est misérable, Voltaire, après avoir crayonné dans sa *Henriade* ce grand et terrible sujet, prédit des temps heureux où il sera transporté sur la scène nationale.[3]

Those people who are upset by this Revolution and who, as I

write, are beginning to raise their heads with an audacity which is nothing other than ridiculous, did not fail to find it appalling that the St Bartholomew's Day Massacre should be shown to the French people; but Voltaire, whose authority is as great as that of those people is contemptible, Voltaire, after drawing a picture of that great and terrible subject in his *Henriade*, predicted happier days when it would be shown on the national stage.

Indeed, Jean-Baptiste Suard, the censor, prohibited the Comédie Française from performing Chénier's play.

It is not difficult to understand Suard's point of view. The monarchy was not, even in 1788, in the healthiest of conditions, and a play which took as its plot the story of the St Bartholomew's Day Massacre of Protestants in 1572 was not likely to strengthen its position. Even in November 1789, when the play was finally performed, it is questionable whether it should have been, in the interests of public order. Jean-Sylvain Bailly, the mayor of Paris, to whom appeal was made on that later occasion, certainly seems to have felt this, but no doubt considered that the public clamour which had been stirred up made it impossible for him to do anything but to allow the production to go ahead.

When Chénier sought to hide behind the precedent of the description of the St Bartholomew's Day Massacre offered by Voltaire in *La Henriade* he was being, to say the least of it, somewhat disingenuous. Jean Gaulmier puts it as follows:

. . . il oubliait qu'une 'représentation' exerce sur le public une influence d'une autre nature et plus brutale qu'un récit inerte. . . . Il oubliait surtout que l'habile Voltaire avait eu soin de placer le récit du massacre dans la bouche de Henri de Navarre: prodigieuse astuce de faire condamner Charles IX par le futur Henri IV, de sorte que les Bourbons puissent se sentir innocents du crime des Valois. Chénier . . . ignore d'aussi subtiles précautions.[4]

. . . he forgot that a performance exerts over the public an influence different in nature from, and more violent than that exerted by a passive narrative. . . . Above all he forgot that the skilful Voltaire had taken care to put the account of the Massacre into the mouth of Henri of Navarre: it was remarkably cunning to have Charles IX condemned by the future Henri IV, so that the Bourbons could feel themselves innocent of the Valois crime. For Chénier . . . there are no such subtle precautions.

In fact, Chénier was well aware how potent theatre can be as a weapon of propaganda. In his *Discours préliminaire* to *Charles IX* he wrote,

> Un livre, quelque bon qu'il soit, ne saurait agir sur l'esprit public d'une manière aussi prompte, aussi vigoureuse qu'une belle pièce de théâtre. . . . Toutes nos idées viennent de nos sens; mais l'homme isolé n'est ému que médiocrement: les hommes rassemblés reçoivent des impressions fortes et durables. Personne, chez les modernes, n'a si bien conçu que M. de Voltaire cette électricité du théâtre.[5]

A book, no matter how good it may be, could not hope to affect the public mind as quickly or as strongly as a fine play. . . . All our ideas come through our senses; but the solitary man is only moderately moved: men in a crowd receive strong and lasting impressions. No one amongst modern writers has so fully appreciated this electricity of the theatre as M. de Voltaire.

Charles IX was not Chénier's first play for the Comédie-Française. Probably helped by the friendship of Palissot, whom he met in his mother's salon, he had succeeded in having a heroic comedy, *Edgard roi d'Angleterre ou le Page supposé* and a tragedy, *Azémire*, produced by that theatre (1785-86). Both were failures.[6] When Suard banned *Charles IX* Chénier embarked upon a campaign, much as Beaumarchais had done in the case of *Le Mariage de Figaro*, of readings of his play in various salons. This he combined with use of the published word, such as his pamphlet on censorship, *De la liberté du théâtre en France*, which appeared in June 1789 and in which he 'plugged' his own play.[7] Certain Revolutionary leaders saw advantages in having *Charles IX* performed and on 19 August a claque including Danton, at the second night of Fontanelle's play attacking the monastic system, *Ericie*, demanded that Chénier's play be performed. The political events of mid-July gave control of the Paris theatres to Bailly, the mayor, who was reluctant to bow to the pressures which were being put upon him to sanction such a performance, no doubt seeing it as a political move by a group less interested in drama for its own sake than in stirring up the feelings of the Parisian mob. He delayed a decision but finally acceded.

Opinion within the company was divided over the play. Many of the Comédiens were less than enamoured of recent political developments, others were in favour of them. It seems that E.-F. Saint-Fal declined to play the part of Charles IX, seeing it as a defamation of the monarchy. The part went instead to a young actor who had never played a leading role at the Comédie-Française but who was to become one of the greatest actors of the French stage, famous for his realistic approach to all aspects of his craft – François-Joseph Talma. He, like Chénier himself, was to become famous overnight as a result of *Charles IX*. When Talma left the company to become a member of the new Théâtre Français in the rue de Richelieu in 1791, the play went with him. It undoubtedly is one of the most significant plays of the period, but it is not insignificant that it has not been performed since the early years of the Revolution. H.C. Ault argues that *Charles IX* 'can now only be regarded as a piece of propaganda, propaganda that was undeniably effective, but also transient. It was out of date within two years'.[8] There is truth in this judgment, but to leave it at that would be unduly dismissive.

As is often the case in such situations, the censorship difficulties experienced by *Charles IX*, skilfully exploited by Chénier himself, proved to be the best kind of publicity, and there was a packed house for the opening night of the play. Many of the leading figures of the National Assembly, including Mirabeau, Danton, and Desmoulins were present. Antoine Arnault reports in his account of the event that Danton was heard to remark, 'Si Figaro a tué la noblesse, Charles IX tuera la royauté'[9] ('If Figaro killed off the nobility, Charles IX will kill off the monarchy'). The controversy continued. Opposed to those who were ardent supporters of the play – and its success can now be seen to have been of rather more political or social than of literary or theatrical significance – were others, some of whom had ideological reasons for opposing it but some of whom were genuinely concerned about the effects which it might have on law and order. Not all the play's opponents were aristocrats of reactionary inclination. Beaumarchais wrote to the Sociétaires of the company on 9 November 1789 that, although *Charles IX* was a play of some merit and had been splendidly produced, en me recherchant sur sa moralité, je l'ai trouvée plus que douteuse. En ce moment de licence effrénée où le peuple a beaucoup moins besoin d'être excité que contenu, ces barbares excès, à quelque parti qu'on les prête, me semblent dangereux à présenter au peuple, et propres à justifier les siens à ses yeux.

when I came to consider its morality, I found it more than suspect. In these days of unbridled licence, when the people are much less in need of being stirred up than of being restrained, these scenes of barbaric excess, no matter to what party one attributes them, seem to me to be dangerous things to offer them, which they are likely to see as justifying their own barbarities.

He went on,

Et puis, quel instant, mes amis, que celui où le roi et sa famille viennent résider à Paris pour faire allusion aux complots qui peuvent les y avoir conduits. Quel instant pour prêter au clergé, dans la personne d'un cardinal, un crime qu'il n'a pas commis (celui de bénir les poignards des assassins des protestants); quel instant, dis-je, que celui où, dépouillé de tous ses biens, le clergé ne doit pas être en proie à la malveillance publique, puisqu'il sauve l'Etat en le servant de ses richesses!

Moreover, what a moment to pick, my friends, but the moment when the King and his family have come to live in Paris, to refer to the intrigues which may have brought them here. What a moment to pick to attribute to the clergy, in the person of a Cardinal, a crime of which they are innocent (that of blessing the daggers of the murderers of the Protestants); what a moment to pick, I say, but the moment when, stripped of their property, the clergy should not be prey to public malevolence, since they are coming to the salvation of the State by the use of their riches.

A little further on in the same letter he wrote,

La pièce de *Charles IX* m'a fait mal . . . et les esprits ardents, Messieurs, n'ont pas besoin de tels modèles! Quel délassement de la scène d'un boulanger innocent, pendu, décapité, traîné dans les rues par le peuple il n'y a huit jours,[10] et qui peut se renouveler, que de nous montrer au théâtre Coligny ainsi massacré, décapité, traîné par ordre de la cour!

Nous avons plus besoin d'être consolés par le tableau des vertus de nos ancêtres qu'effrayés par celui de nos vices et de nos crimes.

The play *Charles IX* distressed me . . . and hotheads, Gentlemen, need no such models! What relaxation after the sight of an innocent baker being hanged, decapitated and dragged through the streets by the people less than a week ago, a sight which may well be repeated, to be shown on stage Coligny being similarly slaughtered, decapitated and dragged through the streets by order of the Court!

We have more need of being consoled by the depiction of our ancestors' virtues than of being terrified by the depiction of our vices and our crimes.

It is not difficult to transpose this argument into modern terms (what should be permitted on the television screen), and if one detects in it the voice of the property-owning middle class, this is not surprising: the Declaration of the Rights of Man of 27 August 1789 was at pains to defend the concept of property (Article II), as were the Constitution of 1791 (Title I), Robespierre's Declaration of Rights of 24 April 1793 (Articles VII, VIII, IX, X), the Constitution of 1793 (Article II) and the Constitution of 1795 (Article I under Rights).

Let us look more closely at the play which caused such a furore. Chénier himself published two versions of *Charles IX*, one in February 1790 and one in An VII of the Republic (1798-99). Chénier had indulged in some fairly considerable rewriting but, as Jacques Truchet says, 'pour des raisons littéraires uniquement: il n'avait rien changé au contenu idéologique'.[11] Certain impressions of the first edition accompanied the text with a considerable number of justificatory pieces by Chénier, reference to some of which will be made in what follows. Charles IX was, as has already been mentioned, played by Talma; Catherine de Médicis, his mother, by Mme Vestris; Henri de Navarre by Saint-Fal; the Cardinal de Lorraine by Saint-Prix; Coligny by Naudet; l'Hôpital by Vanhove. The receipts at the first performance were 5,018 francs; even at the twenty-fourth performance they were still as high as 4,221 francs. The twenty-fifth performance, which was put on for the benefit of the poor, did much less well, largely because only a few hours' notice was given. The next performance, the twenty-sixth did well again, bringing in 4,660 francs. Chénier subsequently withdrew his play from the company, for fear of losing ownership of it, and it was little performed in 1790. When on 13 January 1791 a new law was passed preserving authors' rights, he allowed the play to be acted by Talma's new company at the rue de Richelieu theatre.[12]

In form, there is nothing terribly revolutionary about *Charles IX*. It is a five-act tragedy in verse. True, as a tragedy it is much closer to what Voltaire offered under that label than to what was offered either by Corneille or Racine in the hey-day of French neo-Classicism and monarchical absolutism. For a critic such as H.C. Ault, for whom 'Voltaire's influence was on the whole disastrous to tragedy' and who holds Chénier to be under a 'blind misconception of the very meaning of Tragedy',[13] that is to say everything. Dramatic genres do, of course, change and evolve, and it may well be that some forms of evolution amount to degeneration. Voltaire, however, for all the changes he made in traditional forms, nevertheless remained in many ways essentially classical in his tastes and considered the epic poem and the tragedy to be at the pinnacle of literary genres. His contemporaries and immediate successors hailed him above all because, they believed, he had succeeded in embellishing those two forms. For all that had been done by writers such as Diderot to produce a new dramatic genre in the form of the prose *drame*, the prestige of tragedy remained high. It no doubt was a dying genre, and no doubt its lingering demise was not unrelated to changes in social attitudes and forms which were slowly (and more recently, in Chénier's day, rather more quickly) taking place, but there can be no doubt that both Voltaire and Chénier continued to revere the genre, and thought that tragedy was indeed what they were writing. Chénier's debt to Voltaire was a conscious one, and one which he readily and publicly acknowledged.

Voltaire had introduced a number of changes into French tragedy. Feeling dissatisfaction with the traditional limitations on the choice of plot (classical history and mythology), he had introduced plots from French history as well as plots from more exotic sources. *Zaïre* (1732) is set in the time of St Louis and *Mahomet* (1741) deals with the life of the prophet: both are eloquent pleas for religious tolerance and attacks on fanaticism: one of the major facts about Voltaire's use of the tragic form is that he consistently used it as a vehicle for *philosophe* propaganda, mostly, as Chénier himself pointed out, not of a specifically political kind.[14] He attempted to bring greater flexibility into tragedy as he had inherited it from the seventeenth century, not only in terms of plot but also in terms of the strict observance of the unities, particularly of time and place.

Chénier's *Charles IX* strictly observes the unity of place (the action all takes place in the Louvre) and unity of time (Acts I-IV take place on 23 August 1572, Act V on 24 August) and there can be no criticism of the play in terms of its observance of unity of action. It is classical too in its use of persons in very high places as its characters. It is true that, after the manner of Voltaire rather than the manner of the seventeenth-century tragic playwrights, these characters are drawn from French history. It is also true that Chénier has tinkered with historical facts: at the time of the St Bartholomew's Day Massacre the Cardinal de Lorraine was in Rome and not in Paris, and Michel de l'Hôpital had not been a minister for four years. Chénier candidly admits these changes of historical fact,[15] and it is certainly true that both Corneille and Racine permitted themselves more radical changes in their source material than these. Chénier made much of the fact that he had done away with the confidants of neo-classical tragedy: 'J'ai banni de ma pièce ces confidents froids et parasites qui n'entrent jamais dans l'action et qui ne semblent admis sur la scène que pour écouter tout ce qu'on veut dire, et pour approuver tout ce qu'on veut faire'[16] ('I have banished from my play those cold, parasitical confidants who never become involved in the action and who seem to be allowed on stage only to listen to everything that [the principal characters] wish to say and to approve of everything they wish to do'). On the other hand, in the first few performances of *Charles IX* Henri de Navarre in the best classical tradition, had a dream of the horrors to come: this was subsequently changed to an anecdote involving a game of dice (see III. i. 40-50).

Jacques Truchet is surely right when he suggests that Chénier had no desire to 'democratize' the form of tragedy (although, like Voltaire, he certainly wished to express new ideas through the old forms). The formal differences which do exist in *Charles IX* by comparison with seventeenth-century French tragedy are to be explained in terms of developments which had been slowly taking place throughout the eighteenth century, and which point the way towards Romantic drama. Thus, there are elements which recall Racine (for example the relationship between Charles IX and his mother Catherine de Médicis does to some extent recall that between Agrippine and Néron in *Britannicus*) and Voltaire (much of the anti-clericalism, for instance), whilst other elements look forward to Romantics such as Victor Hugo (perhaps especially the end of Act II and the end of Act IV).[17]

Chénier's justification of his play was, in part, that Greek theatre had been full of praise of Greece and Greek heroes, sometimes even whilst they were still alive.[18] Why should not French theatre, perhaps especially in the dramatic days of the Revolution, do the same thing? He was also determined that tragedy should be freed of the noxious influence associated with what he saw as the trivial aristocratic *galanterie* of writers such as La Calprenède and Mlle de Scudéry which he sees as the scourge not only of the theatre but of the arts in general.[19] He was consciously nationalistic in his approach: after attacking 'les dégoûtantes absurdités du théâtre anglais' ('the disgusting absurdities of English drama' (he no doubt had the Shakespearean mixture of tragic and comic elements in mind here)) and 'les niaiseries burlesques du théâtre allemand' ('the ludicrous silliness of German drama'), he goes on to offer a sort of manifesto:

> Il ne m'appartient pas de juger du mérite de la tragédie de *Charles IX*; et peut-être prouvera-t-elle que mes talents pour exécuter sont très-inférieurs à mes intentions; mais du moins la cour de Charles IX y est peinte de ses véritables couleurs; il n'y a pas une scène dans la pièce qui n'inspire l'horreur du fanatisme, des guerres civiles, du parjure et de l'adulation cruelle et intéressée. La vertu y est exaltée, le crime puni par le mépris et par les remords, la cause du peuple et des lois défendue sans cesse contre les courtisans et la tyrannie. J'ose donc affirmer que c'est la seule tragédie vraiment nationale qui ait encore paru en France; qu'aucune autre pièce de théâtre n'est aussi fortement morale; et, par une conséquence nécessaire de ces deux propositions incontestables, j'ose affirmer qu'il faut être ennnemi de la raison pour craindre la représentation d'une pareille pièce.[20]

It is not my place to evaluate the quality of the tragedy, *Charles IX*; and perhaps the play will demonstrate that my competence in practice is markedly inferior to my intentions; but at least the Court of Charles IX is depicted in its true colours; there is not a single scene in the play which does not inspire a horror of fanaticism, of civil war, of perjury and unfeeling, self-interested adulation. Virtue is exalted, crime is punished by contempt and remorse, the cause of the people and of legality is ceaselessly defended against the courtiers and against tyranny. I therefore make bold to claim that it is the only truly national tragedy thus far to have appeared in France; that no other play is as strikingly moral; and, as an inevitable consequence of these two undeniable propositions, I make bold to claim that, to fear the public performance of such a play, one has to be an enemy of reason.

This view of tragedy, with its mixed stress on a kind of realism and on a brand of moralizing which reveals not only that Voltaire has travelled before Chénier, but that Denis Diderot with his special ideas on drama has been along this road as well, is not exactly the traditional view of tragedy, of course. H.C. Ault remarks, in tones approaching those of despair, 'The sole desiderata for the writing of great Tragedy would seem to be the intention to inculcate virtue and the desire to praise the French nation.'[21] Diderot had written in his *De la Poésie dramatique* that 'tout peuple a des préjugés à détruire, des vices à poursuivre, et a besoin de spectacles, mais qui lui sont propres'[22] ('Every people has prejudices to destroy and vices to prosecute and has need of plays, but plays which are appropriate to that people'), and such was the function of the *drame*, in his view, for his contemporaries.

Chénier is essentially saying the same thing as Diderot, but in terms of the needs of the next generation along. This is the burden of works such as the *Epître dédicatoire à la Nation française*, which opens with the words, 'Français, mes concitoyens, acceptez l'hommage de cette tragédie patriotique. Je dédie l'ouvrage d'un homme libre à une nation devenue libre'[23] ('Frenchmen, my fellow citizens, accept the tribute of this patriotic tragedy. I dedicate the work of a free man to a nation which has become free') and in which he addresses the next generation as follows:

Et vous, enfants, nation future, espérance de la patrie et d'un siècle qui n'est pas encore, vous ne serez pas les hommes des anciens préjugés et de l'ancien esclavage: vous serez les hommes de la liberté nouvelle. C'est à vous surtout que mes écrits conviennent.[24]

And you, the children, the future nation, the hope of the *patrie* and of a century yet to begin, you will not be the men of the old prejudices and the old bondage: you will be the men of the new liberty. It is to you above all that my writings are suited.

The same attitude is also the burden of the *Discours préliminaire*. These are the days of the Enlightenment: Voltaire did not create 'l'esprit philosophique' in France, but 'il sut l'appliquer à tous les genres d'ouvrages littéraires; il le mit à la portée de toutes les classes de la société; il en fit, pour ainsi dire, la monnaie courante'[25] ('He was able to apply it to all kinds of literary works; he placed it within the grasp of all the classes of society; he made it, so to speak, common currency').

What Chénier is offering, then, is certainly not tragedy as it was understood in seventeenth-century France (although there was, despite all the theorizing, no unanimity as to what constituted tragedy in the age of Corneille and Racine), but it was a perfectly coherent view of tragedy and one calculated to appeal at a time when the demythologizing of the old institutions of Church and State was advancing apace. One of the principal weaknesses of *Charles IX* as a tragedy is no doubt that it offers a rather simplistic division of its characters into black and white, good and bad, after the manner of nineteenth-century melodrama or of twentieth-century Western films. And yet stylization of this kind can have a powerful impact, and can linger long in the memory of the members of an audience. This certainly seems to have been the case with Chénier's play which, whatever else may be said of it, was resolutely *engagé*, committed to social change.

First of all, it is important to remember that *Charles IX* had its first performance in the early days of the Revolutionary period. Much more extreme attitudes were later to be expressed (as we shall see) and much more extreme actions were to be taken, but in late 1789 it was still possible to be a revolutionary and a monarchist, and the Jacobin Club was still what its proper title proclaimed it to be, the Society of the Friends of the Constitution, and many of its members were indeed genuine constitutional monarchists. The Constitution which was worked out gradually over the period from 1789 to 1791 and (however reluctantly) accepted by Louis XVI on 13 September 1791 was, of course, a monarchical Constitution, though one which made it clear in the words of Article III of the Declaration of the Rights of Man, which was affixed to the Constitution as a preamble, that sovereignty resided in the nation (and not in the king by divine right). Thus it was that Chénier could preface his play with a verse epistle to the King which contains the following lines:

> Monarque des Français, chef d'un peuple fidèle
> Qui va des nations devenir le modèle,
>
> . . .
>
> Prête à la vérité ton auguste soutien,
> Et, las des courtisans, écoute un citoyen.
>
> . . .
>
> C'est au peuple, en effet, que tu dois ta splendeur,
> Et sa grandeur peut seule affermir ta grandeur.[26]

King of the French, head of a faithful people who are going to become the model for other nations . . ., lend your support to Truth and, weary of courtiers, listen to a citizen. It is to the people, indeed, that you owe your splendour, and it is the greatness of the people alone that can consolidate your greatness.

Chénier goes on in his poem to state that although in his tragedy he has depicted a king who murdered his subjects, it is his earnest wish to write, at the earliest opportunity, of a king who (along with a beloved minister whose passion in life is justice) has given back to the people rights which were usurped from them in the distant past, and of an august Assembly in which the different Estates have abandoned unjust privileges, and so on, and so on. Hopes are high that something approaching Utopia is just around the corner. Let us consider some of the implications which the audiences of the Revolutionary years were likely to derive from *Charles IX*.

The first point to be made here is that, as Jacques Truchet points out,[27] if one simply considers the basic political points being made in the play, there is not much that cannot be found earlier in plays such as De Belloy's *Le Siège de Calais* (1765) or Charles Collé's *La Partie de chasse de Henri IV* (first performed at the Comédie-Française in 1774, after the death of Louis XV). The three plays have in common criticism of aristocratic courtiers for leading the monarch astray, praise of good ministers (l'Hôpital in Chénier's play was equated with Necker, who had been responsible for doubling the representation of the Third Estate at the Estates

General, been dismissed by Louis XVI on 11 July 1789 and recalled immediately after the fall of the Bastille, just as, earlier, Sully in Collé's play had been identified with Turgot, the great reforming Finance Minister dismissed in 1776) and the idea that the king derives his power from the people, whose well-being should be his primary concern. The future Henri IV, of course, appears (as Henri de Navarre) in *Charles IX*. Chénier must have known that he was on to a good thing in this respect, just as Collé had done, as is clearly demonstrated by the opening words of the latter's *avertissement* to *La Partie de chasse*:

> Les noms de Henri IV et de Sully sont si chers à la nation qu'un auteur peut presque se flatter de la réussite d'un ouvrage dans lequel il a le bonheur de rappeler la mémoire adorée de ce grand roi et de ce digne ministre.[28]

> The names of Henri IV and Sully are so dear to the nation that an author can almost rest assured of the success of a work in which he has the good fortune to recall the revered memory of that great King and that worthy Minister.

There was, however, a considerable difference of tone and implication between Chénier's play and the two earlier ones. Like Chénier, De Belloy before him had claimed to have produced the first national tragedy in the history of French theatre,[29] but his *Le Siège de Calais* was dedicated to the King, whereas *Charles IX* (as we have seen) is dedicated to the nation. *Le Siège de Calais* was intended to boost French morale after the unhappy outcome of the Seven Years' War (De Belloy's declared aim was that members of his audience should be led to exclaim, 'Je viens de voir un héros français, je puis être héros comme lui'[30] ('I have just seen a French hero, and I can be a hero like him'). Louis XV gave De Belloy a pension on the strength of it. *La Partie de chasse* had celebrated another French hero, Henri IV. *Charles IX*, on the other hand, attacked one of the most infamous crimes of the French monarchy and invited comparisons between the Court which had urged Charles on to this crime and the Court of Louis XVI who, like Charles, was felt to be lazy, weak-willed, under the evil influence of a woman and inaccessible to his subjects. Hope lay in the fact that he had recently been brought to Paris, where the influence of reactionary courtiers over him should be less strong than had been the case out at Versailles.

Here, then, is one of the genuine marks of originality of Chénier's play. As Truchet observes, if one seeks the first national tragedy on the French stage, there are a number of possible candidates for the title. In so far as henceforth the term 'national' comes to mean 'revolutionary', however, *Charles IX* deserves the title which its author claims for it.[31]

The atmosphere of treachery which pervades the Court is established immediately. Coligny remarks to Henri de Navarre,

> Parmi les courtisans je viens sans confiance;
> De leur génie affreux j'ai trop l'expérience. . .

> (I.i.5-6)

It is without any sense of security that I venture among the members of the Court. I have too much experience of their talent for the frightful.

Coligny still has hopes of the King, however. When he goes on to make it clear that it is the Machiavellian influence of his mother, Catherine de Médicis, which is responsible for the corrupt nature of the royal Court, not only does this invite Chénier's audience to draw a parallel with the foreign female influence at the Court of Louis XVI in the shape of the Austrian Marie-Antoinette but it also gives expression to the growing anti-clericalism of the Revolutionary years which found expression in decisions to sell Church assets (2 November and 20 December 1789), the abolition of the contemplative religious orders and the prohibition of monastic vows (13 February 1790), the civil constitution of the clergy (12 July 1790), and the clerical oath (27 November 1790) by which members of the clergy were required to swear to be faithful to the nation, the law and the king and to accept all decrees of the National Assembly under pain of the full rigour of the law. This was to culminate, after the execution of Louis XVI, in a thorough-going campaign of dechristianization in the latter part of 1793.

It is in the following terms that Coligny describes the Court of Charles IX:

> Si Médicis, fidèle aux mœurs de ses ancêtres,
> Rassemble auprès du roi des flatteurs et des prêtres,
> Si d'une cour perfide il est environné,
> Si de nos ennemis le souffle empoisonné
> Voulut dès le berceau corrompre son enfance,

Je crois, j'aime à penser que, pour notre défense,
Son cœur mieux averti lui parlera toujours.

(I.i.77-83)

If [Catherine de] Médicis, true to the morals of her ancestors, assembles flatterers and priests around the king, if he is surrounded by a perfidious Court, if the poisonous breath of our enemies sought to corrupt his childhood from the cradle on, I nevertheless believe, I like to think, that his more enlightened heart will always speak to him in our defence.

Contrasted with this, in the best late eighteenth-century manner which no doubt owes something to the lucubrations of Jean-Jacques Rousseau, is the rustic upbringing, far from the poisoned atmosphere of the Court, of the future Henri IV. Henri says,

Je ne ressemblais point à ces princes vulgaires
Confiés en naissant à des mains mercenaires,
Enivrés de respects, d'hommages séducteurs,
Livrés aux courtisans, condamnés aux flatteurs,
A l'art des souverains façonnés par des prêtres,
Et sans cesse bercés du nom de leurs ancêtres.
Au lieu de serviteurs à mes ordres soumis,
Je voyais près de moi des égaux, des amis. . .

(I.i.101-7)

I was not like the normal run of princes, who are entrusted from birth to the hands of mercenaries and intoxicated by signs of respect and seductive compliments, abandoned to courtiers, condemned to flatterers, trained in the arts of kingship by priests and unceasingly beguiled by the names of their ancestors. Instead of servants subject to my orders, I had around me equals, and friends. . .

Catherine de Médicis is depicted as a double-dyed villainess. Her Machiavellian cynicism is revealed in her very first words in the play, spoken to that prince of the Church, the Cardinal de Lorraine:

Flattons nos ennemis: ne nous trahissons pas:
Ce jour verra la paix, cette nuit leur trépas.

(I.iii.171-2)

Let us flatter our enemies: let us not give ourselves away. Today shall see peace, tonight shall see their death.

Her view of life was perhaps made a little clearer still in the first version of the play, where she ended Act II, scene iv with, 'Tromper habilement fait tout l'art de régner' ('Skilful deception is the whole art of ruling'). The difference between her view of kingship and the one which Chénier would have his audience accept is demonstrated in her remark to King Charles,

> . . . Il faut bien vous éclairer, mon fils:
> Vous ignorez encor qu'un roi n'a point d'amis.
>
> (II.i.299-300)

. . . I really must enlighten you, my son. You still have not learned that a king has no friends.

Contrast this with the attitude expressed to Charles by Coligny, the representative of the oppressed Protestant minority, in his reference to Philip II of Spain:

> Plaignez, plaignez Philippe: il n'a que des soldats;
> L'amour de ses sujets ne le défendra pas. . .
>
> (II.iii.551-2)

Pity, yes, pity King Philip: he only has soldiers. The love of his subjects will not defend him.

Contrast it too with the advice tendered to his king by Coligny a little later in the play, when he urges him,

> . . . si de vos sujets vous désirez l'amour,
> Soyez roi de la France et non de votre Cour.
>
> (II.iii.647-8)

. . . if you wish to win your subjects' love, be King of France and not King of your Court.

The Chancellor, Michel de l'Hôpital, has the added advantage, from a Revolutionary point of view, of being of humble origin. As he puts it to the villainous Cardinal de Lorraine,

> Le sort m'a refusé, je ne veux point le taire,
> D'un long amas d'aïeux l'éclat héréditaire,

Et l'on ne me voit point, de leur nom revêtu,
Par dix siècles d'honneur dispensé de vertu;
Mais je sais mépriser ces vains droits de noblesse
Que la force autrefois conquit sur la faiblesse.

(III.i.731-6)

Destiny refused me – I make no secret of it – the hereditary brilliance of a long line of forbears, and I am not seen to be exempt from the need to live virtuously because of ten centuries of honour. But I am able to despise those vain aristocratic rights which were won in the past from the weak by the strong.

He insists that if the people are subjects of kings, kings are subject to the law ('Nous sommes leurs sujets, ils sont sujets des lois' (III.i.802)). His function, which he has tried loyally to carry out as the King's minister, is to be both a good subject and a good citizen, 'd'éclairer le monarque, et non pas de lui plaire' (III.i.855), ('to enlighten the monarch rather than to tell him what he wants to hear'), as is the way with courtiers.

The Cardinal de Lorraine puts the Church's position, arguing that 'tout le pouvoir du trône est fondé sur l'autel' (III.ii.922), ('the throne derives all its power from the altar'), which gives l'Hôpital the chance to outline the scandalous history of the papacy (III.ii.931ff.) and to argue that it is this scandalous history which brought about the Reformation: 'Les crimes du Saint-Siège ont produit l'hérésie' (980), ('It is the crimes of the Holy See which brought about heresy'). The play abounds in anti-clericalism, the height of which is reached when, in Act IV, scene v, the Cardinal de Lorraine blesses the murderers' weapons. No playwright in France had previously gone as far as this in an open attack on the Church.

Charles IX throughout shows himself to be weak and vacillating, easily manipulated by his mother, the Cardinal de Lorraine and the Duc de Guise. Chénier sums him up in a passage in the *Discours préliminaire* to the play:

Charles IX, assiégé, flatté, corrompu sans cesse et par sa mère et par les Guises, flotte dans une irrésolution perpétuelle. Il est très-faible, et par conséquent très-facile à émouvoir. . .[32]

Charles IX, beleaguered, flattered, unceasingly corrupted both by his mother and by the Guises, floats in a state of perpetual indecision. He is extremely weak and consequently extremely easy to move. . .

The temptation to see Louis XVI in this portrayal of Charles IX must have been irresistible to the audience of the day (the temptation to see Marie-Antoinette in references such as that to 'Des femmes gouvernant des princes trop faciles' (I.i.121) ('Women controlling princes who are too pliable') must have been equally strong, and the implications for Louis are not comforting. It is true that at the beginning of the play hope is expressed concerning the King, and it is true also that at the end of the play, after the dreadful massacre of the Protestants, including Coligny, has been carried out, the King is overcome by remorse. He says to the Cardinal, Guise and his mother, 'Je ne suis plus un roi; je suis un assassin' (V.iv.1553), ('I am no longer a king; I am a murderer'), but for him it is too late. The closing words are given to him, too:

> J'ai trahi la patrie, et l'honneur, et les lois:
> Le ciel en me frappant donne un exemple aux rois.
>
> (V.iv.1589-90)

I have betrayed my country, honour and legality: Heaven, in striking me, offers a lesson to kings.

The hope that Louis XVI, for one, will profit from this lesson, is there. The relevance of the play to contemporary events is strengthened by the introduction (sometimes, clearly, as last-minute additions to the script) of crystal-clear allusions to contemporary events and aspirations. The play as first performed had l'Hôpital, in Act III, scene i, prophesying the storming of the Bastille (not that that prison, before 1789, had anything like the associations which it acquired afterwards):

> Ces tombeaux des vivants, ces bastilles affreuses,
> S'écrouleront un jour sous des mains généreuses.

These tombs of the living, these frightful bastilles, will be brought crashing down one day by generous hands.

In Act II, scene iii Coligny offers Charles IX a vision of the potential for human development which was to be offered to the world by eighteenth-century Enlightenment. Nowhere is the legacy of the great eighteenth-century *philosophes* more apparent than here. Coligny looks forward to a great flourishing of both commerce and the arts, both of them 'trop longtemps négligés' (579), ('too long neglected'). In what he has to say about the importance of commerce, he is echoing a whole series of writers before him, including the Voltaire of the *Lettres philosophiques* (letter X), who fully saw the importance of the merchant as contributing not only to the prosperity of his own nation but also to the happiness of the whole world, the Beaumarchais of *Les Deux Amis, ou le Négociant de Lyon* (1770), and the Baron d'Holbach of *La Morale universelle* (1776). However, Chénier's Coligny perhaps echoes none more clearly than Michel-Jean Sedaine when he says that

> . . . ramenant les rois à leurs vrais intérêts,
> Le besoin du commerce enfantera la paix,
> Et cent peuples rivaux de gloire et d'industrie,
> Unis et rapprochés, n'auront qu'une patrie.
>
> (II.iii.591-4)

. . . the need for trade will bring back monarchs to an awareness of their real interests and will give birth to peace, and a hundred different peoples, rivals in glory and industry, will be brought together and united and will recognize that they all have but one *patrie*.

Sedaine's M. Vanderk, in *Le Philosophe sans le savoir* (1765), had remarked of the merchant,

> Ce n'est pas un peuple, ce n'est pas une seule nation qu'il sert; il les sert toutes, et en est servi; c'est l'homme de l'univers. . . . Quelques particuliers audacieux font armer les rois; la guerre s'allume; tout s'embrase; l'Europe est divisée; mais ce négociant anglais, hollandais, russe ou chinois n'en est pas moins l'ami de mon cœur. Nous sommes sur la terre autant de fils de soie qui lient ensemble les nations, et les ramènent à la paix par la nécessité du commerce. . .
>
> *Le Philosophe sans le savoir*, II.iv.

It is not one people, it is not a single nation that he serves; he serves them all, and is served by them; he is a man of the universe. . . . A few rash individuals make kings take up arms; war breaks out; everything is in flames; Europe is divided; for all that, the merchant, be he English, Dutch, Russian or Chinese, is none the less the friend of my heart. We are so many threads of silk binding the nations together, and bringing them back to peace through the need to trade. . .

Here we have Chénier transcending nationalism, to reach the internationalism of eighteenth-century *philosophe* thought at its best. This internationalism is to be found in the way in which, in Chénier's tragedy, Coligny is permitted through the power of prophecy to welcome the emergence of a new nation across the Atlantic consequential upon the formulation in Philadelphia in 1787 of the Constitution of the United States. Indeed, it may not be unreasonable to suggest that some of Chénier's contemporaries may have seen a parallel between Coligny and La Fayette. The American connection suggests this (in a note to this part of his play Chénier remarks that Coligny was the first Frenchman to establish a colony in North America.) Certainly, at least one modern critic has suggested such a parallel.[33] What Coligny says here is as follows:

> Ce vaste continent qu'environnent les mers
> Va tout à coup changer l'Europe et l'univers.
> Il s'élève pour nous aux champs de l'Amérique
> De nouveaux intérêts, une autre politique.
>
> (II.iii.583-6)

That vast continent surrounded by the seas will suddenly change Europe and the entire universe. A new set of interests, a new kind of policy is developing for us in the fields of America.

It is no doubt true to say, as John R. Alden remarks in his *History of the American Revolution*, that 'The American Revolution and the French Revolution of 1789 were different in origin, in development and in consequences', but in general terms it is surely equally true to say of the leading figures of the French Revolution what Alden says of the leading, eminently middle-class figures of the American Revolution:

Admittedly, the men who appeared at Philadelphia in the late spring and early summer of 1787 were persons of means, merchants, lawyers and planters rather than mechanics, plain farmers, and teachers. . . . Does it follow that they were not

interested in the economic advance of poorer and less sophisticated Americans, that they were not genuinely concerned for the
establishment of order at home, for national defense? Surely they
had in mind their own interests, their own desire for power, but
they could not forget that their own well-being was ultimately,
even immediately, intermingled with the welfare of humbler
Americans. It will not do to contend that George Washington,
who presided over the convention, and James Madison, who was
the principal architect of the Constitution, were mere selfish
Conservatives. . . . In the main, the delegates displayed an
enlightened, a generous selfishness.[34]

It does not seem unreasonable to suggest a similar definition of
those Frenchmen for whom, in this early phase of the French
Revolution which has been described as 'the Liberal Experiment',[35]
Chénier made himself the spokesman in *Charles IX ou l'Ecole des rois*.

The whole of this powerful speech by Coligny, eloquent as it is
with all the optimism of the belief in human perfectibility
characteristic of the Age of Enlightenment, speaks well for the
Revolutionary spirit. The approach to the arts is more reminiscent
of the Voltaire of works like *Le Mondain* than the Rousseau of the
Discours sur les sciences et les arts. The possibility of educating people
by means of the communication of pleasure through the arts is
expressed enthusiastically (II.iii.595-6), and the importance of
the freedom of the press is stated unequivocally: the press is
important not only for spreading enlightenment throughout the
world but also for encouraging the development of an empirical,
questioning spirit which will, *inter alia*, undermine superstitious
religious beliefs:

> L'art . . .
> D'offrir à tous les yeux tout ce qui fut écrit,
> Renouvelle le monde, et dans l'Europe entière
> Déjà de tous côtés disperse la lumière;
> L'audace enfin succède à la timidité,
> Le désir de connaître à la crédulité.
> Ce qui fut décidé maintenant s'examine,
> Et vers nous, pas à pas, la raison s'achemine.
> La voix du préjugé se fait moins écouter;
> L'esprit humain s'éclaire; il commence à douter. . .
>
> (II.iii.599-608)

The art . . . of offering to the eyes of all everything which has been written is altering the face of the world and is already spreading enlightenment on all sides throughout Europe. Boldness is at last taking the place of timidity, the desire to know is replacing credulity. What used to be taken as read is now being examined and, gradually, rationality is coming closer and closer to us. Less notice is taken of the voice of prejudice; the human spirit is becoming enlightened; it is beginning to doubt. . .

Even in the sixteenth century this is beginning to happen, says Coligny, but

> C'est aux siècles futurs de consommer l'ouvrage.
> Quelque jour nos Français, si grands par le courage,
> Exempts du fanatisme et des dissensions,
> Pourront servir en tout d'exemple aux nations.
>
> (II.iii.609-12)

It will be for centuries to come to complete the work. Some day our Frenchmen, so great in courage, free of fanaticism and discord, will be able to serve as a model for all nations.

This degree of hope, of belief in the possibility of human perfectibility, smacks of the sublime optimism of Condorcet, who died in 1794 in one of the prisons of the Revolution but who nevertheless, in his last work, the *Esquisse d'un tableau historique des progrès de l'esprit humain* (1793), was able to proclaim his intention of demonstrating that nature had set no limit to the development of human faculties and that there is no limit to human perfectibility so long as Earth continues to exist ('. . . la nature n'a marqué aucun terme au perfectionnement des facultés humaines: . . . la perfectibilité de l'homme est réellement indéfinie: . . . les progrès de cette perfectibilité, désormais indépendants de la volonté de ceux qui voudraient les arrêter, n'ont d'autres termes que la durée de la globe où la nature nous a jetés').[36] Chénier was not unaware of the ideas of Condorcet, as he makes clear in a note on this part of *Charles IX*.[37]

Charles IX may not be the most rivetting play one has ever come across. Jean Gaulmier speaks of its 'remarquable clarté', but it has to be conceded that, despite Gaulmier's insistence that this means that interest is sustained throughout the play, aesthetically speaking this 'remarkable clarity' is not necessarily an unmixed blessing. It is this which imparts to the play the too facile division into black and white, good and evil, to which reference has already been made. It is no doubt true that an important part of Chénier's purpose in writing this play was to demonstrate that history is not about the destiny of the Great but about the will and the intelligence of all human beings and that, in Gaulmier's words, 'la tragédie est affaire d'hommes et non de héros fabuleux' ('Tragedy is a matter of men and not of heroes of fable').[38] How successful Chénier was in this endeavour is rather another matter. The way in which Charles is won over first by one side and then by the other is less than convincing and indeed the speed at which he changes his mind runs the risk of creating an unintentionally comic effect on occasion. Chénier shows himself closer to Corneille, who demanded for tragedy 'quelque passion plus noble et plus mâle que l'amour' ('some passion more noble and more manly than love'), than to anyone else when he made it clear in his *Epître dédicatoire à la nation* and in his *Discours préliminaire* that he was concerned with important matters such as the fate of peoples and nations, and when he wrote contemptuously of Racine's public that 'Dans le dernier siècle, *Britannicus* avait cinq représentations; *Bérénice* en avait trente; c'est que les Français de ce temps-là connaissaient mieux *La Princesse de Clèves* que Tacite' ('During the last century Britannicus [which can be said to concern itself with the fate of the entire Roman Empire, as Nero reveals his true nature] had five performances; *Bérénice* had thirty; which shows that at that time the French were more familiar with *La Princesse de Clèves* than with Tacitus'). In the Revolutionary years things have changed:

Vous avez anéanti l'autorité arbitraire: vous aurez des lois et des mœurs. Votre scène doit changer avec tout le reste. Un théâtre de femmelettes et d'esclaves n'est plus fait pour des hommes et des citoyens.[39]

You have destroyed arbitrary authority: you will have laws and customs of your own. Your drama must change along with everything else. A theatre of fops and slaves is no longer appropriate for men and citizens.

There can be no doubt that *Charles IX* is not a tragedy in the French seventeenth-century sense; but nor was it meant to be.

Traditional theatrical values had already undergone considerable modification in the eighteenth century through the work of people like Voltaire and, perhaps especially, Diderot, who had ascribed very firmly to drama a moral aim. In the case of Voltaire this had sometimes taken the shape of a fairly overt attack on religious fanaticism. In the case of both of them and certain of their followers (such as Sedaine, who succeeded in writing a better *drame* than Diderot could ever manage) there were not infrequently implicit political points being made. Chénier added a quite explicit political purpose to drama:

> Je serai toujours persuadé que le but de ce genre si important est de faire aimer la vertu, les lois et la liberté, de faire détester le fanatisme et la tyrannie.[40]

> I shall always remain convinced that the aim of this so important genre is to create a love of virtue, law and liberty, and to create a detestation of fanaticism and tyranny.

This is enough to condemn it out of hand for some critics: H.C. Ault, acknowledging that the revised sub-title, *L'Ecole des rois*, is accurate, adds simply, 'It is hardly a title for a tragedy', and no doubt when one thinks of Molière's *L'Ecole des femmes* or Sheridan's *School for Scandal* one can see what he means. For Ault the main trouble is that 'throughout the five acts Chénier is thinking of the didactic value of his tragedy, not of its drama'.[41]

No doubt tragedy is not an adequate or an accurate description of *Charles IX*, and no doubt that is, in part at least, precisely because it is an early example of a play designed for a society quite different from that in which the theatre-going public had liked to recognize itself in the depiction of the destinies of great princes and princesses, whether this was offered by a Corneille, by a Racine or even by a Voltaire or a Crébillon *père*. Revolutionary theatre it certainly is, though less violent than some plays which were to be set before the French public over the next few years. King Charles feels remorse at the end of the play, no doubt too late, as we have already suggested. But the closing words of the play, as we have seen, do not remove all hope for the monarchy: Heaven offers, through Charles, a lesson to other kings. Chénier's plea to the King in his *Epître dédicatoire à la nation française* is poignant here:

O Louis XVI, roi plein de justice et de bonté! vous êtes digne d'être le chef des Français, mais des méchants veulent toujours établir un mur de séparation entre votre peuple et vous: ils cherchent à vous persuader que vous n'êtes point aimé de ce peuple. Ah! venez au théâtre de la Nation quand on représente *Charles IX*; vous entendrez les acclamations des Français; vous verrez couler leurs larmes de tendresse; vous jouirez de l'enthousiasme que vos vertus leur inspirent; et l'auteur patriote recueillera le plus beau fruit de son travail.[42]

Oh, Louis XVI, monarch full of justice and benevolence! You are worthy of being the chief of the French people, but evil men still wish to set up a dividing wall between your people and you: they seek to convince you that you are not loved by the people. Ah! come to the Théâtre de la Nation when *Charles IX* is being performed; you will hear the cheers of the French people; you will see their tears of tenderness; you will enjoy the enthusiasm inspired in them by your virtues; and the patriotic playwright will gather the finest fruit of his work.

So *Charles IX* is a Revolutionary play but it is not a republican play. That was still to come, not only for Chénier himself, but for other playwrights. With *Caïus Gracchus*, which opened at the rue de Richelieu on 9 February 1792, Chénier seems to have 'achieved the almost impossible feat of being approved by both sides [republicans and monarchists], with only a few extremists demurring'[43] through its appeal to moderation, tolerance and observance of legality. With *Timoléon*, he seems to have come very close to serious trouble with the Revolutionary authorities. It was intended to give the first performance of this play, which depicts in the character of Timophane an oppressive usurper whose brother Timoléon finally decides that there is no option but to assassinate him, on 21 floréal an II (10 May 1794), right at the heart of the Terror: Hébert and eighteen of his principal supporters had been guillotined on 24 March, and fourteen Dantonists, including Danton himself, Camille Desmoulins, and Fabre d'Eglantine followed them to the scaffold on 5 April. According to Etienne and Martainville, a considerable number of members of the Assembly were present at the dress rehearsal and one of them, an ardent supporter of Robespierre, cried out to Chénier, 'Ta pièce est un manifeste de révolte; mais cela ne m'étonne point, tu n'a jamais été qu'un contre-révolutionnaire déguisé'[44] ('Your play is nothing more than a manifesto of revolt; but that does not surprise me. You have never been anything but a secret counter-revolutionary'). The play was banned by the Committee of Public Safety and was not performed until 10 September, well after the fall of Robespierre on 9 thermidor (27 July 1794). As Jean-Alexis Rivoire puts it, the type of patriotism depicted by Chénier in *Timoléon* is a sort of compromise between Girondin and Montagnard concepts: 'Au nom de ce Patriotisme, il faut défendre la Liberté contre le pouvoir arbitraire, mais il faut aussi lutter "pour le peuple et pour l'Egalité"'[45] ('in the name of this patriotism, one has to defend Liberty against arbitrary power, but one has also to fight "for the people and for Equality"'). Increasingly, from this time on, liberty was to be seen as a more immediate need than equality. Chénier, however, retained his republicanism, once acquired, to the bitter end (he died in 1811), in his sobre elegy *La Promenade* (1805) and in works such as his tragedy *Tibère*, which was banned by Napoleon.

4

THE DANGERS OF
LIBERTINAGE

Donatien-Alphonse-François, marquis de Sade, came very close to being one of the handful of prisoners incarcerated in the Bastille when, on the 14 July 1789, that prison fell to the Revolutionary crowd. He was not there, however, having been removed from the Bastille to the lunatic asylum at Charenton on 4 July, in consequence of his behaviour two days earlier. He had entered the Bastille on 29 February 1784, having been transferred there from the prison at Vincennes, where he had been for the previous seven years, not in consequence of any political considerations but because of his scandalous personal behaviour and doubts as to his sanity.

The behaviour which led to his removal to Charenton is briefly described in records of the Bastille under the date of 2 July 1789 as follows:

> Le comte de Sade a crié par sa fenêtre, à diverses reprises, qu'on égorgeait les prisonniers de la Bastille et qu'il fallait venir le délivrer.[1]

> The comte de Sade repeatedly shouted from his window that the prisoners in the Bastille were being massacred and that he needed to be set free.

For this purpose he used an improvised loudspeaker in the form of a metal pipe with a funnel at one end with which he had been provided so that he could empty waste liquids into the moat below. The governor, De Launay, was naturally enough not best pleased by such a demonstration at a time when there was already a good deal of unrest in the streets of Paris and on 3 July he wrote to

86

M. de Villedeuil, the responsible minister, pointing out that in such dangerous times Sade was not a desirable man to have in the Bastille and requesting that he be transferred to Charenton

> ou dans quelque maison de ce genre, ou il ne pourrait pas troubler l'ordre, comme il le fait ici sans cesse. . . . Il est impossible de lui rendre la promenade sur les tours, les canons sont chargés, cela serait du danger le plus éminent.[2]

> or to some other establishment of that type, where he would be unable to disturb the peace as he does here endlessly. . . . It is impossible to renew his permission to take exercise on the towers, since the cannons are loaded and to do so would clearly be highly dangerous.

De Launay added a postscript to the effect that Sade was threatening to renew his shouts to the people outside the prison.

In the event he was indeed removed to Charenton where, as he pointed out to his man of law Gaufridy in a letter written during late May of the following year, his wife's family 'eurent la cruauté de me laisser languir neuf mois au milieu des fols et des épileptiques à qui seuls est consacrée cette maison'[3] ('were sufficiently cruel as to leave me to languish for nine months among the madmen and epileptics to whom that establishment is exclusively devoted'). He was released on 2 April 1790, was legally separated from his wife in June and given his card as an 'active citizen' in the Section des Piques, of which he eventually became secretary and then president. June 1791 saw the publication of *Justine* and Louis XVI's flight to Varennes. In September the Constitution was promulgated and was accepted by the King, whilst on 1 October the Legislative Assembly replaced the Constituent Assembly.

On 22 October Sade's play, *Oxtiern, ou les malheurs du libertinage*, received its first performance at the Théâtre Molière in the rue Saint-Martin. This theatre had been opened on 11 June 1791 by Boursault-Malherbe, who had previously been an actor and the director of the Grand Théâtre in Marseille. On 11 November 1791 *Le Moniteur* wrote of the Théâtre Molière, 'Ce théâtre, depuis son ouverture, s'est distingué par le patriotisme et l'amour de la révolution'.[4] The *Almanach général des spectacles de Paris et de la province pour l'année 1792*[5] contains a manifestly royalist attack on the

Théâtre Molière by Joseph Dubois. The theatre had indeed already acquired a reputation for the production of violently 'patriotic' plays. Dubois argues that the theatre disgraces the name of Molière, the plays performed there are 'incendiaires ou absurdes': Boursault-Malherbe, who has complained that his productions are often ignored by the press, should not be surprised since not only has he attacked the King and Queen, but he has allowed his stage to be used for the expression of 'des idées atroces et sanguinaires' and to preach disorder, licence, murder, hatred and fury under the pretext that this is liberty. For all that Sade was now an 'active citizen' in Revolutionary Paris, it would be a mistake to expect from *Oxtiern*, at any rate in the political sense, atrocious or bloodthirsty ideas. It is, however, a play which has its curiosity value and was the only one of Sade's which was published in his lifetime.

Indeed, only two of Sade's plays, despite the fact that he does seem to have been particularly proud of his efforts as a dramatist, reached the stage. Of these, *Oxtiern* had only two performances in 1791 and one further performance at Versailles in 1799, when Sade himself played the part of Fabrice in the theatre where he was at that time earning a few francs as prompter and after which performance he had the text published, whilst the other, a one-act play in verse entitled *Le Suborneur*, did not even manage one complete performance when it was produced on 5 March 1792 at the Théâtre Italien. *Le Suborneur*, which Gilbert Lély describes as being a play of remarkable platitude ('insigne platitude')[6] was abandoned by the actors when they reached scene iv in the face of a rowdy Jacobin demonstration which seems to have been the first occasion on which the red bonnet was paraded. On 7 April 1792 Sade wrote to Gaufridy,

> La faction jacobite a fait tomber le mois passé une pièce de moi au Théâtre Italien, seulement parce qu'elle était d'un ci-devant. Ils y parurent en bonnet de laine rouge. C'était la première fois qu'on voyait pareille chose. Cette mode a duré quinze jours, au bout desquels le maire en a obtenu l'anéantissement, mais il m'était réservé d'en être la première victime. Je suis né pour ces choses-là.[7]

The Jacobin faction caused the failure of a play of mine last month at the Théâtre Italien, simply because it was by a *ci-devant.* They turned up in red woollen bonnets. It was the first time that such a thing had been seen. That fashion lasted a couple of weeks, at the end of which the mayor had an end put to it, but it fell to my lot to be its first victim. I was born for that sort of thing.

In a footnote to his *Idée sur le mode de la sanction des lois*, which dates from November 1792, Sade rather testily remarks,

> Je ne conçois pas par quelle absurdité on veut absolument que le bonnet de la liberté soit rouge; le blanc était la seule couleur consacrée chez les Grecs et chez les Romains à la déesse de la Liberté, connue et révérée sous le nom d'Eleutherie.[8]

> I fail to comprehend for what absurd reason people will insist that the bonnet of freedom should be red; white is the only colour consecrated by the Greeks and the Romans to the goddess of Liberty, known and revered under the name Eleutheria.

When *Le Suborneur* was performed on 5 March 1792 the political situation, from the point of view of the monarchy, had deteriorated significantly. In November 1791 Louis XVI had vetoed the Assembly's decree that all *émigrés* who remained assembled against the Revolution after 1 January 1792 should be subject to the death penalty and to confiscation of their property. Prospects for the successful establishment of a constitutional monarchy in France were looking increasingly dim. The Girondins were increasing in power and in March 1792 impeached the Foreign Minister and obtained the Interior and Finance portfolios for two of their own, Roland and Clavière.

When *Oxtiern* was premiered in late October 1791, although the flight to Varennes the previous June had plunged France into a major crisis, the King's subsequent (however unwilling) acceptance of the Constitution had brought about an improvement in Louis's popularity and it was still possible to entertain hopes for the establishment of a moderate constitutional monarchy. The Legislative Assembly established at the beginning of October gave no separate representation to clergy or nobility and only a handful of the 745 deputies came from those social groups. The overwhelming majority among the deputies were members of the middle class, and conciliatory Feuillants were markedly more numerous than Jacobins.

Something of Sade's professed political position at this time can be gleaned from his *Adresse d'un Citoyen de Paris au Roi des Français*,[9] which dates from June 1791 and a copy of which Sade later claimed to have thrown into the King's coach as he was brought back into Paris from Varennes on 24 June. The *Adresse* opens with an expression of sorrow and disgust for Louis XVI's betrayal of the French people, and yet from the outset the implication is clear: Louis is being betrayed by those close to him. The people, rightly furious at the abuses committed by the King's ministers, were nevertheless beginning to believe that Louis himself was benevolent:

Il séparait les torts de vos flatteurs des vertus qu'il aimait à reconnaître en vous, et il disait: *Le bien est l'ouvrage de son cœur, le mal est celui de ses ministres.*

They distinguished the wrongs committed by those who flatter you from the virtues which they liked to recognize in you personally, and they said: *The good is the work of his heart, the evil is the work of his ministers.*

If the King wishes to continue to rule over France, it will have to be over a free nation, but there is still hope: every heart is open to hope since the announcement of the King's return to Paris, and everyone is disposed to forgive him:

Ecoutez ce qu'on dit, Sire: ce n'est plus vous qui nous avez trompés; vous l'avez été; cette fuite est l'ouvrage de vos prêtres et de vos courtisans; vous avez été séduit; jamais vous n'auriez conçu ce projet sans eux; saisissez ces dispositions, Sire, pour regagner les cœurs que vous avez aigris, vous le pouvez, tout vous l'assure. Et s'il est vrai, comme cela ne paraît que trop positif, que ce soit la compagne de votre sort qui vous ait donné de tels conseils, ne l'exposez pas plus longtemps à la vengeance des Français; sachez vous en séparer. . .

Listen to what is being said, Sire: it is no longer thought that you betrayed us; you were betrayed; this flight was the work of your priests and your courtiers; you were led astray; you would never have conceived of such a plan without them; take advantage of these good dispositions, Sire, to win back the hearts which you have embittered. You can do that, everything suggests as much. And if it is true, as seems only too certain, that it was the companion of your fate [Marie-Antoinette] who gave you such advice, expose her no longer to the vengeance of the French people; separate from her. . .

Sade concludes his address to the King by saying that no one is more convinced than he that the only form of government possible in France is monarchy, but the monarch, chosen by a free people, must be subject to the law ('. . . il faut que ce monarque, élu par une nation libre, soit fidèlement soumis à la loi'). He expresses the hope that Louis XVI, by his example, will enlighten his contemporaries and his successors on the throne of France, and teach them respect for the people over whom they have the honour of ruling. The reins of power entrusted to monarchs by men who are free and equal by natural law, are like the helm of a ship handed over to a pilot, and monarch and pilot alike are answerable for the way in which they carry out the functions entrusted to them.

And thus it is that in 1792, in his *Idée sur le mode de la sanction des lois*, Sade is able to remark, in words which put us in mind of M.-J. Chénier's *Charles IX*, that Nero, Tiberius, Wenceslaus, Charles IX and Louis XVI spilled blood only because they abused powers which had been delegated to them ('Néron, Tibère, Venceslas, Charles IX et Louis XVI ne répandirent le sang que parce qu'ils avaient abusé d'un *pouvoir délégué*').[10] Before this, however, in a letter to Gaufridy dated 5 December 1791, Sade is to be found explaining that necessity makes him, as a man of letters, write for different parties and that consequently there is a certain flexibility in his way of thinking at the moment. However, he says, he is not totally in tune with any one party and derives elements of his political thinking from a number of quarters:

Je suis anti-jacobite, je les hais à la mort; j'adore le roi, mais je déteste les anciens abus; j'aime une infinité d'articles de la constitution, d'autres me révoltent; je veux qu'on rende à la noblesse son lustre, parce que de le lui avoir ôté n'avance à rien; je veux que le roi soit le chef de la nation; je ne veux point d'Assemblée nationale, mais deux chambres comme en Angleterre, ce qui donne au roi une autorité mitigée, balancée par le concours d'une nation nécessairement divisée en deux ordres; le troisième est inutile, je n'en veux point. Voilà ma profession de foi. Que suis-je, à présent? Aristocrate ou démocrate? Vous me le direz, s'il vous plaît, avocat, car pour moi je n'en sais rien.[11]

I am anti-Jacobin, I have a deadly hatred of them; I adore the King, but I detest the abuses of the past; I like many articles of the Constitution, others of them revolt me; I wish the nobility to regain its old brilliancy, since to have removed it has done no good; I wish the King to be the head of the nation; I do not want a National Assembly, but two Chambers as they have in England, which gives the King a tempered authority, balanced by the cooperation of a nation of necessity divided into two Orders; the third [i.e. the clergy] is useless, and I want to have nothing to do with it. Such is my profession of faith. So what am I? An aristocrat or a democrat? You must tell me, please, lawyer, for as for myself I have no idea.

In the texts referred to above Sade is to be found putting forward a moderate political attitude, many aspects of which were not uncommon at the time and, indeed, one which bears some similarity to the political message which it is possible to discern in Chénier's *Charles IX*. The argument of the *Adresse d'un Citoyen de Paris au Roi des Français*, for example, is quite close to that of Chénier's verse epistle to Louis XVI with which he prefaced his play.[12] The assertion that the King has been led astray by his courtiers, that he derives his authority from the people, and that he has the possibility to become a model for other monarchs, all this is there in common. Similarly, the mistrust of the feminine influence in the life of the King and a marked anti-clericalism are to be found both in Chénier and in Sade.

All the more a pity, then, when we come to examine *Oxtiern*, which does (unlike most of Sade's plays, including *Le Suborneur*, which were written before the Revolution) seem to have been written only very shortly before it was performed, in 1791, to discover there is very little indeed of an overtly political nature in it, despite the views which Sade had expressed in the *Adresse* and despite the already established reputation of the Théâtre Molière for the production of fiery political plays.

Sade's play had a mixed reception. He had submitted the manuscripts of a number of plays to a variety of theatres, always without success. Indeed, before *Oxtiern* was accepted by Boursault-Malherbe for the Théâtre Molière, Sade had submitted it to the Feydeau and there exists a letter dated 25 July 1791 from Miramond on behalf of the selection committee of that theatre turning the manuscript down and in the process making a number of criticisms of the play. It will be appropriate to turn to those criticisms later.

Of the first night of *Oxtiern*, 22 October 1791, Sade himself wrote to Gaufridy a few days later,

> J'ai enfin paru en public, mon cher avocat. On a joué, samedi dernier 22, une pièce de moi dont le succès, grâce aux cabales, aux trains, aux femmes dont je disais du mal, a été *fort balancé*. Elle se redonne samedi vingt-neuf avec des changements; priez pour moi, nous verrons.[13]

> I have finally appeared in public, my dear lawyer. Last Saturday, the twenty-second, one of my plays was performed, the success of which, thanks to cabals, disturbances and women (of whom I had spoken ill) was *very mixed*. It will be performed again on Saturday the twenty-ninth, with alterations. Pray for me: we shall see.

In fact the second performance was postponed until 4 November, and at the end Sade was called on stage to take a bow. Not that this second and, at the Théâtre Molière, final performance of the play was an unqualified success. *Le Moniteur* of 6 November gave a report of the performance which, whilst acknowledging that the play had its good points, went on to say that the central character of Count Oxtiern was revolting ('Il y a de l'intérêt et de l'énergie dans cette pièce; mais le rôle d'Oxtiern est d'une atrocité révoltante. Il est plus scélérat, plus vil que Lovelace. . .'). It is interesting to see that the seducer in Samuel Richardson's *Clarissa*, almost forty-five years after that novel began to appear in London, is still seen as the role model *par excellence* in terms of sexual villainy. *Le Moniteur* goes on to recount how, at the beginning of Act II of *Oxtiern*, a spectator had called out for the curtain to be lowered. Confusion reigned when the curtain was half-lowered. Other spectators demanded that the curtain be raised again and shouted for the spectator who had called out in the first place to be ejected from the theatre. At this point the audience divided itself into two factions, some whistling whilst the others (the majority) applauded and called for the author at the end of the performance.[14] The play was never again performed in Paris, although it was revived on 13 December 1799 (19 frimaire an VIII) at the theatre in Versailles, where Sade, in need of cash, had been employed since the previous February as prompter for 40 sous a day. On this occasion he played the part of Fabrice.

The play is a three-act *drame* in prose, and owes something to the kind of dramatic theory outlined by Diderot, the father of the *drame*, in his three *Entretiens sur le Fils naturel*, published with Diderot's play of that title in February 1757, and in his discourse *De la Poésie dramatique*, published with *Le Père de famille* in November 1758. Jacques Truchet is surely right to place it in the tradition of the 'drame noir, moral et finissant bien, souvent un peu bâclé' which led up to the early nineteenth-century melodramas of Pixerécourt.[15] *Cœlina*, the play by Pixerécourt which Norma Perry describes as 'la pièce-type' of the melodrama, the play with which the genre reached the form which it was to retain with very little change for more than thirty years, received its première at the Ambigu-Comique on 2 September 1800: it had at least 387 performances in Paris and 1,809 in the provinces. This certainly contrasts with the history of *Oxtiern*, which is certainly black, has a good deal of moralizing, a contrived happy ending, and in which the plot and structure are not of the most convincing or the most careful. On the other hand, as Norma Perry points out, the critics were not unduly concerned by the improbabilities in *Cœlina* and any number of other melodramas: Pixerécourt is said to have remarked that he wrote for the people who could not read, the public of the boulevard theatres, the people who, particularly since the Revolution, were avid for sensation and action at any price.[16]

It may be that Sade had similar views of his function as a playwright. However that may be, it clearly was not a view which appealed to the members of the company at the Feydeau theatre in 1791. In returning Sade's manuscript of *Oxtiern* to him on 25 July of that year, Miramond stated his committee's view that they could not hope successfully to produce a play based on such an odious basic situation ('Le comité n'a pas cru qu'on put représenter avec succès une pièce fondée sur la plus odieuse atrocité'). He went on to list some of the comments which had been made about Sade's play by members of the committee: it was not considered probable that Fabrice, as the proprietor of an *hôtel garni* should have sufficient influence to be able to release Herman, Ernestine's beloved, after he had been imprisoned by a man as powerful as Oxtiern, still less that he should have been able to accomplish this in less than twenty-four hours; it was also considered improbable that Ernestine could defend herself for any length of time in the duel against her father who, although elderly, is after all an army officer skilled in arms; it was also felt that 'le style laissait beaucoup à désirer' ('the style left much to be desired'), which comment induced Sade to write in the margin of the letter, 'C'est faux, cela' ('That is not true').[17]

It is, however, difficult not to have some sympathy with Miramond and his committee unless one is an enthusiast for melodrama or unless one is such a fanatical worshipper of the 'divine Marquis' that one is prepared to argue, as Jean-Jacques Brochier is, that it is wrong to criticize Sade for having produced conventional, banal plays and that, to the contrary, the function of Sade's plays is precisely that, although to the naïf reader they might seem unimportant, the total freedom which Sade reveals in his works of prose fiction such as *La Nouvelle Justine* or *L'Histoire de Juliette* could not have existed for him unless, in literary terms, there existed something else, 'le conformisme, la morale convenue' ('conformism, received morality'). For Brochier, it is Sade's theatre which offers this banality and thus serves as a complement to his works of prose fiction and underlines the truth which they express. Brochier himself concedes that this line of reasoning cannot be applied to the moment at which the plays were produced, in that it requires, for an understanding of Sade's theatre, that one is aware of his novels.[18] This was not the position of Sade's contemporaries since they could not know of Sade's curious novels in 1791: Miramond and his committee therefore are perhaps not to be unduly criticized for failing to appreciate that what the Marquis was up to, when he offered them plays like *Oxtiern*, was offering a picture of banality as a foil to his unpublished pornographic novels. Twentieth-century Sadians are differently placed. They may not always be right in their assessments, however.

It is certainly true, as Brochier puts it, that for readers familiar with *Les Cent Vingt Journées de Sodome* or Sade's other works, his plays may seem very disconcerting:

Il n'y a pas de viol ni de torture, on n'y assassine personne, le vice n'y a cours que pour être puni, on y parle de Dieu avec respect, de la société avec vénération, on y est à priori très convenable.[19]

There is neither rape nor torture, no one is murdered, vice appears only in order to be punished, God is spoken of with respect, society with reverence, people are before all else very proper.

That there is a contrast between Sade's prose fiction and his plays is illustrated in a particularly direct way in the case of *Oxtiern*, for this play is (as Sade himself points out in a note to the first edition) taken from one of his short stories about to appear under the title of *Des Crimes de l'amour ou le Délire des passions*.[20] The short story in question is *Ernestine, nouvelle suédoise*, which was indeed published in 1792. The two treatments of the story are intriguingly different.

In the play, Count Oxtiern, a powerful Swedish nobleman and a senator (although this fact seems to be forgotten at one point by Sade, when Ernestine refers to Oxtiern's brother as the senator (I. v)) has taken advantage of Ernestine, the daughter of Colonel Falkenheim, grand-nephew of the great Charles XII of Sweden's confidant. As Ernestine puts it, whereas she was expecting Oxtiern to protect her, he appeared before her dagger in hand, 'voulant mon déshonneur ou ma mort, et ne me laissant pas même la maîtresse du choix' ('seeking my dishonour or my death, and not even leaving me free to make the choice') (I. v). Oxtiern has had Herman, the man Ernestine loves, thrown into prison on a false accusation and abducts Ernestine to a small hotel near Stockholm run by an honest man by the name of Fabrice (there is irony, in view of his own sexual record, in the fact that it was the part of Fabrice which Sade himself played in the production of *Oxtiern* at Versailles in 1799). The elderly Falkenheim arrives at the hotel in hot pursuit of his daughter and her abductor. Ernestine hits on a plan to avenge herself over the man who has wronged her. She sends Oxtiern a note which appears to come from her brother, challenging him to a duel in the grounds of the hotel at eleven o'clock at night with a person who will be dressed in white. Falkenheim also issues a challenge to Oxtiern, who (aware of Ernestine's scheme) hits on the villainous design of bringing about a duel in the darkness between father and daughter. The two do begin to fight, failing to recognize each other in the darkness, but they are separated in the nick of time by Herman, who has been freed from prison in Stockholm by the worthy Fabrice. Herman has already fought and killed Oxtiern before arriving in the hotel garden. Ernestine fears that, dishonoured by Oxtiern, she may be considered no longer worthy of Herman, but he rapidly dispels all such thoughts: 'Ah! les crimes d'un scélérat tel qu'Oxtiern pourraient-ils donc flétrir le plus bel ouvrage de la nature?' ('Ah! could the crimes of a scoundrel such as Oxtiern blight the most beautiful of Nature's works?') (III. vi). He asks Falkenheim for his daughter's hand in marriage.

It cannot be claimed that, within the parameters of this distinctly melodramatic plot, there is much in the way of verisimilitude, psychological or social, although, for the likes of Jean-Jacques Brochier, to look for verisimilitude in Sade's plays is mistaken. Brochier concedes that Sade's theatre, especially his more melodramatic works for the stage, includes a childlike, not to say infantile element ('Le théâtre de Sade, à tout le moins ses drames et ses mélodrames, comporte ce côté enfantin, pour ne pas dire infantile').[21] But to say that is, for Brochier, to miss the point: the important thing is that the sociologically or metaphysically negative cannot exist without the positive, which gives it its value; scandal cannot exist except by reference to a norm. For Brochier it is the function of Sade's plays to offer this norm, and in his view it is failure to realize this that leads that guru of Sadians, Gilbert Lély, into the mistake of likening Sade's plays to those of the worst scribblers of the eighteenth century: for Brochier, what makes the plays important is their role as a sort of foil to Sade's other, libertarian works ('. . . le négatif n'exist[e] pas sans le positif sociologique qui lui donne valeur, . . . le scandale ne [peut] arriver qu'à partir d'une norme. C'est par quoi pèche aussi Gilbert Lély, qui reproche à Sade une théâtre à peine comparable, dit-il, à celui des pires écrivaillons du XVIIIe siècle. C'est parce que ce théâtre faisait fonction de repoussoir qu'il est important').[22] There may seem to be a certain element of desperation in this attempt to elevate the value of Sade's plays, which may well seem to the ordinary reader to be remarkably inept pieces of work, and it will be necessary to come to some considered judgment on *Oxtiern* in this regard in due time. Certainly, the conventionality of the plays does seem to stand in direct contradiction to the rest of Sade's writings.[23] First, however, it is appropriate to make some comments on various aspects of the text of *Oxtiern* before comparing it with the treatment accorded by Sade to the same story in *Ernestine* which, although it was not published until 1792, was written before the Revolution, whilst Sade was in the Bastille.

The play is as ostentatiously moral in its posture as any of the *drames* of the eighteenth century. This moral note is struck from the very outset, with Sade's choice of a line from Act III, scene iii to act as epigraph to the play: 'Malheur aux scélérats que n'arrête point le remords' ('Woe to all scoundrels who are not halted by remorse').[24] A familiar brand of eighteenth-century morality, in which it not infrequently seems that virtue is to be followed for the pleasure which it brings rather than for its own sake, runs throughout the play and is exemplified by Fabrice's observation to Casimir, Oxtiern's manservant:

> . . . secourons l'infortune, lorsque l'occasion s'en présente; il est si doux de faire le bien, mon ami, qu'il ne faut négliger aucun des moyens d'y réussir quand nous sommes assez heureux pour les trouver.
>
> (I. ii. 1086)

> . . . let us help those in misfortune when the opportunity to do so presents itself; it is so sweet, my friend, to perform good deeds, that we should never neglect any means to do so when we are fortunate enough to come across them.

It is there too in Oxtiern's friend and confidant, Derbac, who sees the error of his ways, and decides that a life of virtuous poverty away from Oxtiern is preferable to a life of luxury with him: 'l'infortune m'effraie moins que le crime; à quelque point que souffre un honnête homme, il est consolé par son cœur' (III. iv. 1107) ('misfortune frightens me less than criminality; however much a man of honour may suffer, he is consoled for it by his purity of heart'). This attitude is not unrelated to that of the elderly Falkenheim, who complacently assumes that he is bound to defeat Oxtiern in the duel, since Providence would never allow virtue to succumb to wickedness, a view of life definitively undermined by Sade in his account in his prose fiction of the respective careers of Justine and Juliette:

> Oui, mon triomphe, il est sûr! c'est un monstre que je vais punir, et la Providence est trop sage pour laisser écraser la vertu sous les perfides attentats du vice et de la scélératesse.
>
> (II. xiv. 1103)

Yes, my triumph is assured! he whom I mean to punish is a monster, and Providence is too wise to permit virtue to be crushed by the treacherous plots of vice and villainy.

This contrasts most markedly, of course, with the double-dyed villainy of Oxtiern, of whom it is said that there is no one more dangerous in the whole of Sweden (I. i. 1084) and whose arrival at Fabrice's small hotel is arrogant and noisy and is remarked upon by Casimir, when the sound of a coach drawing in is heard, in the following terms:

Quel tapage! N'en doutons pas, c'est monsieur; le vice devrait-il marcher avec autant d'éclat?

(I. i. 1085)

What a racket! Make no mistake, that is the Count. Should vice create such a stir in its progress?

Although it is Oxtiern's friend Derbac who introduces the first note of what is popularly understood by sadism into the play when he remarks,

Elles sont délicieuses, les femmes, quand des larmes viennent ajouter à leurs attraits tout le désordre de la douleur. . . . Tu es, mon pauvre comte, ce qu'on peut appeler un être bien corrompu. . .

(II. i. 1091)

Women are delicious, when tears add the disarray of suffering to their charms. . . . My poor Count, you can fairly be described as a very corrupt human being. . .

the Count himself remarks that the only way to make women love you is to torment them ('. . . la seule façon de se faire aimer des femmes, c'est de les tourmenter: je n'en connais pas de plus sûres') (II. i. 1093).

Oxtiern sees himself as the torch-bearer of the new philosophy of enlightenment (II. i. 1092) and there can be little or no doubt that Sade's curious form of atheistic determinism derives in no small part from his reading of Diderot, and especially D'Holbach and La Mettrie. There is a sense, of course, in which it is true that many eighteenth-century *drames* present what can broadly be described as *philosophe* attitudes. One may doubt however, whether Diderot, that curious amalgam of rationalism, hedonism and sensibility, would have been at ease with such remarks as those quoted above, despite his manifest dislike for the Christian ascetic ideal, despite the undoubted attraction to him of dynamism for its own sake, despite his oft-stated views about the deterministic nature of the human condition and the view which he attributes to Lui in *Le Neveu de Rameau* that since he can attain happiness through indulgence in vices which are natural to him, it would be very odd if he were to torment himself like a damned soul and morally castrate himself to make himself into something which he is not ('. . . puisque je puis faire mon bonheur par des vices qui me sont naturels . . . il serait bien singulier que j'allasse me tormenter comme une âme damnée, pour me bistourner et me faire autre que je ne suis').[25] Later in the same work, Lui expresses an idea which might well have appealed to the Marquis de Sade, had he been aware of it (the publication history of *Le Neveu de Rameau* is curious and complicated, but no French edition appeared until after Sade's death):

> S'il importe d'être sublime en quelque genre, c'est surtout en mal. On crache sur un petit filou; mais on ne peut refuser une sorte de considération à un grand criminel. Son courage vous étonne. Son atrocité vous fait frémir. On prise en tout l'unité de caractère.[26]

> If there is any matter in which it is important to be sublime, it is above all in evil. People spit on a small-time thief, but they cannot refuse a kind of admiration to a great criminal. His courage astounds you. His atrociousness makes you shudder. People value unity of character in all things.

Sade seems to have been prepared, in his prose fiction at any rate, to go much further than Diderot in this kind of area. If Diderot presents us, in Lui, with a character who is 'malheureuse-ment né', he counterbalances this with the character of Jacques in *Jacques le fataliste*, a man of sunny disposition who behaves in a conventionally moral way, performing good works, no doubt simply because that is how he is made. In Sade things are much more perverse. In conventional moral terms it is no doubt Justine who is 'heureusement née' and her sister Juliette who is 'malheureusement née'. And yet it is Juliette who prospers in this world, and Justine who, for all her innate goodness, suffers torture upon torture and humiliation upon humiliation. Sade was, however, infinitely less adventurous in terms of what he portrayed in his plays. The implications of Diderot's remark in *De la Poésie dramatique*, if taken at face value, that 'Il n'y a rien de ce qui se passe dans le monde, qui ne puisse avoir lieu sur la scène'[27] ('There is nothing which happens in the world which cannot take place on stage'), are very far-reaching indeed. Sade did not seek to exploit this thought of Diderot's in his plays (no doubt, of course, because even in Revolutionary Paris there was no chance that such works would be accepted for performance), although it might be said that he did in a sense do so in a work such as *La Philosophie dans le boudoir* (published in 1795), a work of prose fiction in the form of seven dialogues. Remarks such as those quoted above from Derbac and from Oxtiern himself are isolated exceptions in *Oxtiern*, and represent the extreme limit of that particular form of libertarianism in the play.

Whereas in a *drame* such as Sedaine's *Le Philosophe sans le savoir* (1765) a positive social alternative is suggested to the overweening aristocratic pretensions of the caricatural Marquise, in the form of the bourgeois qualities advocated and indeed consciously adopted by the central character M. Vanderk, such is not the case in Sade's play. It is true that the villainy in *Oxtiern* is associated with wealth and social position. Fabrice remarks, for example, that 'il n'y a rien de si pernicieux que l'or dans la main des méchants' ('Nothing is more pernicious than wealth in the hands of the wicked') (I. i. 1084), and states that he has no desire to be protected by an aristocrat like Oxtiern when this is bound to be at the price of becoming an accomplice of his scandalous behaviour ('. . . je ne veux point de la protection d'un grand seigneur, quand il n'en résulte, comme c'est l'usage, que la complicité de ses désordres') (I. i. 1085). Ernestine herself attacks the corruptions of Court life. She says to her servant, Amélie,

> Je n'irai point chercher près d'une Cour corrompue une protection qui me serait refusée; tu ne sais pas à quel point le crédit et la richesse dégradent l'âme des hommes qui habitent ce séjour d'horreur. Les monstres! je serais peut-être un aliment de plus à leurs affreux désirs!
>
> (I.v.1088)

I shall not go to a corrupt Court to seek the protection which would be refused me. You do not realize the extent to which wealth and influence degrade the soul of the men who inhabit that abode of horror. The monsters! I should perhaps become additional material for their frightful desires!

This is the unsubtle language of melodrama. Ernestine draws the contrast between Oxtiern's villainy, wealth and influence, and her own virtue and that of her father in their poverty (II. ix. 1099), while Oxtiern's man servant (who does not, in fact, share his master's vicious nature) remarks of the worthy hotel proprietor, Fabrice,

> L'honnête homme! voilà pourtant où se trouve la vertu!. . . Dans un être obscur. . . sans éducation; pendant que ceux qui sont nés au milieu de ce que la fortune a de plus brillant n'offrent souvent, à côté de cela, que de la corruption ou des vices. . .
>
> (I.iii.1086)

What a good man! But that is where virtue is to be found! . . . In an obscure fellow . . . without education, whilst those born into the middle of the most brilliant life that fortune can offer often reveal, by contrast, only corruption and vice. . .

There is no substance to this, and things are not helped by the fact that, as Miramond remarked on 25 July 1791 in rejecting Sade's play on behalf of the Théâtre de la rue Feydeau, one remains totally unconvinced that within less than twenty-four hours a person such as Fabrice could have managed to release Herman from the prison in which Oxtiern had had him locked away, thus bringing about the 'happy ending' of the play.[28] This is as unconvincing as to be asked to go along with Falkenheim in his conviction that his triumph in his duel with Oxtiern is assured because virtue is on his side.[29]

In the case of *Oxtiern*, as Truchet does well to point out, although a cultivated twentieth-century reader familiar with other works by Sade will have no difficulty in suspecting mental reservations in the way the play ends, with the good being saved and the wicked Count being punished, no such irony is to be found in the text of the play itself.[30] The play, viewed on its own, has all the appearance today (as it no doubt had for the late eighteenth-century playgoers who were not prepared to give it a significant run, and as it clearly had for those like Miramond at the Théâtre de la rue Feydeau who rejected the manuscript) of a rather poor example of a genre, the *drame*, which did not produce very many distinguished examples in the eighteenth century. The characterization is rudimentary, the plot lacks conviction (improbabilities include not only those mentioned by Miramond, the ease with which Fabrice frees Herman, the way in which Ernestine acquits herself in a duel with her father the colonel, but also such episodes as Ernestine's refusal to run away from Oxtiern (I. v. 1088) and the way in which Falkenheim leaves her where she is rather than extract her from Fabrice's hotel to which Oxtiern has taken her (II. ix. 1100)) and the style is, despite Sade's protest, ham-fisted.

The fact remains, of course, although the 1791 playgoer was not in a position to be acquainted with it, that the short story *Ernestine* did exist, that *Oxtiern* was derived from it, and that there are interesting differences between it and the play.[31] Some of these points of difference are insignificant, such as the fact that although a character by the name of Falkeneim [*sic*] appears in the short story, he is a narrator and not Ernestine's father, which role is filled by a gentlemen rejoicing in the name of Colonel Sanders. Ernestine wears red for the duel in the short story and white in the play, no doubt a sensible change, since the whole point is that she should be readily seen in the dark. Fabrice and his hotel do not appear at all.

Many elements of the story are stronger meat than what is offered in the play. There is some trace of political comment, such as when the point is made that the King of Sweden was on the side of the people in the Revolution of 1772, whilst the senators (such as Oxtiern) were against the King and the people,[32] a point not dissonant with certain elements in Sade's own *Adresse d'un Citoyen de Paris au Roi des Français* of June 1791 or with certain of the attitudes expressed in Chénier's *Charles IX* and the hopes entertained by many a Frenchman in the early years of the Revolution that Louis XVI, freed from noxious Court influences, might yet still prove to be the father of his people. Points made in *Oxtiern* concerning the abuse of rank and privilege are made rather more forcefully in *Ernestine*, as for example when Herman (a much more significant character in the short story than in the play), observes to Oxtiern in positively Rousseauesque tones,

Sénateur, tout homme a droit d'exiger d'un autre la réparation, ou du bien qu'on lui enlève, ou de l'offense qu'on lui fait; le préjugé qui sépare les rangs est une chimère; la nature a créé tous les hommes égaux, il n'en est pas un seul qui ne soit sorti de son sein pauvre et nu [. . .]; je ne connais entre eux d'autre distinction que celle qu'y place la vertu: le seul homme qui soit fait pour être méprisé est celui qui n'use des droits que lui accordent de fausses conventions, que pour se livrer plus impunément au vice.[33]

Senator, every man has the right to demand reparation from another, whether for property taken away from him or for an offence done to him; the prejudice which separates people according to social status is a chimera; Nature created all men equal, and there is not one of them who did not leave her bosom poor and naked . . . ; I recognize no distinction between them other than the one put there by virtue: the only man who is to be despised is he who exploits the rights granted him by false conventions so as to be able to abandon himself to vice with greater impunity.

There is more overt 'sadism' in the short story: Oxtiern not only has Herman imprisoned, but possesses sufficient influence to have him executed and arranges for the execution to take place immediately outside the house to which he has lured Ernestine. When he throws open the window to show Ernestine what is happening outside and offers to spare Herman in return for her favours, Ernestine states that it is wrong to commit one crime to prevent another and expresses the conviction that Herman would not wish to live at the cost of her honour. It is when she subsequently faints that Oxtiern violates her. Characterization is rather more developed than in the play and the partnership between Oxtiern and the atheistic widow Schlotz – she has no time for 'all that religious twaddle' ('toutes ces fadaises')[34] – sometimes puts one in mind of the relationship between the Vicomte de Valmont and the Marquise de Merteuil in Laclos's brilliant novel *Les Liaisons dangereuses* (1782).

The ending of the short story is more complicated and – although technically there is a happy ending in that Oxtiern is brought to a life of radiant virtue – more perverse than that of the play. Sade himself expressed some pride in it, writing in the *Catalogue raisonné des œuvres de M. de S*** à l'époque du 1er octobre 1788*, that it was the best of his collection of short stories, so far as plot and dénouement are concerned ('cette nouvelle est la meilleure du recueil, relativement à la conduite et au dénouement').[35] After Oxtiern has had Herman executed and has violated Ernestine, Ernestine is killed by her father in a duel in mistake for Oxtiern, this case of mistaken identities having been deliberately engineered by Oxtiern himself. Then, however, Oxtiern is brought to justice and sentenced to hard labour for life. Ernestine's father begs for Oxtiern's release and then challenges him to a duel. A repentant Oxtiern refuses to defend himself and gives his sword to Sanders. He then runs on to his own sword. Sanders forgives Oxtiern and gives him his freedom, urging him to change his conduct. The good King Gustav remarks that Oxtiern's rank is surpassed by the virtue displayed by Ernestine's father who, for his part, concludes the story by observing that perhaps all the dramatic events that have taken place were decreed specifically to bring Oxtiern back to the temple of virtue. In this he finds consolation, saying that only he has been hurt by Oxtiern's crimes and that, now that the Count has repented of his wicked ways others will benefit from his virtues ('O vertu! . . . peut-être que l'accomplissement de toutes ces choses était nécessaire pour ramener Oxtiern à ton temple! Si cela est, je me console: les crimes de cet homme n'auront affligé que moi; ses bienfaits seront pour les autres').[36] This is, to put it mildly, breathtaking: after all, far from Colonel Sanders being the only one to have suffered in consequence of Oxtiern's crimes, both his daughter Ernestine and her lover Herman are dead! As Truchet points out, what is happening here, at the end of *Ernestine*, is that we find ourselves faced with a conclusion that is pure blasphemous buffoonery: faith in divine providence is being held up to ridicule. Perceptively, Truchet goes on to suggest a parallel between the ending of Sade's short story and that of Voltaire's *Candide*, when Pangloss, the apostle of Leibnitzian optimism, enumerates the vast series of tragic and ludicrous events which have been necessary in order for Candide and his companions to reach a situation in which they can eat fruit, nuts and sweetmeats. Sade's ending reads rather as a bizarre parody of Voltaire's. As Truchet puts it, 'une telle attitude, amusante chez Pangloss, ne peut que révolter de la part du père d'Ernestine'[37] ('Such an attitude, amusing in Pangloss, cannot but be revolting in Ernestine's father'). Nonetheless, sickening though Ernestine's father's remark may be, there is irony of a kind at the end of the short story.

It is with Sade's play, however, that we are primarily concerned and the absence of any trace of irony in *Oxtiern* is what dooms it to be something worse than mediocre, quite as much as the improbabilities of plot or the lack of characterization. The judgment of Miramond and his committee at the Théâtre de la rue Feydeau in rejecting Sade's manuscript still looks sound two hundred years after it was formulated. The fact that the play only had two performances in Paris in 1791 and another one in Versailles in 1799 suggests that the committee had accurately assessed the taste of the time, too. We know that the audience's reaction to the first performance at the Théâtre Molière was mixed, and we know that the second and final performance at that theatre came only after a delay and that it too was somewhat eventful.

It is not impossible that Boursault-Malherbe, the theatre's director, between the two performances which his company gave, came to a realization that he had perhaps been mistaken in accepting *Oxtiern*. Two days after the première, on 23 October 1791, Boursault-Malherbe wrote to Sade concerning proposals which the latter had made for changes, including changes in the cast. The director pointed out that he could not really be expected to drop the actor playing the part of M. Derbac, since the actor in question was needed for other productions for the next six months; he denied that the costume given to Herman was ridiculous but conceded that changes were possible there, as well as in Fabrice's costume, but pointed out that he could not be expected to spend vast sums of money on costumes for a play which was not a guaranteed success ('Dans l'incertitude d'un succès il serait difficile de faire des dépenses de costumes'). It seems to have been far from certain in Boursault-Malherbe's mind that there should be a second performance at all. At the same time he seems to have resented an inference that he was not doing his best by Sade's play. He continued:

> Si vous le jugez à propos nous tenterons la seconde représenta-
> tion et vous devez sentir, Monsieur, que mon intérêt étant de
> faire de l'argent je suis plus jaloux que vous de faire réussir un
> ouvrage qui pourrait m'en rapporter.[38]

> If you judge it appropriate we shall attempt the second
> performance and you must accept, Monsieur, that since my

concern is to make money I am keener than you to ensure the success of a work which may be capable of making some for me.

It is perhaps disappointing that the play by Sade which Boursault-Malherbe saw fit to produce in the theatre which he had established as a centre of strident patriotism should have proved to be such a damp squib, not only in terms of political and social interest but, quite simply, as a play. What it was that decided him to put on *Oxtiern* we shall probably never know. It is perhaps just as disappointing that Sade who, in his *Adresse d'un Citoyen de Paris*, had published a work in which he adopted a stance in relation to recent political events, should not have offered the Théâtre Molière, given its reputation, a play with greater political content. But perhaps one reason for this was that he did not have Boursault-Malherbe's company particularly in mind, as *Oxtiern*'s rejection by the Feydeau demonstrates. *Oxtiern* is a bad play but it is an example of the fare offered to the theatre-going public in the Revolutionary years, and its author is a figure of some curiosity and indeed importance in the period.

The next play to be examined is, happily, the work of a man who was markedly superior to the Marquis de Sade as a playwright. It is at the same time a play which, for all its differences from *Oxtiern*, derives from the same tradition.

5

A BACHELOR'S LIFE

Jean-François Collin d'Harleville was born plain Jean-François Collin, the son of a Chartres lawyer, in 1755 and died in 1806. He took the *particule* from a property he bought, in the best *Ancien Régime* tradition. His apparently aristocratic name was no more genuine than that of Jean-Baptiste Poquelin de Molière or that of Pierre Caron de Beaumarchais. He was a somewhat ailing bachelor until the end of his days and his most famous play, the play which was seen by his contemporaries not only as his masterpiece but as one of the greatest plays of the eighteenth century, has a bachelor as its central character. This play, *Le Vieux Célibataire*, had its first performance at the Théâtre de la Nation on 24 February 1792 with the great Molé and Louise Contat playing the principal roles.[1] During the Revolutionary years it became markedly less fashionable to sport an aristocratic name, and on the title page of those editions of the play which appeared during this period the author's name is given as Collin-Harleville.

Le Vieux Célibataire was not, however, Collin's first play. Initially, he had followed in his father's footsteps and studied law in Paris, beginning to practise in Chartres in 1780. By that time, however, he had already written his first comedy, *L'Inconstant*. This play had one performance at Court in 1784, but did not receive its première at the Comédie-Française until 1786, when it was a considerable success. The same is true of his next two comedies, *L'Optimiste* (1788) and *Les Châteaux en Espagne* (1789).

The one-act Gascon farce *Monsieur de Crac dans son petit castel* (1791) was equally successful and did something to silence the principal criticism of Collin that was to be heard amongst all the praise, namely that his first three plays were very similar one to another and indeed amounted to one 'comédie en quinze actes'.[2] That he was aware of this accusation is clear from his poem *L'Auteur malade*, published in the *Almanach des Muses* in 1790:

> Que d'égoïsme encor, si l'on veut, on m'accuse;
> Qu'on répète surtout que ma stérile Muse
> (Car je sais qu'on l'a dit en plus d'un bon endroit)
> Va décrivant sans cesse un petit cercle étroit,
> Et que, toujours soumis à mes règles exactes,
> Je n'ai fait jusqu'ici qu'une pièce en quinze actes:
> Je ne me défends point . . .[3]

Let them again, if they wish, accuse me of self-centredness; let them above all repeat that my sterile Muse (for I know that this has been said in more than one place) always describes the same narrow circle and that, always submissive to my precise rules, I have so far only written one play in fifteen acts: I shall not defend myself. . .

More to the point, these early comedies were written by Collin in very stirring times indeed, when an entire society was being turned upside down, but no one would be very aware of any of that simply by examining the text of Collin's plays. The same is more or less true of *Le Vieux Célibataire* which, although it was not first performed until 1792 and not first published until late 1793 in a pirated edition and not published by Collin himself until 1794, was written in 1789 and read to the company at the Comédie-Française in late December 1790. No doubt the reason for the delay in performing was, as André Tissier points out, the internal strife within the company between the 'democrats' and the 'aristocrats' sparked off by M.-J. Chénier's *Charles IX* and which led to the former group, led by Talma, departing to the rue de Richelieu.[4] For all that, it would be quite wrong to suppose that Collin sailed through the Revolution oblivious to what was happening around him. In May 1789 Collin revealed understandable nervousness as to what was going on at the Estates General, expressing in a letter to his friend Louis Le Tellier the fervent prayer, 'Dieu veuille que tout cela tourne bien' ('God grant that all that turns out well'). In his *Epître à ma Muse*, published in the *Mercure de France* on 20 March 1790 he insists that he is no politician but is now sufficiently optimistic to express the kind of mildly monarchical view that it was still possible to put forward five months after Chénier's *Charles IX*:

> Bientôt, sous un bon Roi, l'aimable Liberté
> Ramènera le calme et la félicité.
> Heureux Peuple! heureux Roi! quel avenir s'apprête!

Soon, under a good king, delightful Liberty will bring back calm and felicity. Happy People! Happy King! What a future is being prepared!

No writer who had earned the enmity of Fabre d'Eglantine (himself a playwright but later to become a powerful member of the Committee of Public Safety) as Collin was to do, could possibly afford to ignore what was going on around him in the political sphere. Collin was certainly not a committed Jacobin ideologist like Fabre d'Eglantine. He did, however, play his part in Revolutionary activities – he became an officer in the National Guard – and one likes to think that he sought to act as a moderating influence during those violent years. Unlike Fabre d'Eglantine, who went to the guillotine with the other Dantonists on 5 April 1794, Collin survived the Terror and the reaction after the fall of Robespierre, retaining considerable popularity as a playwright through the Directory and the Consulate and on into the First Empire, until his death in 1806.

The trouble between Collin and Fabre d'Eglantine began before the outbreak of the Revolution and took the form of a dispute over Fabre's play *Le Présomptueux, ou l'Heureux Imaginaire* and Collin's *Les Châteaux en Espagne*,[5] two plays on the same subject. The hitherto unsuccessful playwright Fabre, whose play was first performed on 7 January 1789 in front of a hostile audience, claimed that Collin had plagiarized it for his play, which was premièred on 20 February and which consolidated Collin's reputation. If plagiarism there was, it seems to have been the other way round, in that Fabre benefited from confidences made to him by Collin about the play he proposed to write on the subject of castles in Spain. In any event, Fabre was not to forget that a cabal had been organized against his play on 7 January and remained an enemy of Collin's. The trouble between them was renewed when, after Collin had published some not very good autobiographical verses entitled *Mes Souvenirs*,[6] Fabre circulated a parody of them under the title *Mes Souvenances*.

The *Almanach des Muses* for 1790 published a poem by Collin entitled *A la Simplicité*, a poem liberal in sentiment, the theme of which is an attack on luxury, a common enough theme in the eighteenth century but one which gained, of course, added poignancy in these early years of the Revolution. Collin wrote,

> On gémit de l'abus, l'Etat est surchargé;
> Le passé fait frémir, et l'avenir effraie.
> L'on sonde, l'on découvre une profonde plaie:
> Il était temps, sans doute, et je le sais trop bien.
> J'en gémis et j'espère; au moins bon citoyen,
> Je fais de loin des vœux pour la chose publique;
> Mais homme et campagnard plutôt que politique,
> Je vois que des fléaux déchaînés contre nous,
> Le luxe, notre ouvrage, est le pire de tous.

People groan under abuse, the State is overburdened; the past makes one shudder, the future is frightening. An examination is made and a deep wound is found: it was high time, no doubt – I know that all too well. I groan because of it and I hope; at least as a good citizen from far away I conceive wishes for the public welfare, but as an ordinary man and a countryman at that rather than as a politician, I see that of all the plagues unleashed upon us, luxury, our own creation, is the worst of all.

He goes on to urge the rich man to be just and generous and to share with his less fortunate brother ('Sois juste et généreux, partage avec ton frère').

Matters became worse when, early in 1791, Fabre published the text of his play *Le Philinte de Molière* (first performed at the Théâtre de la Nation on 22 February 1790) along with a preface.[7] Fabre's play was a riposte to Collin's *L'Optimiste, ou l'Homme content de tout* of 1788, and in particular Act II scene ix of Fabre's work shows Philinte offering an outrageously cynical version of the all-is-for-the-best-in-the-best-of-all-possible-worlds philosophy of M. de Plinville, the central character of *L'Optimiste*. The purpose of Fabre's extravagant preface is to represent Collin's play as being counter-revolutionary *avant la lettre*, to suggest that it was commissioned, or at any rate suggested ('sinon commandé, du moins conseillé') by the Establishment under the *Ancien Régime* to transmit the message that, far from ignoring the miserable and the downtrodden, they were guided by virtue and love of order alone ('la vertu seule et l'amour de l'ordre guident les gens en place'): never was anything written that was more politically foolish and false or more barbarously lacking in humanity ('En fait de politique, a-t-on jamais écrit de naiserie plus fausse? en fait d'humanité, de maxime plus barbare?').[8] This was a grotesque over-reaction to Collin's light-weight comedy and smacks not only of the humourlessness which so often characterizes the political ideologist but also, of course, of personal resentment.

In his *Epître à ma Muse* Collin had insisted both upon the validity of appealing through the heart to men's sense of morality rather than through reason to effect political change and upon the importance of not being so solemn as to frown upon a little entertainment. His antipathy to excessive stress on political ideology and to the puritanical spirit which often accompanies it is apparent:

> Quand on rirait un peu, voyez! le grand malheur!
> Qu'on réforme l'Etat, j'y consens de bon cœur.
> L'utile, j'en conviens, l'utile est préférable;
> Mais à l'utile on peut allier l'agréable.
> Les plaisirs purs et vrais sont toujours de saison.

If people laugh a little, come now, what harm is there in that! Let the State be reformed, I readily agree to that. The things which are useful, I agree are preferable, but the agreeable can be joined to the useful. Pure and true pleasures are always in season.

In his poem *Les Muses délaissées*, however, which appeared in the *Almanach des Muses* in 1791, he clearly considered that a rather different tone was required. Whereas he had earlier been inclined to put more emphasis on aesthetic rather than on political values, he now writes,

> Aveugles! quoi, nous gémissons
> De voir l'art que nous chérissons,
> Paraître un moment inutile!
> Si Quatre-vingt-neuf fut stérile
> En bagatelles, en chansons,
> Contemplez tant d'autres moissons:
> Fut-il année aussi fertile?

Are we blind? What, do we complain to see the art which we

love seem useless for a short while! If '89 was sterile in trivia, in songs, just consider all its other harvests. Was there ever so fertile a year?

This can have done Collin no harm at all in the eyes of those in influential places.

In 1791 Fabre d'Eglantine did not have the power which he was later to acquire when, on 25 March 1793 he became a member of the Committee of Public Safety, and it would not be unreasonable to suppose that Collin felt increased nervousness during the period after that date until the day on which, just over a year later, Fabre went to the guillotine. In fact, however, performances of *L'Optimiste*, as Tissier has pointed out, were allowed on 12 June, 25 July and 22 August 1793, when Fabre d'Eglantine was at his most powerful.[9] No doubt Fabre had bigger fish to fry. In any event, shortly after this, on 3 September, the *Paméla* affair led to the closure of the Théâtre de la Nation and the imprisonment of virtually all the members of the company.[10]

Collin's own edition of his masterpiece *Le Vieux Célibataire* was published early in 1794, although it had been premièred, as we have seen, about two years earlier, on 24 February 1792. Although it is true that Fabre d'Eglantine was arrested on charges of corruption on 13 January 1794, the fact remains that this was a period when literature had to celebrate the Revolution if authors wished to avoid imprisonment and, quite possibly, death. André Chénier was to go to the guillotine on 25 July. Collin published with the text of his play a preface, which he concluded with a defence of his loyalty to the Revolution:

... j'espère bientôt mêler ma voix à celle des écrivains patriotes. Car c'est être véritablement patriote que de prêcher la morale; et, en un sens, je crois l'avoir été dès avant la Révolution. Cette Révolution va donner à nos accents plus de ton, à nos pensées plus d'énergie, et plus de développement à nos moyens; mais j'aime à croire que la décence et le goût auront toujours leur prix, et qu'avec des intentions droites et franches, un style pur et un but constamment moral, les auteurs dramatiques mériteront bien de la Patrie, et serviront aussi une République qui se fonde sur le patriotisme ardent, mais ne se soutient que par les mœurs et la vertu.[11]

... I hope soon to mingle my voice with the voice of the patriotic writers. For to preach morality is to be truly a patriot and, in a sense, I believe that I have been one since even before the Revolution. This Revolution will give greater quality to our voices, greater strength to our thoughts, and greater development to our methods; but I like to believe that decency and taste will always have their value and that, given upright, honest intentions, a pure style and a constantly moral aim, playwrights will deserve well of the Fatherland and will, furthermore, be of service to a Republic which is founded on burning patriotism but which is sustained only by morality and virtue.

Seeking to refute the charges which had been brought against him by Fabre d'Eglantine he produced a one-act sequel to *L'Optimiste*, entitled *Rose et Picard*, showing M. de Plinville living under the Revolution, still imbued with the spirit of optimism but now also full of the Revolutionary spirit and grateful that he already enjoys the happiness which will soon be the lot of the nation as a whole. With Robespierre in power, Collin included references to the cult of the Supreme Being in this sequel and wrote a *Hymne à l'Etre Suprême* which, on 10 June 1794 was recited on the stage of the Théâtre de la République. This hymn, which is anything but great poetry, was published in the *Journal de Paris* on 25 prairial an II (13 June 1794). In part, however, it is a plea for moderation and tolerance, as the following brief extract shows:

> Et surtout aimons-nous comme un peuple de frères.
> Plus de sectes, de lois l'une à l'autre contraires.
> Ne séparons jamais la fière Liberté,
>   La Justice et l'Humanité;
> Et que l'Etre Suprême avec plaisir contemple
> La France, qu'il chérit, devenue un beau temple,
> Où d'une voix on chante: honneur au Dieu du Ciel!
> Bénissons notre Père, adorons l'Eternel.

And above all, let us love one another like a people of brothers. No more internal divisions, no more contradictory laws. Let us never separate proud Liberty, Justice and Humanity; and let the Supreme Being with pleasure contemplate the France which it loves, now become a beautiful temple in which with one voice the people sing, 'Honour to the God of Heaven! Let us bless our Father. Let us adore the Eternal Being.'

On 16 June his sequel to *L'Optimiste* had its first performance at the Théâtre de la République, full of topical allusions, in which M. de Plinville, now called Agathon, gave plentiful proof of his – and therefore Collin's – patriotism.[12] Collin continued to write occasional verse of a patriotic character, such as a dialogue for the proposed inhumation of the remains of the young heroes of the Revolution, Barra and Viala, in the Pantheon (although in the event the arrest of Robespierre led to the cancellation of this ceremony).

What, however, was the state of affairs in France in February 1792, when the Théâtre de la Nation gave the first performance of *Le Vieux Célibataire?* By this stage in the development of the Revolution the prospects for the successful establishment of a constitutional monarchy were looking very slim indeed. The previous November, by vetoing the Assembly's decree which applied the death penalty and confiscation of property to all *émigrés* who remained assembled against the Revolution, the King had seemed to place himself openly on the side of the *émigrés*. When, on 29 November, the Assembly voted repressive measures against the refractory clergy, Louis XVI again used his veto. In March 1792, the month after Collin's play was first performed, the Girondins impeached the Foreign Minister and, under Dumouriez, obtained the Ministries of the Interior and of Finance for two of their number, Roland and Clavière. In April Louis was constrained upon, after a good deal of Girondin war propaganda, to declare war on Austria and, subsequently, Prussia. In June Louis vetoed a bill against the clergy and another one seeking to establish a camp near Paris for 20,000 National Guards from the provinces. Roland announced that the King must choose between the Revolution and those opposed to it. In consequence, on 12 June, Louis dismissed the Girondin ministers. Eight days later an armed mob attacked the Tuileries and threatened the royal family. On 11 July a state of emergency ('La patrie en danger') was declared and by the end of the year the King had been indicted on a charge of treason. There is precious little sign of such heady goings on in *Le Vieux Célibataire* (the play had, admittedly, been written a good deal earlier, but Collin was perfectly capable of introducing topical elements into his work when it suited him, as we have already mentioned).

The plot is thin and, in certain respects, calls for a fairly considerable degree of suspension of disbelief. The old bachelor of the title, M. Dubriage, has fallen under the influence of his housekeeper Mme Evrard, who has recently become a widow. She has introduced the unscrupulous Ambroise into the household as steward and the two of them have been working together to deprive their employer of his wealth. Were it not for the existence of a nephew, Armand, they would have things entirely their own way and Mme Evrard has sought to estrange Armand from his uncle by slandering him and his marriage to Laure, and by being selective and, on occasion, positively mendacious when it comes to reading Armand's letters to the old man. M. Dubriage has in consequence disowned his nephew, thus becoming isolated in his own house. Mme Evrard hits upon the scheme, as an answer to his avowed loneliness, of marrying M. Dubriage and in the process, of course, cutting Ambroise out of things and taking all her employer's wealth for herself. Meanwhile, the one loyal member of this *ménage*, the porter George, has succeeded in introducing Armand into the household as a servant, under the name of Charle: he also arranges the arrival of Armand's wife Laure, as an assistant to Mme Evrard. M. Dubriage is charmed by Laure, even when he knows her identity (he had been led to believe that his nephew had married a woman no better than she ought to be), and has already been charmed by Charle who (in due time) he is delighted to discover is his nephew. Mme Evrard and Ambroise are both discomfited and have to go away. Nothing very original here!

On the other hand, it would be quite wrong to suggest that *Le Vieux Célibataire* is a play which is totally divorced from the times in which it was written. There are, as we shall see, respects in which it belongs very clearly to the neo-classical tradition of comedy going back through Regnard to the greatest French comic playwright of them all, Molière. However, there are equally ways in which it belongs very much to its own day: for all its formal old-fashionedness, its characters, its setting, and its themes belong to a France which has seen the development, through Diderot, Sedaine, and Mercier, of the *drame*. What *Le Vieux Célibataire* is not, however, is a piece of political propaganda. This is not to say that its author has no values to express. He certainly has, but these are moral and social values rather than ideas peculiar to a given political ideology.

The play is formally traditional in that it is a five-act comedy, observing the unities, particularly those of time and place, and written in verse. The verse, it has to be admitted, is less than impressive much of the time: one cannot dissent from André Tissier's summary when he says, 'C'est souvent de la prose rimée dans un style facile, mais assez plat' ('It is often rhymed prose of a fluent style, but rather commonplace').[13] The subject matter itself cannot be said to be original: in his *avertissement* to the 1794 edition Collin himself recognized that Dubuisson's comedy *Le Vieux Garçon* (1782) supplied him not only with the basic subject but with a number of points of detail, and that Dorat's *Le Célibataire* (1775) and Regnard's *Le Légataire universel* (1708) amongst other plays might be seen as precedents, 'sans vouloir rappeler ici tous les vieux garçons qu'on a mis sur la scène, ce qui serait un peu long' ('without wishing to recall here all the old bachelors who have been portrayed on stage, which would take rather a long time'). He goes on specifically to deny any prior knowledge of Etienne Avisse's virtually forgotten comedy *La Gouvernante* (1737), although he admits that when the text of this play was drawn to his attention the similarities with his own play at first alarmed him.[14] As for the idea of a central character's wealth being pillaged by those around him, this is no uncommon situation in comedy: perhaps one of the most obvious examples is that of Lesage's five-act prose comedy *Turcaret* (1709), but the tone and implications of that 'ricochet de fourberies'[15] are quite different from those of *Le Vieux Célibataire*.

And yet Collin's play is far from being merely another literary comedy. If the device of having not only Armand but also his wife Laure incognito in M. Dubriage's household suggests a certain lack of realism about the situation which we are offered in the play (not quite as improbable, perhaps, as the double disguise which is at the heart of Marivaux's *Le Jeu de l'amour et du hasard* (1730), but not an unrelated device) and if M. Dubriage's gullibility in allowing Mme Evrard to read – and distort – his nephew's letters rather than taking the trouble to read them for himself is marginally less extreme than that of Bartholo in Beaumarchais's *Le Barbier de Séville* (1775), who is in turn blind and deaf as the twists of the plot and Almaviva's wooing of Rosine dictate, such elements in *Le Vieux Célibataire* are traditional to the point of being hackneyed. Nonetheless, there is more to Collin's work than this.

If Collin remains faithful to the traditions of seventeenth-century comedy in still writing in verse, it is nevertheless the case that he both avoids the kind of preciosity which Molière both used and satirized and the new preciosity of which the eighteenth century was fond. In his own day, it was said of Collin's style by *La Décade philosophique* for 10 frimaire an XII (2 December 1803) that 'c'est la conversation des honnêtes gens', and indeed what he somehow succeeds in offering us is what André Tissier describes as 'une conversation familière en vers' ('a colloquial conversation in verse').[16] It may be the case that for the purist, as he eyes the printed page of Collin's text, the verse seems very fractured. And so it is. And yet most of the time it has about it, for all that, a ring of authenticity as casual conversation which the prose of Diderot's *Le Fils naturel* (published in 1757) or *Le Père de famille* (1758) can by no means always be said to possess. There are no long, melodramatic tirades in *Le Vieux Célibataire*: to the contrary one has an impression of everyday, broken conversation, full of the common tricks of ordinary speech. Much of Collin's vocabulary consists of the kind of brief words and interjections which one might hear in relaxed conversation any day of the week: André Tissier has counted in this play 69 examples of 'ah!', 78 of 'eh!', 36 of 'oh!', 9 of 'quoi!', 7 of 'ô ciel!', 15 of 'bon!', 110 of 'oui', 52 of 'non', 23 of 'allons!', and so on.[17] It is true that some of these expressions are used on occasion to pad out lines of verse but the overall effect is of remarkably fresh and convincing dialogue, much more 'realistic' than the plot in which it is used. This is in harmony with the aims of Diderot in developing the theory of the *drame*, or with the views of Jean-Jacques Rousseau, who wrote of the great neo-classical playwrights of the seventeenth century (he was thinking particularly here of Racine and Corneille),

> Communément, tout se passe en beaux dialogues, bien agencés, bien ronflants, où l'on voit d'abord que le premier soin de chaque interlocuteur est toujours celui de briller. . . Tout cela vient de ce que le Français ne cherche point sur la scène le naturel et l'illusion et n'y veut que l'esprit et des pensées. . .[18]

> Usually, everything happens in fine dialogues, well constructed, very high-sounding, and one sees straight away that the prime aim of each speaker is always to stand out. . .
> All that stems from the fact that the French do not seek in the theatre that which is natural or its illusion and only want wit and ideas. . .

Le Vieux Célibataire parts company too from the seventeenth-century tradition of comedy in that it does not set out to examine a great, universal type such as the misanthropist or the miser. In his thin plot and his excellent dialogue what Collin studies is in many ways much closer to the 'condition' advocated by Diderot and as exemplified in the titles of Diderot's two plays *Le Fils naturel* and *Le Père de famille*.[19] The old bachelor is just as much a 'condition' as either of these two states, and it is certainly the case, as we shall see, that Collin is trying to make a general point about the unmarried condition (which was a topical issue of the day) quite as much as he is trying to portray an individual bachelor in M. Dubriage. At the same time it has to be conceded that Diderot is, in the end, making a false distinction when he seeks to separate 'caractère' from 'condition', and it is certainly true that the characters in *Le Vieux Célibataire* – especially M. Dubriage and Mme Evrard – are markedly more interesting than the artificial, conventional situation in which they are placed. It is not going too far to say that, despite its old-fashioned, seventeenth-century structure (especially in its observation of the unities and the retention of the alexandrine rhyming couplet, in however adulterated a form), *Le Vieux Célibataire* contains many of the essential themes and much of the tone of the *drame*: the emphasis on the bourgeois milieu and values (especially the defence of marriage and the family), the lack of class-consciousness between master and servants (abused by Mme Evrard and Ambroise but not by George), a stress on honesty and honest work as anything but demeaning, a certain implication that the provinces are perhaps less corrupt than Paris, an implied belief in natural religion, and a marked emphasis on sensibility and pathos which points the way towards nineteenth-century melodrama.

Like that other (and far greater, no doubt) eighteenth-century writer of sensibility, Jean-Jacques Rousseau, Collin did not enjoy good health (some would suggest that the pair of them enjoyed ill health) and manifested a certain misanthropy. In this respect it is interesting to speculate as to how far the portrait offered of M. Dubriage is autobiographical and how far it expresses Collin's regret at having missed the joys of conjugal life as described by both Armand in his role as Charle and by George. Certainly M. Dubriage makes much of the loneliness which is his in his celibate state:

M. DUBRIAGE

Je n'ai pas un ami dans toute la nature,
Pour verser dans son sein les peines que j'endure
(I. viii. 321-2)

I have not a single friend in the whole of Nature into whose
bosom I could pour out the sufferings which I undergo.

Tu le vois, je suis seul sur la terre,
Triste. . .

CHARLE

Seul, dites-vous?

M. DUBRIAGE

Oui, je suis solitaire.
Ah! pourquoi, jeune encore, au moins dans l'âge mûr,
Ne faisais-je pas choix d'une femme?
(I. viii. 325-8)

M. DUBRIAGE As you see, I am alone in the world. Sad. . .
CHARLE Alone, you say?
M. DUBRIAGE Yes, I am a solitary being. Ah! Why, when I
was still young – or at least when I reached mature years – did I
not choose a wife?

M. Dubriage tries to console himself with the thought that
marriage is a tie. He is not allowed to get away with this, however:
Charle (Armand) points out to him that it can be a pleasant tie
and tellingly draws his uncle's attention to the fact that by
avoiding the bonds of matrimony one sometimes places oneself in a
worse form of servitude (I. viii. 347-50). M. Dubriage says that
married life is too full of worries, to which his nephew replies that,
along with the responsibilities of marriage goes its pleasure, which
is lacking in a purely mercenary household ('un alentour
mercenaire, étranger') such as that of M. Dubriage (I. viii. 363-9).
This theme of praise of married life is taken up by the porter
George, a happily married man with two children, in Act II. When

M. Dubriage complains to George of his loneliness, George says that he is always happy (a fact which his employer has observed) and attributes this to matrimony and goes on to point out that there is no need for M. Dubriage to remain in his sorry state:

GEORGE

Pourquoi rester garçon? Il ne tenait qu'à vous,
Dans votre état, avec une grosse fortune,
De trouver une femme, et dix mille pour une.

M. DUBRIAGE

Que veux-tu?. . . J'ai toujours aimé le célibat.

GEORGE

Célibat, dites-vous? C'est donc là votre état?
Triste état, si par là, comme je le soupçonne,
On n'entend n'aimer rien, ne tenir à personne!
Vive le mariage! Il faut se marier,
Riche ou non; et tenez, je m'en vais parier
Que si quelqu'un offrait au plus pauvre des hommes
Un hôtel, une carrosse, avec de grosses sommes,
Pour qu'il vécut garçon, il dirait: 'Grand merci;
Plutôt que d'être riche, et que de l'être ainsi,
J'aime cent fois mieux vivre, au fond de la campagne,
Pauvre, grattant la terre, auprès d'une compagne.'

M. DUBRIAGE

Assez.

GEORGE

Ce que j'en dis, c'est par pure amitié;
C'est que vraiment, monsieur, vous me faites pitié.

M. DUBRIAGE

Pitié!

GEORGE

Je suis honteux de voir qu'un misérable,
Que moi, qui près de vous ne suis qu'un pauvre diable,
Sois plus heureux pourtant; c'est chagrin que j'ai.

M. DUBRIAGE

De ta compassion je te suis obligé;
Mais changeons de sujet.

(II. ii. 492-513)

GEORGE Why remain a bachelor? It was entirely up to you, in your station in life, with a great fortune, if you wanted to find a wife – any one of ten thousand.

M. DUBRIAGE What do you mean? I have always liked celibacy.

GEORGE Celibacy, you say? So that is the name of the state you are in? It is a sad state if, as I suspect, it means not loving anyone, not belonging to anyone! Long live marriage! Everybody should marry, whether they are rich or not. I'll tell you something: I am prepared to bet that if the poorest of men was offered a mansion, a coach and lots of money provided that he lived a bachelor's life, he would say, 'No thanks! Rather than be rich, in that way, I would a hundred times sooner live in the depths of the countryside, poor, scratching the earth for a living, with a wife by my side.

M. DUBRIAGE That is enough.

GEORGE What I say is out of pure friendship. The truth of the matter, sir, is that I pity you.

M. DUBRIAGE Pity!

GEORGE I am ashamed to see that a miserable fellow like me, who by comparison with you am nothing but a poor devil, should for all that be happier than you are. That upsets me.

M. DUBRIAGE I am obliged to you for your compassion. But let us change the subject.

By the end of the play, faced with the spectacle not only of George's happy marriage but also of that of Armand and Laure, M. Dubriage comes to a full appreciation of what he has missed in his bachelor life:

En m'isolant ainsi, je sens que j'ai perdu
Plus d'une jouissance et plus d'une vertu.
Trop juste châtiment! Quiconque fut rebelle
Aux lois de la nature en est puni par elle.

(V. ix. 1863-6)

By isolating myself in this way, I feel that I have lost many a pleasure and many a virtue. The punishment is only too just! Whoever rebels against the laws of nature is punished by her.

This passionate defence of conjugal bliss would not have been out of place in a *drame* and certainly M. Dubriage's observation about the laws of nature could have been written by Diderot himself. One is put in mind of his remark on the subject of the ascetic Christian ideal which was so contrary to his own nature:

C'est le comble de la folie, que de se proposer la ruine des passions. Le beau projet que celui d'un dévot qui se tourmente comme un forcené pour ne rien désirer, ne rien aimer, ne rien sentir, et qui finirait par devenir un vrai monstre s'il réussissait![20]

To seek the destruction of the passions is the height of folly. What a fine plan is that of the devout person who torments himself like a madman so as to desire nothing, to love nothing, to feel nothing, and who would end up by becoming a real monster if he succeeded!

M. Dubriage has not, of course, come to this extremity, and as a substitute for what he has missed, he in effect adopts Armand and Laure as his own children, refusing to allow them to call him 'Uncle': 'Dites *mon père*; moi, je dis bien *mes enfants*' ('Call me "Father"; as for me, I shall certainly say, "My children"')(V. ix. 1880). In the closing lines of the play M. Dubriage makes it clear that what he has learned is intended to have a general application in society:

Si quelque chose manque encore à mon bonheur,
C'est ma faute; du moins mes regrets salutaires
Seront une leçon pour les célibataires.

(V. ix. 1884-6)

If there is still anything lacking for my happiness, the fault is mine; at least my salutary regrets will serve as a lesson for all unmarried people.

In eighteenth-century France opposition to celibacy in all its forms was a part of enlightened thinking for a variety of reasons, one of which was that it was thought (mistakenly) that France was undergoing a crisis of depopulation. In fact the opposite was true and France was at the beginning of a population explosion. Thus Diderot is by no means alone in attacking celibacy at this time. The idea that the doors of the convents and monasteries should be thrown open and their denizens be let out to do something practical about this fancied crisis of depopulation is quite a favourite cry of Voltaire's, too. These themes of Collin's play, then, fitted in with the spirit of the times. On 13 February 1790 the National Assembly had passed a decree prohibiting monastic vows and stipulating (Article 2) that individuals of either sex at present in monasteries might leave them by making a declaration before the local municipality.[21] The Convention, which succeeded the National Assembly with effect from 21 September 1792, went so far as to offer cash incentives to parents of potential defenders of the homeland.[22]

That the question of celibacy was indeed a matter of some topicality is indicated by a work entitled *Réflexions philosophiques sur le plaisir; par un célibataire*, usually attributed to Grimod de la Reynière, a friend of Collin's.[23] Tissier argues that celibacy had come to be fashionable in eighteenth-century society outside the religious orders in consequence of the immorality of the Regency and the reign of Louis XV, because it made it possible for the man of fashion to satisfy all his whims and sexual instincts without let or hindrance.[24] Whatever the truth of this, the *Réflexions philosophiques* has a number of alarming things to say about the sexual mores of the latter years of the *Ancien Régime*. Convent education is blamed for the unpreparedness of young girls for life in the outside world (p. 26), of women it is said that 'amour-propre' is almost universally their dominant passion (p. 21) and that it has to be agreed that they are in large measure responsible for contemporary dissoluteness ('Convenons . . . que les femmes sont en grande partie cause de la dissolution des mœurs actuelles')(p. 31). This low view of women is certainly shared up to a point by Collin's M. Dubriage, although he is reluctant to believe that they are quite as black – or as scarlet – as they are sometimes painted. The following exchange between him and his disguised nephew gives a fair flavour of this aspect of the play:

M. DUBRIAGE

Les femmes (sans parler ici de leur vertu:
J'aime à croire qu'à tort souvent on les décrie),
Mais conviens qu'elles sont d'une coquetterie,
D'un luxe!. . . Telle femme est charmante, entre nous,
Dont on serait fâché de devenir l'époux;
Tel mari semble heureux, qui, dans le fond de l'âme,
Gémit. . .

CHARLE

Mais en revanche il est plus d'une femme,
Modeste en ses désirs et simple dans ses goûts,
Qui met tout son bonheur à plaire à son époux.

M. DUBRIAGE

Il en est, mais bien peu.

(I. viii. 352-61)

M.DUBRIAGE   Women (Let us not discuss their virtue here: I like to think that they are often wrongly disparaged), well you must agree that they are so coquettish, so fond of luxury!. . . Between you and me, there is many a charming woman whose husband one would hate to be. Many a husband seems happy who, in his heart of hearts, is bemoaning his fate. . .
CHARLE   On the other hand, there is more than one woman, modest in her desires and simple in her tastes, who derives all her happiness from pleasing her husband.
M. DUBRIAGE   There are some, but very few.

Charle's attitude may not seem very attractive in the twentieth century, but it is at least less positively anti-feminist than that expressed by M. Dubriage or that of the *Réflexions philosophiques sur le plaisir*.

In the section of the *Réflexions* which deals specifically with marriage, the influence of Rousseau is manifest (although the author is not afraid to differ from 'l'éloquent Citoyen de Genève' on occasion) and the similarity with what M. Dubriage says about deviation from the laws of nature in the closing scene of *Le Vieux Célibataire* is striking: 'Plus [l'homme] s'est éloigné de la Nature, plus il s'est écarté du bonheur' (p. 49) ('The further man has moved away from Nature, the more he has distanced himself from happiness'). In Paris, largely in consequence of the system of arranged marriages, wedlock is no more than a commercial agreement in which each partner seeks his or her own advantage: 'les mariages d'inclination sont aujourd'hui fort rares: ils jettent une sorte de ridicule sur ceux qui les contractent. . .' (pp. 50-1) ('love matches are extremely rare these days: those who enter into them are seen as ridiculous in a way'). In the light of statements such as this, backed up by the example of the unhappy marriage of a colleague witnessed by M. Dubriage, one can well understand Collin's character's reluctance to embark on matrimony: 'la Société n'est plus qu'un échange d'infidélités réciproques' (p. 55) ('Society these days is nothing other than an exchange of reciprocal infidelities'). In the *Réflexions* this view of society (which has a good deal in common with the view propounded by Chamfort, who mixed in Girondin circles and was put in charge of the Bibliothèque Nationale in August 1792 by Roland), that 'l'amour, tel qu'il existe dans la Société, n'est que l'échange de deux fantaisies et le contact de deux épidermes' ('love, as it exists in Society, is no more than the exchange of two fantasies and the contact of two skins')[25] does not speak well for the aristocracy under the *Ancien Régime*, whatever the degree of truth it may be thought to express. The author of the *Réflexions* contends that it is almost only amongst the middle classes that the domestic virtues are to be found: 'ce n'est presque jamais que dans la Bourgeoisie, et surtout dans le Commerce, qu'on trouve l'exemple des vertus domestiques' (p. 58).

In that part of the *Réflexions* which deals specifically with celibacy (pp. 60-78) we are assured that about 100,000 of the 700,000 inhabitants of Paris are not married and that there are 40,000 prostitutes in the city, this flourishing of the oldest profession being seen as a direct consequence of the fashion for celibacy. The causes underlying this fashion are the expense: two certainly cannot live as cheaply as one, since women are so obsessed by the luxuries of life. As old age approaches, we are told, many a bachelor dreads being robbed by his servants and feels the need of company and of children (the parallel with Collin's play is very clear here): he therefore marries. More marriages take place between the age of 50 and 65 than between 30 and 40, and some of these marriages unite old men with young girls:

> Quoi de plus ridicule, de plus odieux même, que de voir une jeune personne de 18 ans devenir la proie d'un vieillard de 60?. . . Ces sortes d'unions ne sont cependant pas rares.
>
> (*Réflexions*, p. 69)

What is there more ridiculous, more odious indeed, than the sight of a young girl of 18 years of age becoming the prey of an old man of 60?. . . And yet these sorts of unions are not rare.

In *Le Vieux Célibataire*, M. Dubriage is too sensible to make that kind of mistake. Referring to the thought he had had of marrying Mme Evrard, he says at the end of the play,

> Me mariant si tard, comme tant d'autres font,
> Pour réparer un tort j'en avais un second.
>
> (V. ix. 1875-6)

Marrying so late, as so many others do, I would have committed a second wrong whilst trying to right the first.

It seems clear that in tackling the question of celibacy Collin was taking up a theme which reflected badly on the society of the *Ancien Régime* and that, in approaching it in the way he did, he was doing something which was likely to appeal to the Revolutionary authorities. There are a couple of other aspects of *Le Vieux Célibataire* which the playwright could hope might appeal to those in charge of the new political order of things. The first of these amounts to an anticipation of legislation which the Convention was to bring in on 7 March 1793 abolishing the right to dispose as one wished of one's property either by gift whilst living or by last will and testament after death: all heirs were to have an equal share of the estate of the deceased. The sentiments expressed by M. Dubriage in Act IV of *Le Vieux Célibataire* are very much in harmony with this later legislation. M. Dubriage says that despite the complaints he has against his nephew Armand he has never felt it proper to disinherit him. Indeed, he has never made a will at all:

> Mais, malgré mes griefs contre Armand,
> Je répugnai toujours à faire un testament:
> Je ne sais. . . de tout temps je m'en suis fait scrupule.
> Je trouve un testament injuste et ridicule.
> Disposer de ses biens en mourant, c'est vouloir
> Au-delà de sa vie étendre son pouvoir.
>
> (IV. ii. 1223-8)

And yet, despite my grievances against Armand, I always felt reluctant to draw up a will: I don't know. . . I have always had scruples about it. I find a will unjust and ridiculous. To dispose of one's property when one dies is to wish to extend one's power beyond the end of one's life.

M. Dubriage was less rigorous, however, than the Convention was to prove to be: the decree of March 1793 banned the distribution of one's property in the form of gifts during one's lifetime, but M. Dubriage sees nothing wrong with that. He goes on:

> Que l'on donne ses biens, soit; alors on s'en prive;
> Mais être généreux lorsque la mort arrive!. . .
> On ouvre un testament; ces premiers mots sont lus:
> 'Je veux. . .' On dit encore *je veux* quand on n'est plus!
>
> (IV. ii. 1229-32)

If people wish to give their property away, all well and good: then they are making a sacrifice, but to be generous when death comes along! . . . The will is opened and it begins with the following words: '*I wish* . . .' You are still saying I wish when you are dead!

The other aspect of *Le Vieux Célibataire* which might be thought likely to appeal to the Revolutionary authorities is to be found in the very next scene, where the newly arrived Laure meets M. Dubriage for the first time and is immediately seen by her husband's uncle to be a woman of honour and candour. Laure attributes these qualities to the upbringing which she has received from her parents. M. Dubriage says that she must have had 'd'honnêtes parents' and this remark gives rise to what Jacques Truchet suggests must be one of the last examples of the opposition of two senses of the word 'honnête', the one being found in the almost untranslatable expression 'honnête homme', a purely social concept dear to the French seventeenth century, and the other being the moral sense of 'honest'. The concept of 'honnêteté' was an essentially aristocratic one and had no essentially moral content: in no sense did it equate with the notion of 'honesty' but rather referred to the qualities necessary for a gentleman to integrate himself as elegantly as possible into polite society. The 'honnête homme' was a gentleman, and a gentleman in the seventeenth century (and no doubt at any time) did not seek to detach himself from polite society around him: the desire to integrate with society as opposed to standing outside it or in opposition to it is central to the concept. The Duc de la Rochefoucauld defined the 'honnête homme' as the man who preens himself on nothing: 'celui qui ne se pique de rien'.[26]

This is one of the main reasons why, for a seventeenth-century audience, Alceste, in Molière's *Le Misanthrope*, who behaves in a manner directly opposed to what is appropriate to an 'honnête homme', insisting on being recognized as a special individual ('Je veux qu'on me distingue'),[27] was a comical figure, and why Rousseau, that moralistic man not over-endowed with humour, attacked Molière so roundly in his *Lettre à M. d'Alembert sur les spectacles* (1758) for having poked fun at such a virtuous man as Alceste, that 'véritable homme de bien'. In what he writes Rousseau signals the imminent arrival of the Romantic hero who, far from integrating into society, is very much at odds with it, and also expresses the same opposition between two senses of the word 'honnête' which we find in Collin's play. Rousseau writes as follows:

Je trouve que cette comédie [*Le Misanthrope*] nous découvre mieux qu'aucune autre la véritable vue dans laquelle Molière a composé son théâtre. . . . Ayant à plaire au public, il a consulté le goût le plus général de ceux qui le composent: sur ce goût il s'est formé un modèle, et sur ce modèle un tableau des défauts contraires, dans lequel il a pris ses caractères comiques, et dont il a distribué les divers traits dans ses pièces. Il n'a donc point prétendu former un honnête homme, mais un homme du monde; par conséquent il n'a point voulu corriger les vices, mais les ridicules. . . . Ainsi, voulant exposer à la risée publique tous les défauts opposés aux qualités de l'homme aimable, de l'homme de Société, après avoir joué tant d'autre ridicules, il lui restait à jouer celui que le monde pardonne le moins, le ridicule de la vertu: c'est ce qu'il a fait dans le *Misanthrope*.[28]

I consider that this comedy [*Le Misanthrope*] shows us better than any other the true intent with which Molière wrote his theatrical works. . . . Having to please the public, he consulted the most widely held taste of those of whom it is composed: he built a model on the basis of that taste, and on the model he constructed a tableau of the contrary faults and from this he took his comic characters, distributing their various traits throughout his plays. And so he did not lay claim to forming an honest man, but a man of the world. Consequently, he did not wish to correct vices but what were considered ridiculous ways. . . . Thus, wishing to hold up to public mockery all the faults opposed to the qualities possessed by the agreeable man, the Society man, having made fun of so many other ridiculous ways, it was left to him to make fun of the one of which society is least forgiving, the ridiculous behaviour called virtue: that is what he did in *Le Misanthrope*.

What we find in *Le Vieux Célibataire* is the following piece of dialogue:

M. DUBRIAGE

Vous devez donc le jour à d'honnêtes parents?

LAURE

Honnêtes? Oui, monsieur; mais non pas dans le sens
Que lui donnait l'orgueil; dans le sens véritable.
Mes père et mère étaient un couple respectable,
Placé dans cette classe où l'homme dédaigné
Mange à peine un pain noir de ses sueurs baigné,
Où, privé trop souvent d'un bien mince salaire,
Un ouvrier utile est nommé *mercenaire*,
Quand on devrait bénir ses travaux bienfaisants;
Mes parents, en un mot, étaient des artisans.

M. DUBRIAGE

Artisans! Croyez-vous qu'un riche oisif les vaille?
Le plus homme de bien est celui qui travaille.

(IV. iii. 1263-74)

M. DUBRIAGE   So you were born of honest parents?
LAURE   Honest? Yes, sir, but not in the sense which pride
gives to that word; in the true sense. My father and mother were
a respectable couple placed in that scorned class where a man
may have barely more to eat than black bread soaked in his own
sweat; where a useful worker, too often deprived of his tiny wage,
is called a *mercenary*, when his useful work should rather be
blessed. My parents, in short, were working people.
M. DUBRIAGE   Working people? Do you believe that a rich
idler is worth as much as they? The best man is the man who
works.

Not only does Laure here indulge in praise of the lower orders such
as is to be found in so many eighteenth-century *drames*, but, as
Truchet points out,[29] she makes it pretty clear that the concept of
the 'honnête homme' so valued in the society of the likes of La
Rochefoucauld is a thing of the past, killed off by the Revolution
with the society based on pride which gave it birth.

None of this, of course, is enough for us to hail *Le Vieux Célibataire*
as a masterpiece of Revolutionary drama. And indeed it is nothing
of the sort. Such factors as we have suggested might appeal to the
Revolutionary authorities are peripheral to the main plot and the
main themes of the play. The heart of the play is certainly not
Revolutionary ideology or propaganda. Nevertheless, although
Collin's play cannot be seen as a masterpiece of Revolutionary
drama, it has frequently been hailed as the best comedy of the
Revolutionary years. This was certainly the view of many of
Collin's contemporaries. That it was in its own day a great success
is undeniable: Tissier points to the 245 performances of *Le Vieux
Célibataire* in Paris between 1792 and 1886, to the number of
editions and translations published in France and abroad, and to
the curiously unanimous praise which the play received in the
closing years of the eighteenth century.[30] On 6 March 1792, just a
few days after the opening night, the *Journal des théâtres* declared
that *Le Vieux Célibataire* confirmed its author's talent ('Nous

regardons cette comédie comme celle qui prononce le talent dramatique de M. Collin d'Harleville') and on 4 April 1792 *Les Petites Annonces* described it as his best play. On 1 March 1794 the *Journal de Paris* judged that whilst Collin's earlier plays had already guaranteed him a distinguished reputation amongst modern writers, *Le Vieux Célibataire* took him to the very first rank, and on 18 June of the same year *La Décade philosophique* was prepared to compare him with Terence. Tissier notes that with Collin's friend Grimod de la Reynière enthusiasm became delirium and in January 1798 in *Le Censeur dramatique* he spoke of *Le Vieux Célibataire* as the placing of the seal of genius on Collin's reputation; in February he was claiming it as one of the best plays produced in the eighteenth century ('l'une des meilleures pièces dont le dix-huitième siècle ait droit de s'honorer'); after a performance of the play on 13 May 1798 Grimod was so ecstatic that he concluded that, after having seen the play performed so brilliantly, the only thing left to do was to die ('Il n'y a plus qu'à mourir après avoir ainsi vu jouer la comédie').[31] And so the chorus of praise went on, into the early years of the nineteenth century, until the first signs of the end of the period of adulation came in 1811, when in the 3 October number of the *Journal de l'Empire* Geoffroy attacked the central character in Collin's play as caricatural: 'ce n'est point là un caractère, c'est une caricature'. *Le Vieux Célibataire* was revived in 1859, but was a failure. Its high reputation, that of Collin d'Harleville and (it has to be admitted) that of the theatre of the Revolutionary period was from that point on more or less dead.[32]

In purely literary or theatrical terms one cannot seriously quarrel with the judgment passed on *Le Vieux Célibataire* by succeeding generations since the latter part of the nineteenth century. The play's historical interest is perhaps a different matter. But the truth is that *Le Vieux Célibataire*, endowed in the fashion of the day with a greater dosage of sentimentality than finds favour with modern audiences, is none the less a well made play. It is certainly no better than that. It really cannot any longer be regarded as one of the best plays of the eighteenth century. It is difficult to conceive of anyone giving it the advantage over the best of Marivaux's comedies or over Beaumarchais's great pre-Revolutionary comedies, *Le Barbier de Séville* and *Le Mariage de Figaro*, although it would stand up favourably to comparison with Beaumarchais's third Figaro play produced during the Revolution,

La Mère coupable, which flopped at the Théâtre du Marais on 26 June 1792. Lesage's *Turcaret* is surely a better play than *Le Vieux Célibataire* by most criteria. So, the present author would argue, is Sedaine's *Le Philosophe sans le savoir* (1765), although perhaps not by much.

The problem is rather less to explain the oblivion into which Collin d'Harleville and *Le Vieux Célibataire* have fallen than to explain the great success which they enjoyed in their own day. No doubt the success of Collin's play in his own lifetime is to be explained by the fact that it appealed to many of the attitudes and values which were popular in the closing years of the eighteenth century – the sentimentality, the fondness for drawing a moral lesson, a certain brand of realism (the bourgeois· interior, M. Dubriage's walks in the Luxembourg gardens). Something of this appeal can still be felt, despite a lack of verisimilitude in some aspects of the plot. The severely fractured alexandrine rhyming couplets (perhaps in consequence of the fact that they *are* fractured) can be seen as offering quite lively and convincing colloquial dialogue. This does not, however, explain the inordinate praise which was heaped upon it. To have managed to combine many of the themes which were already common in the *drames* of the late eighteenth century with a thin plot and a form which was in so many ways very old-fashioned, looking back to Molière and the seventeenth century, in a play which has a certain life is, no doubt, an achievement of a kind and it is certainly one which Collin could claim.

It is not easy to explain the astonishing success of *Le Vieux Célibataire*. Certainly it is not enough to say, as does L.H. Skinner, that 'The strong character study of the· scheming housekeeper constitutes the play's most valid claim to first rank in the period,[33] or to rhapsodize nonsensically, as does Lenient, about Mme Evrard as an 'Agrippine de la domesticité'.[34] Mme Evrard has precious little in common with the daunting mother-figure of Racine's *Britannicus*. On the other hand, the skill of the actress who played Mme Evrard, Mlle Contat, may well have made a considerable contribution to the remarkably high esteem in which Collin's play was held in the latter years of the eighteenth century. A clue to at least part of the answer may indeed be found in the rapturous remark by Grimod de la Reynière quoted on page 132: 'Il n'y a plus qu'à mourir après avoir ainsi vu jouer la comédie'.

The emphasis here is on the brilliance of the performance, and Collin does indeed seem to have been well served by his actors.[35] In particular he was well served by Molé, who twenty-seven years earlier had played the younger Vanderk in *Le Philosophe sans le savoir* and who since then had become 'l'idole du public',[36] in the part of M. Dubriage, and by Louise Contat in the part of Mme Evrard. Tissier argues convincingly that it is a common phenomenon in periods of what he calls 'indigence littéraire' that, in the absence of any great new plays, the public dotes on a given actor or actress (one might be tempted to add 'or director') to the extent of going to see not a particular play but something in which that particular actor or actress (or director) is involved. And Tissier draws our attention to an interesting passage in *La Décade philosophique* for 23 October 1803 (30 vendémiaire an XII):

> L'art dramatique n'est plus l'art de composer la tragédie ou la comédie; c'est l'art de la jouer. . . . Les auteurs n'étant rien et les comédiens étant tout, il est naturel qu'il se forme des acteurs, mais fort peu de poètes dramatiques. Ce dernier métier est mis trop au-dessous de l'autre.[37]

> Dramatic art is no longer the art of writing tragedy or comedy; it is the art of acting them. . . . Authors counting for nothing and actors counting for everything, it is natural that actors should flourish and that there should be very few playwrights. This latter profession is placed too far below the other.

This no doubt does not approach a total explanation of the astonishingly eulogistic reaction to Collin d'Harleville and to *Le Vieux Célibataire* in particular but it is surely an important factor. Did the public go to see Chénier's tragedies or to see Talma? Did they go to see Collin's comedies or Molé and Mlle Contat? One must be careful not to oversimplify – but one cannot doubt the capacity of great actors to make a success of relatively undistinguished material and this is, as Tissier suggests, all the more likely to happen when there is a famine of really first-class playwrighting talent.

For the most part, the plays written by Collin d'Harleville after *Le Vieux Célibataire* were markedly less successful, with the exception (up to a point) of *Les Mœurs du jour*, premièred on 26 July 1800.[38] He was, however, anything but forgotten in his final years.

On 14 December 1795 he was elected to the Institut National, which body had been created that year by the Directory as a replacement for the Académies which had been abolished in 1793. The Legion of Honour was conceived of under the Consulate but by the time the first Chevaliers were sworn in the Empire had been inaugurated. Collin d'Harleville's name was on the first list of those to receive this decoration, but it is not known whether he was well enough to be present to receive the award in person from the Emperor in the ceremony held in the chapel of the Invalides on 15 July 1804. He died, at the age of fifty, on the fourteenth anniversary of the first performance of *Le Vieux Célibataire*.

Whatever the liberal attitudes one may detect in *Le Vieux Célibataire*, one cannot reasonably describe it as a piece of political propaganda. The same is by no means true of the next two plays to be examined, Laya's *L'Ami des lois* and Maréchal's *Le Jugement dernier des rois*.

6

LIBERTY AND LICENCE

Jean-Louis Laya (1761-1833), in collaboration with his friend Gabriel Legouvé, himself to become a tragic playwright, first went into print in 1786 with a collection of elegies. After the beginning of the Revolution he experienced success as a playwright, first of all with his tragedy *Jean Calas* (1789) and then with a *drame* entitled *Les Dangers de l'opinion* (1790). Both of these plays were, it is fair to say, *pièces à thèse*. Voltaire had made Jean Calas into an archetypal victim of oppression and a number of playwrights in the Revolutionary years were to treat the subject;[1] *Les Dangers de l'opinion*, whilst it avoided tendentious topicality, nevertheless dealt with the risks of stigmatizing the innocent. As the *Gazette nationale* for 4 January 1793 put it, in a favourable but perhaps not entirely objective review of Laya's third play, which is to be our subject in this chapter,

> Dans un pays où il existe des citoyens, où le mot de patrie offre un sens, la première idée, le premier désir de chacun doit être de chercher les moyens de se rendre utile à tous.
>
> L'un de nos auteurs dramatiques, le citoyen Laya, s'est constamment proposé, dans ses productions, ce but honorable. *Le* [sic] *Danger des opinions* attaquait ce préjugé cruel qui rendait commune à des parents vertueux l'infamie dû au seul coupable; *Jean Calas* montrait la barbarie et le danger de nos lois criminelles. Le troisième ouvrage qu'il vient de donner, *L'Ami des lois*, tend à éclairer le peuple sur ses vrais intérêts, à lui montrer les maux et les crimes qu'entraînent la licence et l'anarchie, à ramener tous les citoyens vers un centre commun, le bonheur public, qui n'existera jamais sans gouvernement, sans ordre, sans respect des lois.

In a country in which there are citizens, in which the word fatherland has meaning, the prime notion, the prime desire of everyone should be to seek means of being useful to all.

One of our playwrights, Citizen Laya, has always set himself this honourable goal. Le [sic] Danger des opinions attacked the cruel prejudice whereby the infamy appropriate to a guilty person is extended to that person's virtuous relations; Jean Calas depicted the barbarity and the dangers of our criminal laws. The third work which he has just presented, L'Ami des lois, seeks to enlighten the people as to their real interests, to show them the evil and the crimes which follow in the train of licence and anarchy and to lead all citizens towards a common focus, public happiness, which will never exist without government, without order, without respect for the law.

L'Ami des lois had its first performance on 2 January 1793 at the Théâtre de la Nation, well known for the conservative sympathies of its troupe of actors (although prior to putting on Laya's play it had sought to avoid politically controversial productions).

It could scarcely have appeared at a more emotional moment in the history of the Revolution: Louis XVI's trial before the Convention was under way. A résumé of the disturbances occasioned by the production of L'Ami des lois has already been given,[2] but some particulars will have to be dwelt on here. The play became part of a power struggle between the Girondins and the Montagnards in the Convention and between the Convention and the much more radical Commune of Paris. The troubles which marked the play's performances were the beginning of a series of events which culminated, six months later, in the closure of the Théâtre de la Nation and the imprisonment of the members of its company.

The Montagnards accused the Girondins of being lukewarm in their attitude to the Revolution and of being federalists whilst they, the Montagnards, were sublimely loyal to the 'République une et indivisible'. The Girondins, as is implicit in the title of Laya's play, accused the leaders of the Montagne, especially Robespierre, of lack of respect for the law and of dictatorial tendencies. L'Ami des lois is unmistakably a Girondist play. In 1802, there was no doubt about it:

Tout le monde reconnut Robespierre dans Nomophage, et Marat dans Duricrâne.[3]

Everyone recognized Robespierre in Nomophage, and Marat in Duricrâne.

There is little question that many people saw Robespierre in Nomophage, the principal villain of the play and Marat, editor of *L'Ami du peuple*, in his accomplice, the journalist Duricrâne, although, as Truchet points out, there was some hesitation over the keys to the real-life identity of the characters (with Marat being suggested as the original for the character of the 'enragé' Plaude, who was also said to have been inspired by the leaders of the Commune, Hébert and Chaumette).[4] At the time, of course, Laya coyly insisted,

> Non, je n'ai point fait, comme on ose le dire, de mon art, qui doit être l'école du civisme et des mœurs, la satire des individus.[5]

> No, I have not, as some have dared to say, made of my art, which must be a school of civic virtue and morality, a satire of individuals.

Truchet is right to remind us that although Laya was praised throughout the nineteenth century as a courageous Girondin standing up to the wicked Jacobin brigands,[6] and although in the event the Girondins lost the struggle with their more extreme opponents, it was not self-evident in January 1793 that this would be the outcome, and Laya was not taking up the cudgels on behalf of the oppressed citizenry as much as playing the part of a committed political propagandist taking sides in an ideological battle which the Girondins hoped and intended to win.[7]

The form in which Laya set his propaganda was anything but original. He takes the basic situation of Molière's comedy *Les Femmes savantes* (1672) and reworks it for his own purposes. If, in Molière's verse comedy, Chrysale's wife Philaminte is, to her husband's exasperation, besotted with the foppish *beaux esprits* Vadius and Trissotin, in Laya's verse comedy Mme de Versac[8] is equally besotted with the two Revolutionary militants, the 'eater of laws' Nomophage, described in the manuscript as a 'grand démagogue', and the journalist Duricrâne. Philaminte appears as the head of a literary and intellectual salon and Mme de Versac appears at the head of a Revolutionary salon. She can not bear the thought of Forlis marrying her daughter because he has failed to place himself at the head of a Revolutionary faction. In effect, she considers that Forlis's prospects are not good, since he appears to have missed the Revolutionary boat. She says to him,

Avec tous vos talents, chef d'une faction,
Vous eussiez agrandi vos biens et votre nom;
Quand l'audace est encor la vertu de votre âge,
Quand il fallait oser, vous avez fait le sage;
Faux calcul! vous voyez, avec tous vos talents
Vous restez de côté, tandis que d'autre gens,
Moins forts que vous peut-être, auront sur vous la pomme.

(I. iv. 199-205)

With all your talents, as the leader of a faction, you would have enhanced both your fortune and your reputation. When boldness was the virtue of your age, when you should have dared, you were docile. What a miscalculation! You see, for all your talents, you remain to one side whilst other people, quite possibly less gifted than you, will carry off the prize.

So just as Clitandre is out of fashion in *Les Femmes savantes*, so Forlis (who, in Girondin terms, represents the true patriot) is, in a very different way and in a very different world, out of fashion in *L'Ami des lois*. And of course, the salon favourites in the two plays get their come-uppance and the reasonable man takes the centre of the stage for the final bow. The love theme, however, has become so insignificant by comparison with Molière's play, in which we are given the views of two daughters of Philaminte concerning the relationship between the sexes, that in *L'Ami des lois* M. and Mme de Versac's daughter does not even appear on stage: her parents simply agree in the final scene of the play that there is no one other than Forlis to whom they would wish to see her married (V. vi. 1455).

It is remarkable to see just how long a shadow was cast by Molière. Laya's play stands as perhaps even more striking an example of this than that offered by Fabre d'Eglantine's *Le Philinte de Molière*. The debt is clear, not only to *Les Femmes savantes*,[9] but also to *Le Misanthrope* and, inevitably, to *Tartuffe*. In the discussion at the Convention of *L'Ami de lois* and the attempt by the Montagnards and the Commune to have it banned, one unnamed speaker saw the comparison with Molière and made the point that

Lorsque Molière voulut faire jouer son *Tartuffe*, tous les

hypocrites et les hommes qui y étaient joués s'opposèrent à la représentation de cette pièce; cependant elle fut jouée et c'était sous le règne de Louis XIV.[10]

When Molière wished to have his *Tartuffe* performed, all the hypocrites and all those who were made fun of opposed this play's being staged; nonetheless it was performed, and that was in the reign of Louis XIV.

If this could happen under the absolute monarch *par excellence*, surely the new order could afford to put on Laya's play?

Laya himself, in the preface in which in 1793 he dedicated the published text of his play to the members of the Convention – his *Epître dédicatoire aux Représentants de la Nation* – drew the comparison between himself and the great master of French comedy:

Molière, dans *Tartuffe*, n'a fait de son vrai dévot qu'un moraliste. Ce grand homme nous a donné dans le personnage de Cléante, la théorie de la véritable piété. Quelque humoriste du temps eût pu élever des doutes sur la tenue de son caractère dans les applications de la vie. Mais ici [in the case of Forlis] c'est un philosophe pratique; ce n'est pas seulement par des discours, c'est par ses actions qu'il prêche et qu'il persuade.[11]

Molière, in *Tartuffe*, made his genuine devout man merely a moralist. The great man, in the character Cléante, gave us the theory of true piety. Some humourist of the time might well have raised doubts as to the behaviour of his character in everyday life. But here [in the case of Forlis] is a practical philosopher: it is by his actions that he preaches and persuades.

A little later on in the *Epître dédicatoire* Laya offers what he says are lines from an unfinished prologue to his play in the form of a dialogue between the author and a friend. Here too he makes a comparison with Molière and says he intends to show as much courage as his great predecessor. The friend asks whether Laya has Molière's genius and Laya modestly accepts that he has not:

> Moi suivre ce géant dans sa course infinie!
> Jamais! Très faible auteur, mais très bon citoyen,
> Je borne ici ma gloire à faire un peu de bien.[12]

I? Follow that giant in his boundless course! Never! As a very poor writer but a very good citizen I limit my claim to glory here to that of having done a little good.

The mark of the Molière tradition on *L'Ami des lois* is clear, not only in particular points of resemblance with particular plays, but also in the fact that this is a five-act verse play, with the alexandrine couplet still the chosen form, with unity of time, place and action pretty well adhered to.

But this no doubt is the mark of the seventeenth-century neo-classical tradition in general rather than that of Molière. The concentration on a crisis within the lives of the characters is as much a feature of seventeenth-century tragedy as of comedy and the same is true of the absence of action on stage. At the end of Act IV Filto is sent out to report on what happens to Forlis when he bravely goes to meet the angry mob, and his lengthy account in Act V, scene iii of the grandeur of Forlis on the one hand and that of the people of Paris on the other hand has rhetorical aspirations which put one in mind of Racine: Filto may be given a function not entirely dissimilar to that of Théramène in the final act of *Phèdre*, but there the resemblances between the poetic brillance of Racine and the verse of Laya end. Where Racine achieves grandeur, Laya only achieves the grandiose. Ignoring for the moment the political point which is being made in the following lines, they do perhaps reveal something of the essential difference of tone and outlook between the seventeenth century and the eighteenth. Filto is asked by Versac by what prodigy Forlis was saved from the rage of the crowd, and he replies,

> Un prodige chez lui de grandeur, de courage;
> Chez le peuple un prodige à jamais répété.
> De justice, d'égards, de sensibilité!
> Tout ce qu'on vit jamais de noble et d'équitable,
> Tout ce qui fut jamais et grand et respectable,
> A paru dans une heure entre le peuple et lui;
> Ils ont lutté tous deux de vertus aujourd'hui.
> L'un était digne enfin d'être sauvé par l'autre.
>
> (V. iii. 1296-1303)

On his part a prodigy of greatness, of courage; on the part of the people an ever-repeated prodigy. Of justice, respect and sensibility. All the nobility and equity that was ever seen, all that was ever both great and worthy of respect was there in an hour between the people and him. Today they vied in virtue with each other. In short, the one was worthy of being saved by the other.

The reference to sensibility is important here. It is in its emphasis on sensibility – not to say sentimentality – that *L'Ami des lois* reveals the other great literary influence which it has undergone (that of the *drame*) and shows the imminence of the melodramas of Pixerécourt and his nineteenth-century successors.

Sensibility, of course, is not all that there is to the *drame*, but it is undoubtedly one characteristic of that genre. And sensibility there is in plenty in Laya's play. Sensibility and, on occasion, sententiousness. Forlis, of course, lays claim to being a rationalist: rationalism is the basis of his political system and it is because of his faith in the power of reason that he is able to remain optimistic about the future of his friend Versac, a *ci-devant* baron who is proud of his aristocratic blood and titles, a state of mind of which Forlis is certain that his friend will be cured:

> Je réponds à présent de votre guérison.
> Vous raisonnez; c'est être à moitié démocrate.
>
> (I. i. 132-3)

Now I am certain of your cure. You are being rational; that is halfway to being a democrat.

And there is plenty of rational discussion in this play, to which we shall return in due course. But there are other factors which will play a part in effecting Versac's cure and one of these is the qualities within the true revolutionaries which appeal to his better nature. This is particularly true, of course, of Forlis, and by the end of the play Forlis's virtue has almost won Versac over to the Revolution:

VERSAC

> Ce diable d'homme en soi je ne sais quoi renferme
> Qui, si je m'oubliais, si je n'étais pas ferme,
> Me ferait presque aimer sa Révolution!

FORLIS

> Vous l'aimerez.
>
> (V. vi. 1447-50)

VERSAC This devil of a man contains within himself something or other which, if I were to forget myself, if I were not firm, would almost make me love his Revolution!
FORLIS You will love it.

The process, however, starts much earlier in the play. When the villainous Nomophage and Duricrâne arrange for the arrest of Forlis, the principal officer sent to carry out this task is so impressed by Forlis's demeanour and respect for the law that he proposes to leave him on parole in the care of Versac or, as he puts it, to make him a prisoner of the friend who loves him ('Vous faire prisonnier de l'ami qui vous aime') (III. v. 772). Versac is very impressed by this and is promptly assured that this is normal Revolutionary behaviour:

VERSAC

Quel noble procédé! je ne l'attendais pas.

L'OFFICIER

Vous avez tort, messieurs: nos citoyens soldats
Ont tous le même cœur, ont tous le même zèle.
Ces cœurs n'admettent point une vertu cruelle;
Et, jamais endurci d'insensibilité,
Le courage est toujours chez eux l'humanité.

(III. v. 777-82)

VERSAC What noble behaviour! I was not expecting that.

THE OFFICER You are wrong, gentlemen: our citizen soldiers all have the same heart, all have the same zeal. These hearts do not accept that virtue can be cruel and, since they have never been made hard by lack of sensibility, for them courage is always synonymous with humanity.

Filto, Nomophage's friend, is weak rather than wicked and has been said to be based on Prieur de la Marne,[13] a member of the Convention and of the Committee of Public Safety. He has a certain nostalgia for virtue and innocence, as his rather Diderotian – or even Sadian – debate (to which we shall return) with Nomophage as to whether virtue can exist in the world in which they find themselves, or whether Nomophage's view of humankind is a blasphemy against nature reveals (IV. i-ii). It is in connection with Filto that much of the sensibility, indeed the mawkishness, of the play finds expression. He is most impressed by the courage and virtue shown by Forlis as he faces up to the mob and by the way in which he brings that mob back to the kind of virtuous behaviour which, we are to believe, is the norm for the people ('Peuple juste et d'un crime incapable' (V. iii. 1315)), as he recounts in the long narrative to which we have already referred. He seeks to make his evil life with Nomophage a thing of the past. In the final scene, when Mme de Versac wishes to send Filto away, Forlis will have none of it. He insists that Filto has been led astray by evil men and tells him,

> J'ai lu dans votre âme,
> Elle est droite.
>
> (V. vi. 1436-7)

I have examined your soul. It is a straightforward one.

And, a little later,

FORLIS

> Vous avez dû rougir quand vous étiez coupable.
> Le repentir, monsieur, fait de vous mon semblable.
> Donnez-moi votre main.

FILTO

> Sous le crime abattu,
> Je puis près de vous seul renaître à la vertu.

FORLIS

> Vous la sentez déjà.

FILTO

> Votre voix consolante
> Rassure et raffermit mon âme chancelante;
> Au sentier des vertus j'ai besoin d'un soutien.
> Je réponds de mon cœur, si vous êtes le sien.
>
> (V. vi. 1439-46)

FORLIS You must have blushed in the days of your guilt.
Your repentance, monsieur, makes you a man like me. Give me
your hand.
FILTO Laid low by crime, only by your side can I be reborn
to virtue.
FORLIS You can feel it happening already.
FILTO Your consoling reassures and strengthens my wavering
soul. I shall need a support along the path of virtues. I will
answer for my heart, if you are its support.

And so the play ends in a welter of mawkishness, with Versac
being told that not only will he come to love the Revolution but
that he will do so 'à l'adoration' (V. vi. 1450), and with Mme
Versac coming to a view of life not dissimilar from that of
Henriette in *Les Femmes savantes* and deciding to devote herself
henceforth to her family, since that is the way in which a woman
can love and serve the fatherland ('C'est ainsi qu'une femme aime
et sert la patrie' (V. vi. 1468)).

The last lines of the play are Mme de Versac's words of thanks
to Forlis,

> Puisque dans vos leçons vous nous montrez si bien
> Que le seul honnête homme est le vrai citoyen.
>
> (V. vi. 1469-70)

Since in your lessons you show us so clearly that only the honest
man is a true citizen.

It is clear that the sense of 'honnête homme' here is moral and not
social. The opposition between the two senses which is referred to
in Collin d'Harleville's *Le Vieux Célibataire*[14] is clearly a thing of the
past.

The point has already been made, however, that sensibility
lurching into sentimentality is by no means the only distinguishing
mark of the *drame*, although it tends to appear there with fair
frequency. Nor, for that matter, is it exclusive to that genre. There
are other aspects of *L'Ami des lois*, however, which can be seen to
relate to the *drame*. No doubt the 'ami des lois' is as much a
'condition' as the 'philosophe sans le savoir'. Sedaine's play has it
in common with Laya's that, whilst both eschew aristocratic
values, each has a person of noble birth as the central character:
M. Vanderk is 'titré de chevalier, d'ancien Baron de Savières,

de Clavières, de. . .'[15] and Forlis, we know, is a *ci-devant* marquis. The *drame* is a prose genre, and the alexandrine verse of the epic, tragic and high comedy traditions seems in Laya's play perhaps even more inappropriate than in *Le Vieux Célibataire*, for here we have a play which sets out to show us something of what contemporary life in Paris was really like. That picture is clearly far from an objective one in some ways (in so far as the political propaganda is concerned), but there can be no doubt that we derive from *L'Ami des lois* a clear conviction that the characters live in a Paris which is rent by dissension, in which crowds on occasion roam the streets and burn down houses (Forlis's house suffers this fate) and in which one can be hauled off to court as a counter-revolutionary at any moment. This aspect of the play can, up to a point, be said to fulfil the demand for realism made by Diderot for the *drame*. Diderot, after all, had insisted that there was nothing which happened in this world which could not be depicted on stage ('Il n'y a rien de ce qui se passe dans le monde, qui ne puisse avoir lieu sur la scène').[16] On the other hand, none of the dramatic moments, such as the burning of Forlis's house, or his facing up to the crowd in the street, or his triumphant appearance in court, is actually seen on stage: they are all narrated, in the best tradition of the seventeenth century. The dialogue, it has to be said, is markedly more stilted and considerably more overblown than that in *Le Vieux Célibataire*. Collin d'Harleville, in some measure by fracturing the alexandrine couplet, produced convincing colloquial dialogue; Laya produces clumsy alexandrines which are trying to be as rhetorical as those of a Corneille or a Racine (Filto's narrative in Act V is a particularly clear example of this). The way in which the characters are for the most part divided into black and white, into opposing stereotypes of good and evil (although in Laya's case this is done primarily to make his political point) helps to link the *drame* with the melodrama which was to flourish in the nineteenth century.

There are, quite apart from the links with the *drame*, other connections between *L'Ami des lois* and Denis Diderot. In particular, there is a relationship between Laya's play and the works of Diderot to which Truchet points when he suggests that Nomophage, for all his coarseness, has a certain panache and attains in his downfall a kind of grandeur even, as is indicated by his final words in the play,

Adieu, monsieur Forlis. Vous pouvez l'emporter;
Mais j'étais avec vous digne au moins de lutter

(V. iv. 1405-6)

Farewell, Monsieur Forlis. You may have won the day, but at
least I proved worthy to do battle with you.[17]

It is no doubt true that this is an indication of the imminence of
full-blown melodrama in the French theatre but, in terms of
Diderot, it is an indication of more than that. Nomophage may put
one in mind of the double-died villain of melodrama, but there is
more to him than that, something which suggests a relationship
between him and the 'malheureusement né' individual in Diderot's
determinist universe, such as the character Lui in *Le Neveu de
Rameau* (perhaps Forlis can be seen as one who is 'heureusement
né', such as Jacques in *Jacques le Fataliste*).

Filto, in his soliloquy in Act II, scene iv, is perhaps the first to
nudge us towards such a comparison and to encourage us to think
of Laya's play in terms of one of the central Diderotian themes,
namely consideration of the nature of genius and the fear of
mediocrity. Filto observes of Nomophage and Duricrâne,

Ces deux enragés-là, Nomophage surtout,
Ont fait un intrigant de moi, contre mon goût.
J'étais né pour la vie honnête et sédentaire.
C'est le plus grand des maux qu'être sans caractère.
Dans les nœuds des serpents je suis pris. . . aujourd'hui.
Remplissons notre sort, je n'ai qu'eux pour appui.
Hélas! que ne peut-on, d'une marche commune,
En restant honnête homme aller à la fortune!

(II. iv. 509-16)

Those two fanatics, especially Nomophage, have made a plotter
of me against my wish. I was born for an honest, sedentary
existence. To be lacking in character is the greatest of
misfortunes. I am caught up in the snakes' coils . . . today. Let
us fulfil our destiny. They are my only support. Alas! why can
one not, keeping step with one's fellows, make one's fortune
whilst remaining an honest man!

These thoughts certainly have something in common with the
tensions between Lui and Moi, the two speakers in Diderot's great

dialogue work, but the relationship between Laya's play and aspects of Diderot's thinking becomes more strongly marked when Nomophage, Filto's mentor in villainy, says to him,

> Sachez qu'un scélérat, mais grand, mais prononcé,
> Vaut mieux que l'être nul dans son néant fixé,
> Honnête sans vertu, criminel sans courage,
> Et qu'il faut être enfin Forlis ou Nomophage.

> (IV. i. 843-6)

Appreciate that a villain, a great one, an outstanding one, is worth more than the worthless human being stuck in his nothingness, honest without virtue or criminal without courage, and that in fact what you need to be is either a Forlis or a Nomophage.

The parallel is striking between this statement and that of Diderot's Lui, that

> S'il importe d'être sublime en quelque genre, c'est surtout en mal. On crache sur un petit filou; mais on ne peut refuser une sorte de considération à un grand criminel. Son courage vous étonne. Son atrocité vous fait frémir. On prise en tout l'unité de caractère.[18]

If it is important to be sublime in any way, it is above all in evil. People spit on a petty rogue, but they cannot refuse a certain respect to a great criminal. His courage amazes you. His atrociousness makes you tremble. People value unity of character in all things.

Not only is the basic point similar, but the melodrama is there too.

The whole of this first scene of Act IV hammers home Nomophage's message: God is dead and therefore everything is permissible (the play antedates by more than a year the Robespierrean cult of the Supreme Being). At times things become almost Sadian, although more often than not one can find Diderotian precedents for the attitudes expressed. Laya is clearly well acquainted with the liberal thinkers of the French Enlightenment. Nomophage's

> Les formes ne sont rien, le grand but c'est la vie.
> Pourvu qu'au mouvement la matière asservie

148

Dans son cours productif roule éternellement,
Elle vit, elle enfante, il n'importe comment.

(IV. i. 881-4)

Forms count for nothing, the great aim is life. Provided that
matter, subject to movement, rolls eternally onward on its
productive course, it lives, it gives birth, and matters little.

and his 'Rien ne se perd, s'éteint, tout change seulement' (IV. i.
891) ('Nothing is lost or extinguished, it is simply that all things
change') have something in common with the following passage
from Diderot's *Le Rêve de d'Alembert* (written in 1769, published
1830),

Je suis donc tel, parce qu'il a fallu que je fusse tel. Changez le
tout, vous me changez nécessairement; mais le tout change sans
cesse. . . . L'homme n'est qu'un effet commun, le monstre qu'un
effet rare; tous les deux également naturels, également nécessaires, également dans l'ordre universel et général. . . . Et qu'est-
ce qu'il y a d'étonnant à cela? . . . Tous les êtres circulent les uns
dans les autres, par conséquent dans toutes les espèces . . . tout
est en un flux perpétuel. . . . Tout animal est plus ou moins
homme; tout minéral est plus ou moins plante; toute plante est
plus ou moins animal. Il n'y a rien de précis en nature. . .[19]

So I am thus because it was necessary that I be thus. Change the
whole and of necessity you change me; but the whole is changing
unceasingly. . . . Man is simply a common effect, the monster a
rare effect: both are equally natural, equally necessary, equally
in the general, universal order of things. . . . And what is there
surprising about that?. . . All beings circulate the ones in the
others, and consequently in all species . . . everything is in
perpetual flux. . . . Every animal is more or less man; every
mineral is more or less plant; every plant is more or less animal.
There is nothing precise in nature. . .

A little further on in the same work we read,

Naître, vivre et passer, c'est changer de formes. . . Et qu'importe
une forme ou une autre? Chaque forme a le bonheur et le
malheur qui lui est propre.[20]

To be born, to live and to pass away, is to change forms . . . And what does one form rather than another matter? Each form has the good fortune and the misfortune which is proper to it.

Not that such ideas were original to Diderot, who was something of an intellectual magpie, although an astonishingly creative one (and it is less than likely that Laya was intimately acquainted with many of Diderot's ideas at first hand, since so many of the great *philosophe's* works were not published in his lifetime, or indeed for some time thereafter, although a few fortunate individuals could read them in manuscript versions which were circulated). In the passages quoted immediately above, the influence of Buffon and of La Mettrie is particularly clear. What is interesting is that the villainous Robespierre figure in Laya's piece of propaganda theatre seems well versed in the radical views of the *philosophes* and shows a certain kinship with the Marquis de Sade. Something very akin to Diderot's determinism in Nomophage's attitude to life is pointed out by Filto (who seeks, weakly, to challenge it): 'Ainsi point de vertus, voilà la conséquence?' (IV. i. 909) ('And so there is no such thing as virtue, that is the consequence?'). In *Le Rêve de d'Alembert*, Dr Bordeu is made to argue that,

> On est heureusement ou malheureusement né; on est insensible-ment entraîné par le torrent général qui conduit l'un à la gloire, l'autre à l'ignominie.[21]

> One is born either fortunate or unfortunate; one is imperceptibly carried along by the general torrent which leads this individual to glory and that one to disgrace.

And the best that Bordeu (and Diderot) can do, not very convincingly, is to suggest that the word 'virtue' ('vertu') be replaced by the word 'charity' ('bienfaisance'). The eminently 'heureusement né' Jacques is taken to task by his master when he voices a determinist view of things and is told that if one accepted his line of argument there would be no crime which one could not commit without remorse and he remarks cheerily,

> Ce que vous m'objectez là m'a plus d'une fois chiffonné la cervelle; mais . . . puis-je n'être pas moi? Et étant moi, puis-je faire autrement que moi? . . . Prêchez tant qu'il vous plaira, vos raisons seront peut-être bonnes; mais s'il est écrit en moi ou là-haut que je les trouverai mauvaises, que voulez-vous que j'y fasse?[22]

What you put forward there has bothered my brain more than once; but . . . can I not be me? And, being me, can I behave other than as me? . . . Preach as much as you like, your reasons may be good ones; but if it is written within me or on high that I should find them bad, what do you expect me to do about it?

If Jacques represents the sunnier expression of eighteenth-century determinism, Laya's political enemy under the guise of Nomophage, not to mention any number of Sade's monsters, represents its black side.

One should not seek to make too much of Nomophage as a character, however, or indeed of the other characters in *L'Ami des lois*. The truth of the matter is that they are pasteboard characters representing different political positions, black and white stereotypes. Nomophage and Duricrâne are the Montagnards, represented in this play quite simply as scoundrels masquerading as patriots, prepared to use Machiavellian methods to further their own personal ambitions, prepared to say anything to bring about the downfall of those who oppose them and to fall back on the argument, if their plans should go wrong, that 'We may have made a mistake but it was sincerely done, in the best interests of the people', a spine-chilling prognostication of the kind of cynicism which has characterized the representatives of more than one political ideology since Laya's day. Perhaps the best example of this in *L'Ami des lois* comes in the opening scene of Act III, when Filto urges caution on Nomophage in respect of Forlis. Nomophage is sublimely confident, assuring his acolyte that there is nothing to fear from Forlis:

> Sottes alarmes!
> Car enfin, contre lui n'avons-nous pas des armes?
> Je mets la chose au pis, et ma haine y consent:
> Forlis est cru coupable et se trouve innocent.
> Bon! ses accusateurs ont tort? Erreur nouvelle.
> Ils se sont égarés, oui, mais c'était par zèle;
> Leur terreur, quoique fausse, était un saint effroi,
> Et le salut du peuple est la suprême loi.
>
> (III. i. 519-26)

Foolish fears! For, after all, do we not have weapons against him? I postulate the worst scenario, and my hatred concedes that it might come about: Forlis is believed guilty but is then found to be innocent. Right! So his accusers were at fault? Wrong again. They were misguided, yes, but it was through zeal; their terror, although mistaken, was a holy fear, and the safety of the people is the supreme law.

Laya's position in his play is that the rule of law is the supreme law and cannot be over-ridden on the pretext that public safety demands it. Thus it is that Forlis insists on the all-importance of obeying the laws:

> ... sans leurs saintes entraves
> La liberté, monsieur, est le droit du brigand.
> Le plus libre est des lois le moins indépendant;
> Malheur à tout état où règne l'arbitraire...
>
> (III. iv. 696-9)

... without their sacred constraints, freedom, sir, becomes the right of the brigand. He who is most free is he who is least independent of laws. Woe betide any state subject to arbitrary rule.

There is perhaps more than a hint here of the doctrine expounded by Rousseau in the *Contrat social* and based, apparently paradoxically, on the notion of the sovereignty of the people, of forcing people to be free.[23]

Forlis, of course, represents the Girondin position, and it is the Girondin position which triumphs. The enemies of the Girondins are accused of failing to respect the law: above all else, Forlis is 'l'ami des lois'. His enemies are also accused of wishing to dismember France: it is, as J.-A. Rivoire has pointed out, a telling device to find Laya accusing the Montagnards of such intentions, since it was they who presented themselves as champions of the one, indivisible Republic and accused the Girondins of federalism.[24] On the other had, it has to be admitted that the way in which this is done is more than a little melodramatic, with Nomophage uttering the following remarkably cynical statement of policy,

> Il faut qu'avant huit jours ce Forlis qui nous nuit
> Tombe, ou nous: de sa fin notre règne est le fruit;
> Et de l'ordre et des lois ces fidèles apôtres
> Sont les amis du peuple, et ne sont pas les nôtres.
> Un Forlis, dégagé de toute ambition,

Ivre de son pays pour toute passion,
Ne doit être à nos yeux qu'un monstre en politique.
Ces prôneurs d'unité dans une république
Sont des fléaux pour nous; un état démembré
Seul à l'ambition offre un règne assuré.

(II. ii. 349-58)

Within a week either this man Forlis who does us harm must fall, or we must fall: our reign will be the fruit of his defeat, and these faithful apostles of order and legality are the people's friends, not ours. A man like Forlis, devoid of all ambition, whose only passion is that he is intoxicated by his country, can only be in our eyes a political monster. These advocates of unity in a republic are plagues upon us: a dismembered state alone can offer ambition certain rule.

The theme of national dismemberment is hammered home in a comical manner when Nomophage and Filto, fantasizing about their futures, see the daughter of the *ci-devant* baron de Versac as beneath them:

NOMOPHAGE

L'empereur du Poitou, digne allié des rois,
Ne pourra plus descendre à ces liens bourgeois.

FILTO

Monsieur le gouverneur de l'un et l'autre Maine
Peut trouver dans les cours quelque infante, et sans peine

(II. ii. 397-400)

NOMOPHAGE The Emperor of Poitou, worthy of a royal alliance, will no longer be able to sink to such bourgeois connections.
FILTO His Excellency the Governor of both the Maines will be able to find in one of the Courts some Infanta, without any difficulty.

Another concept discussed in Laya's play which can be said to have overtones of Rousseau about it, is the concept of property. It is, of course, true that Rousseau began the second part of his discourse on the origins of inequality with the statement that

153

Le premier qui ayant enclos un terrain, s'avisa de dire, *ceci est à moi*, et trouva des gens assez simples pour le croire, fut le vrai fondateur de la société civile. Que de crimes, de guerres, de meurtres, que de misères et d'horreurs, n'eût point épargnés au Genre humain celui qui arrachant les pieux ou comblant le fossé, eût crié à ses semblables, 'Gardez-vous d'écouter cet imposteur; Vous êtes perdus, si vous oubliez que les fruits sont à tous, et que la Terre n'est à personne . . .'[25]

The first person who closed in a piece of land, took it into his head to say, 'This is mine', and found people simple-minded enough to believe him, was the true founder of civil society. From how many crimes, wars, murders, miseries and horrors might humanity have been saved by the man who, pulling up the fencing-stakes or filling in the boundary ditch, had cried out to his fellows, 'Beware of listening to this impostor; you are lost if you forget that the fruits of the earth belong to everybody and the earth itself to nobody.'

For Plaude, in Laya's play, the sole cause of France's problems is property: he has written a treatise to demonstrate this fact (III. iii. 600-20). The whole of his speech on this subject is distorted Rousseauism, directed towards justifying the unscrupulous criminality of the opportunists which Rousseau was so determined to control through such concepts as that of the General Will, the sovereignty of the people, and respect for the law. Says Plaude,

> Tout est commun; le vol n'est plus vol, c'est justice.
> J'abolis la vertu pour mieux tuer le vice.
>
> (III. iii. 619-20)

Everything is in common. Theft is no longer theft: it is justice. I abolish virtue in order the better to put an end to vice.

Forlis's reply to Plaude's tirade is the ironical statement that moderation is not his weakness ('La modération n'est pas votre défaut'), to which Nomophage responds by saying that moderate people are not what France needs ('Tant mieux; les modérés ne sont pas ce qu'il faut') (III. iii. 621-2).

Here Laya is to be found tackling another aspect of the political debate of the day between Montagnards and Girondins. As Rivoire points out, the two principal charges made against the Girondins by the Montagnards were *fédéralisme* and *modérantisme*.[26] We have already seen that Laya's response on behalf of the Girondins to the first of these charges was to turn it round and suggest that it was in fact the Montagnards who wished to split up the country. Let us see how he responds to the second charge. He (or Forlis on his behalf) makes it clear that he has no time for those who are moderate only in the sense that they have no opinions,

> Ces égoïstes nuls, ces hommes sans élans
> Endormis dans la mort de leurs goûts nonchalants
> (III. iii. 625-6)

Those worthless egotists, those men without drive, quiescent in the death of their unconcerned tastes.

But such are not the real moderates:

> Mais si vous entendez par ce mot l'homme sage,
> Citoyen par le cœur plus que par le langage,
> Qui contre l'intrigant défend la vérité,
> En dût-il perdre un peu de popularité,
> Sert, sachant l'estimer et parfois lui déplaire,
> Le peuple pour le peuple et non pour le salaire,
> Patriote, et non pas de ceux-là dont la voix
> Va crier *Liberté* jusqu'au plus haut des toits,
> Mais de ceux qui sans bruit, sans parti, sans systèmes,
> Prêchent toujours la loi qu'ils respectent eux-mêmes;
> Si fuir les factions, c'est être modéré,
> De cette injure alors j'ai droit d'être honoré.
> (III. iii. 631-42)

But if by that word you mean the sound fellow who is a citizen through what he feels in his heart more than through the words he utters, who defends truth against schemers even at the cost of a little popularity, who serves the people for the people's sake and not for the money, knowing how to value the people and when it is necessary to displease them, and who is a patriot – not one of those who shouts *Freedom* from the highest rooftops, but rather one of those who, quietly, without party prejudice, without theorizing, always speak up for the law which they themselves respect. If to flee from faction is to be moderate, then I am entitled to be honoured with that insult.

He tells Nomophage that there are others to be feared rather than the moderates thus defined. Nomophage asks whether he means the haughty powers, those heroes across the Rhine ('Ces héros d'outre-Rhin, ces puissances altières' (III. iii. 651)), but Forlis says there is no need to go looking outside France's borders to find the really dangerous enemies, and he makes a vigorous attack on those who have distorted the word 'freedom' and have made it as bloodthirsty as they are ('sanguinaire comme eux' (III. iii. 662)). He ends,

> Guerre, guerre éternelle aux faiseurs d'anarchie!
> Royalistes tyrans, tyrans républicains,
> Tombez devant les lois, voilà vos souverains!
>
> (III. iii. 668-70)

War, eternal war to the creators of anarchy! Royalist tyrants, republican tyrants, fall down before the laws: they are sovereign!

Law, once again, is the ultimate value for Forlis.

In *L'Ami des lois* it is the Girondist Forlis, the defender of legality, who wins the day, whilst the self-seeking Montagnard schemer Nomophage is the one who is condemned by the justice of the people. Historically, of course, things happened rather differently. The distinctions were by no means as black and white as Laya makes them in his play and, although horrible things were to be done by the likes of Robespierre and Marat in the name of liberty, we do well to remember, as Truchet reminds us, that Laya was not simply a disinterested defender of the oppressed but a committed propagandist writing on behalf of a party which still hoped to win the political struggle for power going on at the time.[27] Nonetheless, in this play sweetness and light triumph, however partial the way in which they are depicted. The same is certainly not true of the next play to be examined, Maréchal's *Le Jugement dernier des rois*.

7

A *SANS-CULOTTE* VERDICT ON MONARCHY

Of the Revolutionary credentials of the author of the next play to be considered there can be no doubt. Indeed, the credentials of Sylvain Maréchal (1750-1803), the author of *Le Jugement dernier des rois (Day of Judgement for the Kings)*, a one-act play in prose which was performed for the first time at the Théâtre de la République in the rue de Richelieu on 17 October 1793, the day after the execution of Marie-Antoinette, and less than a month before the celebration of the Festival of Reason in Notre Dame (10 November) are those of a republican and atheist (although his major work in the context of atheism, his *Dictionnaire des athées*, was not to be published until 1802). However, both his republicanism and his atheism are readily discernible in the play. Under the Directory, Maréchal was involved in the Conspiracy of the Equals, a group of egalitarians who demanded the abolition of the 1795 Constitution and a return to the Montagnard Constitution of 1793, demanded the total destruction of the existing social order and the confiscation of all private property. He managed, however, to avoid being arrested along with Babeuf and other leaders of the conspiracy, in May 1796. Babeuf was guillotined on 27 May 1797.

As Maurice Dommanget puts it, if Chénier's *Charles IX* characterizes the earliest stage of the French Revolution and Laya's *L'Ami des lois* the supreme but vain effort of the moderate party ('le suprême et vain effort du parti modéré'), Maréchal's *Le Jugement dernier des rois* characterizes the Terror.[1] As such, it met with considerable adverse criticism throughout the nineteenth century and, indeed, on into the twentieth. Etienne and Martainville, in 1802, described the play as

... de tous les ouvrages joués pendant la terreur ... sinon la plus atroce, du moins la plus propre à faire connaître jusqu'à quel point on avait dégradé l'art dramatique.[2]

. . . of all the works performed during the Terror, if not the most atrocious, at least the one most suited to demonstrate just how far the art of the theatre had been degraded.

They suggested that the kindest thing that could be said about Maréchal was to see him as a madman ('un homme tourmenté d'un délire continuel').[3] Henri Welschinger, in 1880, remarked that whereas Etienne and Martainville had shuddered with horror in writing about Maréchal's play,

Pour nous cette farce immonde nous fait lever les épaules. Si une semblable pièce était jouée aujourd'hui, elle tomberait à la première représentation devant le mépris public.[4]

As for us, this squalid farce merely makes us shrug our shoulders. If such a play were to be put on nowadays, it would flop at the first performance in the face of the public's contempt.

In 1896, Hippolyte Lucas saw *Le Jugement dernier des rois* as an utterly burlesque concept, the strangest of the plays of the Revolutionary period, and the one which best expresses the disorder of that time.[5]

Not many twentieth-century commentators have been kinder to Maréchal and his play. Félix Gaiffe, in 1931, wrote that *Le Jugement dernier des rois* reaches the ultimate extremes of coarseness in comedy ('les dernières limites de la grossièreté dans le comique').[6] In 1966 Marvin Carlson described it as 'one of the most infamous plays of the Revolution', to be lambasted by Daniel Hamiche in 1973 in a violent and lengthy footnote in which Carlson is accused *inter alia* of not having even taken the trouble to read Maréchal's play.[7] Dommanget, in trying to situate the play in the times in which and for which it was written, is something of an exception in attempting a sympathetic and yet objective evaluation of it. For him, this play is politics in action:

Pour bien comprendre l'émotion soulevée par la pièce de Maréchal, il faut se reporter dans ce milieu de sans-culottisme frémissant dont elle n'a fait que traduire les aspirations.

En 1794, peu importe au public la valeur littéraire d'une œuvre; si elle répond au sentiment général, elle est bonne, elle réussit. Que veut faire Maréchal? Faire du théâtre une tribune.[8]

In order properly to understand the emotions aroused by Maréchal's play, we must transport ourselves back to the passionate *sans-culotte* environment whose aspirations it simply expressed.

In 1794 the literary value of a work was of little interest to the public: provided that it responded to the general feeling of the day, it was good and it succeeded. What is Maréchal seeking to do? To make the theatre into a political platform.

Daniel Hamiche's espousal of the cause is as passionate as Maréchal himself could have hoped for, part of a continuing class war. For him, the criterion by which one judges whether a play is revolutionary or counter-revolutionary, is the effect which the work has on the masses, on society ('l'effet produit par l'ouvrage sur les masses, sur la société'), and by August 1793

l'époque où le théâtre pouvait impunément servir de tribune aux ennemis avoués du peuple et de la Révolution était enfin close . . .[9]

the era when the theatre could with impunity serve as a platform for the avowed enemies of the people and of the Revolution was finally over . . .

In September the reactionary members of the Théâtre-Français were arrested and imprisoned, as we have already seen.[10] In October, *Le Jugement dernier des rois*, conceived as a piece of Revolutionary propaganda, was performed for the first time. Daniel Hamiche expresses his view of the significance of this event in the following terms:

Ce serait . . . ne pas comprendre grand-chose à la pièce de Maréchal que de vouloir principalement la situer dans un courant littéraire ou une thématique dramatique, alors qu'elle est avant tout une rupture et qu'elle ouvre la voie à un théâtre dont l'aspect essentiel n'est plus la théâtralité, mais la matérialisation sur la scène d'une idéologie dont l'expression didactique est propre à favoriser l'éducation politique du spectateur.[11]

It would be . . . to understand little about Maréchal's play if one's principal desire were to situate it in a literary tradition or a dramatic thematic, when it is above all a break with the past and when it opens the way to a theatre the essential aspect of which is no longer theatricality but the materialization on stage of an ideology of which the didactic expression is favourable to the advancement of the spectator's political education.

Whatever one may think of the implications of the above passage, there can be no doubt that, in October 1793 and for some little time thereafter, *Le Jugement dernier des rois* was a considerable popular success.

Its author was the son of a Paris wine merchant who, after studying law, turned his attention to journalism and other forms of writing. He had come to republican views before 1789. Indeed, as early as 1781 he was writing verse attacking the whole notion of monarchy, which he considered to be neither legitimate nor necessary:

> Malheur plutôt à vous, ô souverains!
> Si l'état assemblé pesait vos droits divins;
> Si, recourant enfin aux sages lois d'un code,
> Il ne voyait en vous qu'un rouage incommode,
> Un ressort superflu pour régler les états,
> Qui, sans rois, n'ont besoin que de leurs magistrats.[12]

Woe betide you, rather, oh sovereigns! If the assembled state weighed your divine rights, if, having recourse at last to a codified set of wise laws, it saw in you nothing but a useless cog-wheel, a spring which is not necessary in order to control states which, without kings, need only their magistrates.

In 1784 Maréchal produced his *Livre échappé au Déluge*, a work which cost him his job as an assistant in the Mazarine library, in which he wrote amongst other things,

> Père de la Nature, rappelle à toi tes enfants; ramène-les à leurs premières habitudes.... Tu ne les avais soumis qu'au pouvoir paternel.... S'ils s'en fussent toujours rapportés à la loi du Dieu de la Nature, ils ignoreraient encore ce que c'est que la puissance absolue et l'autorité arbitraire.... Dieu de mes pères, fais reprendre à l'homme sa dignité première; et apprends-lui à se gouverner lui-même. Fais-lui ressouvenir que tu ne l'avais pas créé pour servir ni pour se faire servir. Les enfants du Père de la

Nature doivent être tous libres. Le Père de la Nature n'a point fait d'esclaves.[13]

Father of Nature, recall your children to you; bring them back to their original habits. . . . The only power to which you subjected them was paternal power. . . . If they had always relied on the laws of the God of Nature, they would still be unaware of the notion of absolute power and arbitrary authority. . . . God of my fathers, make man take on again his original dignity; and teach him to govern himself. Make him remember that you created him neither to serve nor to make others serve him. The children of the Father of Nature must all be free. The Father of Nature created no slaves.

In 1788 there came Maréchal's highly revolutionary *Premières leçons du fils aîné d'un roi*, a violently anti-monarchical work containing such sentiments as the following:

Malheur au peuple dont le roi est généreux! Le roi ne peut donner que ce qu'il a pu prendre à son peuple. Plus le roi donne, plus il a pris au peuple.[14]

Woe to the people whose king is generous! The king can give away only that which he has managed to take away from his people. The more the king gives away, the more he has taken from the people.

The downfall of kings is not enough: he seeks their death. In Lesson XXVIII he tells the story of a visionary's dream:

En ce temps-là, revenu de la Cour bien fatigué, un visionnaire se livra au sommeil, et rêva que tous les peuples de la terre, le jour des Saturnales, se donnèrent le mot pour se saisir de la personne de leurs rois, chacun de son côté. Ils convinrent en même temps d'un rendez-vous général, pour rassembler cette poignée d'individus couronnés, et les reléguer dans une petite île inhabitée, mais habitable; le sol fertile n'attendait que des bras et une légère culture. On établit un cordon de petites chaloupes armées pour inspecter l'île, et empêcher ces nouveaux colons d'en sortir. L'embarras des nouveaux débarqués ne fut pas mince. Ils commencèrent par se dépouiller de tous leurs ornements royaux qui les embarrassaient; et il fallut que chacun, pour vivre, mit la main à la pâte. Plus de valets, plus de courtisans, plus de soldats. Il leur fallait tout faire par eux-mêmes. Cette cinquaintaine de personnages ne vécut pas longtemps en paix; et le genre humain, spectateur tranquille, eut la satisfaction de se voir délivré de ses tyrans par leurs propres mains.[15]

At that time, returning very tired from Court, a visionary abandoned himself to sleep and dreamed that all the peoples of the earth, at the Saturnalia, passed the word round that they should each of them separately seize hold of the person of their king. At the same time they agreed on a general meeting, to bring together this handful of crowned individuals and consign them to a small island, uninhabited but habitable: its fertile soil needed only a little physical effort and light cultivation. A cordon of small armed boats was established to keep an eye on the island and prevent these new colonists from leaving. The confusion of the newly landed monarchs was not slight. They began by stripping themselves of all their royal adornments, which got in their way: it was a question of everyone having to lend a hand, if they were to survive. No lackeys, no courtiers, no soldiers. They had to do everything themselves. The fifty or so personages did not live together in peace for long; and the human race, tranquil spectators, had the satisfaction of seeing themselves freed of their tyrants by the tyrants' own hands.

As is clear from this, Maréchal had no time for the concept of the good king, which Chénier was prepared to tolerate in his *Charles IX*, and it is not surprising that the *Premières leçons* were banned by the authorities. The passage quoted above contains, however, the broad outline of the plot of *Le Jugement dernier des rois*, and Maréchal reproduced it at the head of the published text of his play in Year II of the Revolution (1793-94).

This dream seems to have been a recurring one with Maréchal: it reappears, between the *Premières leçons* and *Le Jugement dernier des rois*, in his *Dame Nature à la barre de l'Assemblée nationale* in 1791, a work in which Mother Nature asks the Deputies what the Revolution has achieved so far, and in which she argues that the answer to that question is, 'Precious little':

Et ne voyez-vous pas que cette révolution qui agite vingt-cinq millions d'hommes ressemble à ces changements de position que les malades incurables se procurent sur leur lit de douleur. . .?[16]

And do you not see that this revolution which is stirring up twenty-five million people is like the changes of position which terminally ill patients seek on their bed of pain. . .?

They insist on retaining a king, an individual who is where he is merely by the chance of birth and yet without whom their decrees have not the force of law. Why do they not rid themselves of this 'fétiche'? There is still a royal court, which is to nature and to liberty what a brothel is to a virgin who respects herself ('qui est pour la nature et la liberté ce qu'est un lieu de prostitution pour une vièrge qui se respecte').[17] The Bourbons must be removed: the other nations of Europe will not be slow to follow such an example. As Dommanget puts it, Mother Nature in Maréchal's work envisages, quite simply, a total and immediate social transformation on the European scale.[18]

Maréchal's propaganda play had very considerable popular success. It had twenty-five performances in Paris, according to the calculations of Beatrice F. Hyslop, an impressive number, as Truchet points out, for a play of this type.[19] It also seems to have done well in the provinces: performances are referred to in Rouen, Lille, Grenoble, Le Mans, Metz, Beauvais, and Compiègne: Dommanget goes so far as to suggest that *Le Jugement dernier des rois* was performed in most of the major towns of France. It also found a provincial publisher in Vienne in 1793 in the shape of 'le citoyen J. Labbé, imprimeur du district'.[20] Maréchal had certainly caught the spirit of the day and, by contrast with the sour critiques of the play published in the nineteenth century, there was no shortage of favourable notices in the periodical press immediately after it first appeared on the stage. These good notices were paralleled by signs of considerable official favour.

The *Révolutions de Paris* (to which, it should be noted, Maréchal was for some years one of the principal contributors, and in which he waged a vigorous anti-clerical campaign, as well as campaigns against Louis XVI and Marie-Antoinette and in favour of the creation of a suicide battalion of Tyrannicides)[21] said on 28 October 1793 that although patriots had recently had cause to complain that on stage at the Opéra all the characters were monarchs, no such complaint could be levelled at the Théâtre de la République:

Tous les monarques de l'Europe à peu près y figurent, il est vrai, sur la scène; mais pour ainsi dire muselés, comme les ours que les montagnards de la Savoie faisaient jadis danser dans nos carrefours pour amuser la multitude.

More or less all the monarchs of Europe do appear on stage there, it is true; but, as it were, muzzled, like the bears that the mountain dwellers of Savoy used to make dance at crossroads to entertain the crowds.

The article concludes by embracing one of the principal ideas underlying Maréchal's play, the possibility of the Revolution becoming internationalized:

Il ne manque à cette pièce que de pouvoir être représentée en présence de tous les sans-culottes de l'Europe. La fiction théâtrale ne tarderait pas à devenir un fait historique.[22]

It only remains for it to become possible for this play to be performed before all the *sans-culottes* of Europe. The theatrical fiction would not be slow in becoming historical fact.

Evidence of the popularity of *Le Jugement dernier des rois* is offered by other journals of the time. The *Petites Affiches* (19 October 1793) reported that the piquant title of the play had drawn a packed house who received it with much laughter and applause. The *Feuille du Salut public* (20 October) confirmed that Maréchal's play was received 'avec enthousiasme' at the Théâtre de la République,

. . . parce qu'on ne traita jamais de sujet plus à l'unisson des désirs des spectateurs, aussi glorieux pour les Français, et d'un intérêt plus général. . . le parterre et la salle entière paraissaient composés d'une légion de tyrannicides, prêts à s'élancer sur l'espèce léonine, connue sous le nom de rois.

. . . because never was there a subject more in harmony with the desires of the spectators, as glorious for the French, and of more general interest . . . the stalls and the whole house seemed full of a legion of tyrannicides, ready to throw themselves upon the leonine species, known by the name of king.

On 31 October the *Abréviateur universel* was still writing about the full houses which were showing by their applause the extent to which the play was to their taste. Hébert, in issue 310 of the *Père*

Duchesne, made Duchesne say to his wife that he would take her to the theatre which was rightly called the Théâtre de la République:

> . . . tu verras *Le Jugement dernier des rois*, tu verras tous les brigands couronnés la corde au col, jettés dans une île déserte, tu verras le pape faire amende honorable, et obligé de convenir qu'il n'est qu'un joueur de gobelets; tu verras tous les tyrans de l'Europe obligés de se dévorer eux-mêmes, et engloutis, à la fin de la pièce, par un volcan. Voilà un spectacle fait pour des yeux républicains.

> . . . you will see *Day of Judgement for the Kings*, you will see all the crowned brigands with a rope round their necks, deposited on a desert island, you will see the Pope make public amends for his sins and obliged to admit that he is only a conjurer; you will see all the tyrants of Europe obliged to devour one another and swallowed up, at the end of the play, by a volcano. There's a show made for republican eyes.[23]

The play met with a good deal of official support, as has already been mentioned. According to certain versions of events, this official support was there from the outset, in that three members of the National Convention accompanied Maréchal when he went to read the script of his play to the members of the Théâtre de la République, and when one of the actors, Grandménil (who eventually played the part of Stanislas of Poland), expressed a certain nervousness of being hanged should the monarchy be re-established, one of the members of the Convention enquired as to whether he would prefer to be hanged for having refused to accept *Le Jugement dernier des rois*.[24] There exists other evidence to suggest that the Revolutionary government was well aware of the value which Maréchal's play offered. Maurice Dommanget draws attention to the fact that the Committee of Public Safety on 14 November agreed to pay for three thousand copies of the text of *Le Jugement dernier des rois* and the Ministry of War paid for a further six thousand for distribution among the troops. Daniel Hamiche points out that the conscription ordered by the National Convention on 23 August 1793 had resulted in the creation of an army six hundred thousand strong and goes on to suggest that the ordering of one copy of the play for every hundred soldiers is an eloquent expression of the propaganda value attached to the play.

Dommanget calculates that this was worth eleven thousand francs to Maréchal.[25]

Perhaps the most astonishing proof of the official favour accorded to Maréchal's play, however, is the fact that the Théâtre de la République, aware that much of the dramatic effect of Maréchal's play turns on the eruption of the volcano which, at the end, consumes the crowned heads of Europe together with the Pope, appealed successfully for help in creating a sufficiently impressive effect to the Committee of Public Safety. In its session held on 19 November 1793, the Committee decreed as follows:

> Vu la pétition des entrepreneurs du théâtre de la République qui représentent qu'il leur est impossible de donner des représenta-tions de la pièce patriotique et républicaine intitulée: *Le Jugement dernier des rois*, s'ils n'obtiennent pas vingt livres de salpêtre et vingt livres de poudre, l'artifice indispensable dans cette pièce, le Comité, prenant en considération les avantages qui peuvent en résulter pour la propagation des principes républicains, arrête que la régie des poudres et salpêtres fera délivrer 20 livres de salpêtre et 20 livres de poudre aux entrepreneurs du Théâtre de la République, qui en payeront la valeur.[26]

> In view of the petition from the management of the Théâtre de la République pointing out that it is impossible for them to give performances of the patriotic, republican play entitled *Day of Judgement for the Kings* unless they can obtain twenty pounds of saltpetre and twenty pounds of gunpowder for the ingenious device essential to the play, the Committee, taking into consideration the advantages to be derived in terms of the propagation of republican principles, decrees that the Depart-ment of Gunpowder and Saltpetre shall arrange for the delivery of 20 pounds of saltpetre and 20 pounds of gunpowder to the management of the Théâtre de la République, who shall meet the cost thereof.

Daniel Hamiche reminds us that at this time there was war within the boundaries of France as well as on her frontiers and that gunpowder and saltpetre were in short supply for the army: the decision taken by the Committee of Public Safety therefore underlines the importance attached by the government to propa-ganda as a Revolutionary tool.[27]

Yet further evidence of the continuing popularity of *Le Jugement dernier des rois* is offered by the fact that at a meeting of the Jacobin Club held on 20 January 1794 Louis Sentex proposed that on the following day, to commemorate the first anniversary of the execution of Louis XVI, all the Paris theatres be required to stage Maréchal's play.[28] This proposal may well have served as evidence of the republican purity of Sentex, as well as of Momoro (who supported him), but it was, of course, ludicrously impractical and no attempt was made to act upon it.

Let us now examine this one-act play which had such an impact and which was so much an expression of the times in which it appeared, a utopian piece of republican wish-fulfilment. The published version[29] bore the epigraph 'Tandem!. . .' ('At last!. . .') and the subtitle *Prophétie*. It is a prophecy, of course, in that although the French had abolished their monarchy, the pan-European upsurge of republicanism in emulation of France's achievement depicted in the play and in the visionary's dream from the *Premières Leçons du fils aîné d'un roi* which was also used as a sort of preamble to the play, had not yet taken place. In Maréchal's preface, 'L'Auteur du *Jugement dernier des rois* aux spectateurs de la première représentation de cette pièce', extracted from Prud-homme's periodical, the *Révolutions de Paris*, to which, as has already been pointed out, he was a major contributor, the playwright at once makes clear the gulf which separates him from writers such as Laya, whose *L'Ami des lois* was written in the hope that moderation would win the day and the Revolution would go no further. It is worthwhile to give the text of this preface *in extenso*:

Citoyens, rappelez-vous donc comment, au temps passé, sur tous les théâtres on avilissait, on dégradait, on ridiculisait indigne-ment les classes les plus respectables du peuple souverain, pour faire rire les rois et leurs valets de cour. J'ai pensé qu'il était bien temps de leur rendre la pareille, et de nous en amuser à notre tour. Assez de fois ces *messieurs* ont eu les rieurs de leur côté; j'ai pensé que c'était le moment de les livrer à la risée publique, et de parodier ainsi un vers heureux de la comédie du *Méchant*:

Les rois sont ici-bas pour nos menus plaisirs.[30]

GRESSET

Voilà le motif des endroits un peu *chargés* du *Jugement dernier des rois*.[31]

Citizens, now remember how, in the past, in all the theatres they used to debase, degrade and ignobly ridicule those classes of the people most worthy of respect, in order to amuse kings and their court lackeys. I thought it time to give them some of their own medicine, and for us to amuse ourselves with them for a change. Those *gentlemen* too often had the laughs on their side; I thought now was the time to make them into a public laughing stock, and to parody in the following way a felicitous line from the comedy *Le Méchant*:

Kings are here on earth for our amusement.[32]

GRESSET

That is the motive behind those parts of *Day of Judgement for the Kings* which are a little *strong*.

Maréchal certainly practised what he preached. His play has an astonishingly distinguished cast. In addition to an old Frenchman, savages of various ages and both sexes, a *sans-culotte* from every nation in Europe, there appear the Empress Catherine the Great of Russia, the Emperor Francis II of Austria (the last Holy Roman Emperor), King George III of England, King Charles IV of Spain, King Stanislas II of Poland, King Frederick-William II of Prussia, King Ferdinand IV of Naples, King Victor Amadeus III of Sardinia, a number of other, unspecified kings, and Pope Pius VI. Maréchal gives detailed descriptions of the costumes and decorations to be worn by each of these characters, as well as notes concerning physical appearance: thus, the king of Spain has a large false Bourbon nose made of flesh-coloured taffeta and George III of England has a false belly. The part of Catherine the Great was played by a man, the comic actor Antoine Michot who was at the time an ardent revolutionary, but who subsequently was to support in turn the First Empire and the restoration of the monarchy.[33] All this, as Jacques Truchet points out, makes the play smack of masquerade.

The action takes place on a volcanic island. The stage directions at the beginning inform us that a volcano can be seen in the background and, throughout the duration of the play, it spits out flame from time to time. A cabin nestles under some trees close to a great white rock on which is inscribed in charcoal the legend,

Il vaut mieux avoir pour voisin
Un volcan qu'un roi.
Liberté. . . . . . . Egalité.

> It is better to have as your neighbour
> A volcano rather than a king.
> Liberty. . . . . . . Equality.

Some figures have also been inscribed on the rock by the old Frenchman as he counted the time he has been on the island. There is a stream with a waterfall, and a view of the sea. There are reminders of Rousseau and Defoe amongst others from time to time throughout the play.

Scene i of *Le Jugement dernier des rois* reveals the old Frenchman, alone, counting the time that has elapsed since he was banished to the island. We learn that he has been there for precisely twenty years. Jacques Truchet points out, perhaps a little unnecessarily, that twenty years before the première of Maréchal's play was 1773, when the despot responsible for the fate of the old man would have been Louis XV, whose Queen, Maria Leczinska, had died in 1768. This makes nonsense of the reference to the Queen in scene iii, Truchet points out, adding that in any case there was no reason for Maréchal to attack Louis XV's Queen. Truchet continues,

> . . . il ne faut pas oublier qu'il s'agit d'une 'prophétie': l'action se joue dans le futur, après la victoire totale de la République sur les rois; or il suffisait d'attendre le mois de mai 1794 pour que le souverain régnant vingt ans plus tôt devînt Louis XVI, et la reine Marie-Antoinette.[34]

> . . . it must not be forgotten that we are dealing with a 'prophecy': the action takes place in the future, after the total victory of the Republic over the kings; one had only to wait until May 1794 for the sovereign on the throne twenty years earlier to be Louis XVI, and for the queen to be Marie-Antoinette.

This is all a little laborious, since the point is clear from the text of the play and there is no reason to suppose that the propagandist Maréchal was thinking in terms of such mathematical precision when he wrote his play, even though he does make the old Frenchman say that it is precisely twenty years since he was marooned on the island. The audience would be in no doubt as to whom they considered to be the French King and Queen in question. This is no doubt careless writing by Maréchal. It is not the only example to be found in this play: Truchet himself refers to another one in relation to the Pope and Cagliostro.[35] Political polemic is by no means always noted for its accuracy of detail.

The old man, it is revealed in this opening scene of the play, is to represent not only the victims of arbitrary despotism but also the sterling revolutionary qualities of the ordinary man. He remarks that the island's volcano, the wild beasts and the savages who regularly visit the island seem to have shown respect over the period of twenty years for the victim of a king's tyranny ('Le volcan, les animaux carnassiers, les sauvages, semblent avoir respecté jusqu'à ce jour la victime d'un roi' (i. 1310)), and he says, as he sees a boat containing white people approaching the shore, that even if the King is dead and his successor wishes to offer him clemency, as is the way at the beginning of a new reign, he will have none of it:

> Je ne veux point de la clémence d'un despote: je resterai, je mourrai dans cette île volcanisée, plutôt que de retourner sur le continent, du moins tant qu'il y aura des rois et des prêtres.
>
> (i. 1310-11)

I wish to have nothing to do with the clemency of a despot: I shall remain on this volcanic island and I shall die here, rather than return to Europe, at least so long as there are still kings and priests there.

Right from the very outset the twin themes of the play, its militant republicanism and its equally militant anti-clericalism (and indeed atheism), are established. This was very much in the spirit of the times: as part of the movement against the Catholic religion, the Paris Commune under the leadership of Hébert and Chaumette took the initiative against the church and on 14 October 1793 all religious symbols, statues and crosses were ordered to be removed and replaced by busts of Marat (who had been murdered by Charlotte Corday on 13 July) and of Lepelletier de Saint Fargeau (who had been murdered by a member of the King's bodyguard on 20 January 1793, the eve of Louis XVI's execution).[36] In scene ii, twelve or fifteen *sans-culottes*, one from each nation in Europe, disembark on the island. The old man watches them and listens to them from a hiding-place behind the white rock. We learn that this is the third island which they have visited in their search for a suitable place in which to dump the monarchs of Europe. The French *sans-culotte* suggests that this one looks to be a very likely place, not least because it has an active volcano:

Tant mieux! le globe sera plus tôt débarrassé de tous les brigands couronnés dont on nous a confié la déportation.

(ii. 1311)

So much the better! the earth will all the more quickly be rid of the crowned bandits with whose deportation we have been entrusted.

He is obligingly supported in this view by his English and his Spanish comrade. The English *sans-culotte* says that, through the agency of the volcano,

La main de la nature s'empressera de ratifier, de sanctionner le jugement porté par les sans-culottes contre les rois, ces scélérats si longtemps privilégiés et impunis,

(i. 1311)

The hand of nature will speedily ratify and sanction the verdict brought in by the *sans-culottes* against the kings, those villains who have for such a long time enjoyed privilege and gone unpunished,

and the Spaniard expresses the hope

qu'ils éprouvent ici tous les tourments de l'enfer, auquel ils ne croyaient pas, et qu'ils nous faisaient prêcher par les prêtres, leurs complices, pour nous *embêter*.

(ii. 1311)

that here they will experience all the torments of hell, which they did not believe in themselves but which they had their accomplices, the priests, preach about to us, in order to brutalize us.

These attitudes are not to be seen as in contradiction to the humanity of the *sans-culottes* (by contrast with the inhumanity of the despots) with which some play is made later in the play. Nature is left to purify herself and the world. It is, of course, the case that the French revolutionaries had not left it to Nature to deal with Louis XVI or his Queen.

The *sans-culottes* read the old man's inscription on the white stone, realize that it must have been put there by 'quelque martyr de l'ancien régime', and cheer. The old man emerges from his hiding-place at the beginning of scene iii, rejoices to see fellow

Frenchmen again and offers them fruit and drinking-water. They ask him for his story, and so it is that we learn that he is a Parisian who used to live near the royal park at Versailles. One day his land was invaded by the royal hunt (there is perhaps a touch of La Fontaine about this, although Truchet suggests that Maréchal may have devised this anecdote in order to give the lie to Collé's *La Partie de chasse de Henri IV*, which had often been performed since the beginning of the Revolution and which had served the royalist cause). The old man's daughter was abducted and when the father went to the château to protest the King laughed in his face; the Queen referred to him as 'cet ennuyeux personnage' ('this tiresome person') and had him banned from her presence,[37] and a minister (who was also a bishop) had him thrown into a cell and subsequently deported in the hold of a ship to the island. The French *sans-culotte* assures him that he is well avenged: there are now no kings left in the whole of Europe. He adds that he is not teasing the old man, as the latter suspects:

> De vrais sans-culottes honorent la vieillesse, et ne s'en amusent point . . . comme faisaient jadis les plats courtisans de Versailles, de Saint-James, de Madrid, de Vienne.

> True *sans-culottes* honour old age and do not make fun of it . . . as the obsequious courtiers of Versailles, of Saint James's, of Madrid and of Vienna used to do.

The European monarchs are now languishing in the hold of a ship, much as the old man had done twenty years earlier. The following dialogue ensues:

> UN SANS-CULOTTE . . . Tu vas les voir tous ici, un pourtant excepté.
> LE VIEILLARD   Et pourquoi cette exception? Ils n'ont jamais guère mieux valu les uns que les autres.
> LE SANS-CULOTTE   Tu as raison . . . *Excepté un*, parce que nous l'avons guillotiné.
> LE VIEILLARD   *Guillotiné*! . . . Que veut dire?
> LE SANS-CULOTTE   Nous t'expliquerons cela, et bien autre chose; nous lui avons tranché la tête, de par la loi.
> LE VIEILLARD   Les Français sont donc devenus des hommes!

LE SANS-CULOTTE   Des hommes libres . . .

(iii. 1313)

A SANS-CULOTTE   . . . You will see them all here. With one exception, however.

THE OLD MAN   Why with one exception? It was surely never the case that any one of them was worth any more than the others.

THE SANS-CULOTTE   You are quite right. . . . With one exception, because we have guillotined him.

THE OLD MAN   Guillotined!. . . What does that mean?

THE SANS-CULOTTE   We'll explain that to you, and many other things; we cut off his head, in the name of the law.

THE OLD MAN   So the French have become men!

THE SANS-CULOTTE   Free men. . .

The old man expresses his delight that he has lived to see such a great day and asks whether it is really true that the whole of Europe has freed itself from the contagion of monarchy. This serves as an opportunity for the representatives of other European nations to develop Maréchal's piece of wish-fulfilment in terms of the rest of the continent. The German *sans-culotte* is the first to speak, beginning 'L'exemple des Français a fructifié' ('The French example was a fruitful one'). Signs of the debates within the French Revolution are there, as the German recounts the attempts made to undermine 'cette nation généreuse', France: the monsters who impudently called themselves the sovereigns did everything in their power to destroy the liberty created in France:

> . . . on a voulu la modérantiser, la fédéraliser, l'affamer, l'asservir de plus belle, pour dégoûter à jamais les hommes du régime de l'indépendance.

(iii. 1314)

> . . . they tried to impose moderantism on her, and federalism, they tried to starve her, they tried to subjugate her still more thoroughly than in the past, so as to make people disgusted with the system of independence for all time.

But, whatever the designs of the monarchs of the other European nations, the ordinary people refused to go along with them and sought to fraternize with their 'aînés en raison, en liberté' ('their elders in rationalism and liberty'). In consequence of this,

173

. . . chaque section de l'Europe envoya à Paris de braves sans-culottes, chargés de la représenter. Là, dans cette diète de tous les peuples, on est convenu qu'à certain jour toute l'Europe se lèverait en masse. . . et s'émanciperait. . . . En effet une insurrection générale et simultanée a éclaté chez toutes les nations de l'Europe; et chacune d'elles eut son 14 juillet et 5 october 1789, son 10 août et 21 septembre 1792, son 31 mai et 2 juin 1793. . .

(iii. 1314)

. . . each section of Europe sent honest *sans-culottes* to Paris to represent it. There, at a Congress of all the peoples, it was agreed that on a certain day the whole of Europe would rise up en masse . . . and free itself. . . . And indeed a general, simultaneous insurrection broke out in all the European countries, and each one of them had its 14 July and 5 October 1789, its 10 August and 21 September 1792, its 31 May and 2 June 1793 . . . [38]

In the published version of the play these remarks by the German *sans-culotte* are soon followed by a speech by his English counterpart, in which the English *sans-culotte* speaks of a *Convention européenne* held in Paris, the capital city of Europe ('chef-lieu de l'Europe'), which proceeded to the 'dernier jugement des rois' and condemned them to exile on an island until the death of the last of them (iii. 1315). This speech, however, was omitted from the staged version of the play.

In both the staged and the published version, however, the old Frenchman seeks a definition of the term *sans-culotte*, which he has heard used so frequently. It is the French *sans-culotte* who claims the right to supply this definition:

Un sans-culotte est un homme libre, un patriote par excellence. La masse du vrai peuple, toujours bonne, toujours saine, est composée de sans-culottes. Ce sont des citoyens purs, tout près du besoin, qui mangent leur pain à la sueur de leur front, qui aiment le travail, qui sont bons fils, bons pères, bons époux, bons parents, bons amis, bons voisins, mais qui sont jaloux de leurs droits autant que de leurs devoirs. Jusqu'à ce jour, faute de s'entendre, ils n'avaient été que des instruments aveugles et passifs dans les mains des méchants, c'est-à-dire des rois, des nobles, des prêtres, des égoïstes, des aristocrates, des hommes d'Etat, des fédéralistes, tous gens dont nous t'expliquerons, sage et malheureux vieillard, les maximes et les forfaits. Chargés de tout l'entretien de la ruche, les sans-culottes ne veulent plus souffrir désormais, au-dessus ni parmi eux, de frelons lâches et malfaisants, orgueilleux et parasites.

(iii. 1315)

A *sans-culotte* is a free man, a patriot above all else. The mass of the real people, always good, always healthy, is made up of *sans-culottes*. They are pure citizens, close to the poverty line, who gain their bread by the sweat of their brow, who like work, who are good sons, good fathers, good husbands, good relatives, good friends, good neighbours, but who are as jealous of their rights as of their duties. Up to now, in consequence of their failure to come to an agreement amongst themselves, they had been merely blind and passive instruments in the hands of the wicked, that is to say of the kings, the nobles, the priests, the self-seeking, the aristocrats, the statesmen, the federalists, the maxims and infamous crimes of all of whom we shall explain to you, wise and unfortunate old man. Now that they have been made responsible for the upkeep of the entire hive, the *sans-culottes* henceforth do not intend to tolerate, either above them or amongst them, lazy, harmful, overblown, parasitical drones.

This idealistic definition of the *sans-culotte* and the spirit of optimism which goes with it cause the old Frenchman to cry out, '*avec enthousiasme*', 'Mes frères, mes enfants, et moi aussi je suis un sans culotte' ('My brothers, my children, I too am a *sans-culotte*'). The idealism and the optimism chime in with the feelings experienced both by S.T. Coleridge,

> When France in wrath her giant-limbs upreared
> And with that oath, which smote air, earth, and sea,
> Stamped her strong foot and said she would be free. . .
> And when to whelm the disenchanted nation,
> Like fiends embattled by a wizard's wand,
> The Monarchs marched in evil day,
> And Britain joined the dire array . . .[39]

and by William Wordsworth, for whom

> Bliss was it in that dawn to be alive,
> But to be young was very heaven!

and for whom it seemed that

> Not favoured spots alone, but the whole earth,
> The beauty wore of promise . . .[40]

Both English poets, of course, were to experience disillusionment with the French Revolution, and were by no means alone in that. None the less, however tainted the ideals were to become, expressions of hope for the future such as those which are to be found in Maréchal's play speak eloquently to us even today, two centuries later, and justify the beliefs of those of us who hold that the French Revolution, for all its shortcomings, is arguably the greatest single expression of that which is best in the human spirit to have been experienced by Europe or indeed the world.

The old man asks why the *sans-culottes* went to all the trouble of bringing the monarchs to his island, and suggests that it would have been more expedient to hang the lot of them. The French *sans-culotte* rejects this:

> Non, non! Leur supplice eût été trop doux et aurait fini trop tôt; il n'eût pas rempli le but qu'on se proposait. Il a paru plus convenable d'offrir à l'Europe le spectacle de ses tyrans détenus dans une ménagerie et se dévorant les uns les autres, ne pouvant plus assouvir leur rage sur les braves sans-culottes qu'ils osaient appeler leurs sujets.
>
> (iii. 1315)

> No, no! their death would have been too painless and too quickly over; it would not have served the intended purpose. It seemed more appropriate to offer Europe the spectacle of its tyrants detained in a menagerie, devouring one another, since they were no longer able to assuage their rage on the honest *sans-culottes* whom they dared to call their subjects.

One has a sense of being involved with a sort of republican *Robinson Crusoe* as the old man tells the *sans-culottes* that although the island is, apart from himself, uninhabited, it is regularly visited by savages of whom he was at first afraid but who have proved to be imbued with sweetness and light: they gave him a warm welcome and promised to keep him regularly supplied with fruit, fish and meat, since they visited the island daily to pray to the volcano. The old man, without wishing to undermine their worship of the volcano, urged them to pay homage too to the sun. At one point the savages had shown signs of wishing to make the old Frenchman their king, but when he had explained his own past to them they swore never to have either king or priests. The old man judges that his island is an admirable place in which to deposit the crowned heads of Europe,

> ... d'autant mieux que depuis quelques semaines le cratère du volcan s'élargit beaucoup et semble menacer d'une éruption prochaine. Il vaut mieux qu'elle éclate sur des têtes couronnées que sur celles de mes bons voisins les sauvages, ou de mes frères les braves sans-culottes.
>
> (iii. 1316)

> ... all the more so since for the past few weeks the crater of the volcano has been growing considerably and seems to be threaten-ing an imminent eruption. It is better that it erupts on the crowned heads of Europe rather than on the heads of my good neighbours the savages, or the heads of my brothers the honest *sans-culottes*.[41]

And so a signal is sent to the fleet, instructing it to spew out the poison it is carrying ('pour . . . qu'elle vomisse les poisons dont elle est chargée') (iii. 1316-17).

The good savages arrive and much fraternization ensues between them and the *sans-culottes*: as the old man points out, they do not understand each other's languages, but 'le cœur est de tous les pays' ('the heart is international') (iii. 1317). The monarchs and the Pope are brought ashore, dressed in full regalia and with an iron chain round their necks, the end being held by a *sans-culotte*. In a vaguely Rousseauesque style, the old man points out to the *sans-culottes* that the savages have a longer history of freedom than they: 'Nés libres, ils vivent et meurent comme ils sont nés' ('Born free, they live and die as they were born') (iv. 1317).

In scene v the prisoners are brought ashore. The Emperor Francis II is accused of absolutist activities such as suppression of freedom of thought, and of having outdone in Austria what Marie-Antoinette had sought to do in France: he exhausted the country's finances, caused the death of many of its inhabitants, neglected agriculture and trade, and ravaged the Polish borders, having not done as well as he wished in the partition of that country. Over and above that, he was a false friend, a perfidious ally, and a man who delighted in doing evil for its own sake: a real monster ('Faux ami, allié perfide, faisant le mal pour mal faire; c'est un monstre'). The Emperor seeks to defend himself by putting the blame on Kaunitz, Cobourg and Brunswick (v. 1317-18).

Then an English *sans-culotte* brings in George III whom he accuses of having, with the aid of the 'génie machiavélique de M. Pitt', emptied the English Exchequer in order to foment civil war in France and to encourage anarchy, famine and federalism, this last being the worst of all. George III pleads insanity: 'Punit-on un fou? On le place à l'hôpital' ('One doesn't punish a madman. One puts him in an asylum.') (v. 1318). Frederick-William II of Prussia is brought on and accused of the deaths, for no good reason, of countless soldiers. Charles IV of Spain is brought on next. The Spanish sans-culotte says of him,

> Il est bien du sang des Bourbons: voyez comme la sottise, la cagoterie et le despotisme sont empreints sur sa face royale.
>
> (v.1318-19)

> You can see he is of Bourbon blood: see how stupidity, religious fanaticism and despotism are printed on his royal face.

Charles obligingly agrees that he is only a fool who has always been led by priests and dominated by his wife and therefore feels entitled to ask for mercy (v. 1318-19). Ferdinand of Naples says that he had no choice but to join in with the other monarchs in their anti-revolutionary policy and introduces a note of grim humour by saying that one volcano is as good as another and therefore the *sans-culottes* might just as well have left him with his own Mount Etna ('Volcan pour volcan, que ne me laissiez-vous là-bas!') (v. 1319). The next royal personnage to be produced is the lethargic, priest-ridden, inadequate Victor of Savoy, King of Sardinia, more stupid than wicked most of the time. Next comes Catherine the Great of All the Russias, referred to scabrously as Madame de l'Enjambée ('Madame Leg-over'):

> Sans mœurs et sans vergogne, elle fut l'assassin de son mari, pour n'avoir pas de compagnon sur le trône, et pour n'en pas manquer dans son lit impur.
>
> (v. 1319)

Without morals and without shame, she murdered her husband so as to have no one beside her on the throne and so as not to be short of people beside her in her impure bed.

Stanislas of Poland follows, to be accused (accurately enough) of having been one of Catherine's lovers: it was she who had put him on the Polish throne. Next comes a *sans-culotte* holding several chains attached to the necks of several monarchs:

Tenez! voici le fond du sac. C'est le fretin: il ne vaut pas l'honneur d'être nommé.

(v. 1319-20)[42]

Here you are! Here is the bottom of the barrel. The small fry: they don't deserve the honour of being named.

But if that is the end of the procession of secular princes and princesses, it is not the last of the *sans-culottes'* prisoners. There is still the Pope to be reviled, Giannangelo Braschi, Pope Pius VI (1717-99), who had seen in the early days of the Revolution Church property confiscated and himself burned in effigy at the Palais-Royal. A republican agent, Hugo Basseville, had been murdered in the streets of Rome in January 1793, adding to the tension between Revolution and Papacy. The French charged the Pope with being implicated in the murder.[43] The attack on the Pope in Maréchal's play is a violent one. The Roman *sans-culotte* who leads him in says that there has been no odious plot in which the priests and their chief, the Pope, have not been involved:

C'est ce monstre à triple couronne qui, sous main, provoqua une croisade meurtrière contre les Français, comme jadis ses prédécesseurs en avaient conseillé une contre les Sarrasins. Après les rois, les prêtres sont ceux qui firent le plus de mal à la terre et à l'espèce humaine.

It is this monster with the triple crown who, covertly, provoked a bloody crusade against the French, just as in the past his predecessors called for crusades against the Saracens. After the kings, the priests are those who have done most harm to the world and to humankind.

The French are to be congratulated for having remembered the patriotism of Brutus, the founder of the Roman republic, and having been the first among modern nations to unmask the hypocrisy of the priests. The Pope responds by saying that he has been more moderate than any of his predecessors would have been: in such circumstances they would all have placed France under an interdict. He concludes by saying that, if spared, he will spend the rest of his days praying to God for the *sans-culottes* ('Ecoutez; faites-moi grâce; tout le reste de ma vie je prierai Dieu pour les sans-culottes') (v. 1320). The Roman *sans-culotte* will have none of this, however:

> Non, non, non! Nous ne voulons plus de prières d'un prêtre: le Dieu des sans-culottes, c'est la liberté, c'est l'égalité, c'est la fraternité! Tu ne connus et ne connaîtras jamais ces dieux-là. Va plutôt exorciser le volcan qui doit dans peu te punir et nous venger.
>
> (v. 1320-1)

> No, no, no! We want no more priests' prayers: the god of the *sans-culottes* is Liberty, is Fraternity, is Equality! You did not recognize those gods and you never will. You would do better to go and exorcize the volcano, which shortly will punish you and avenge us.

A French *sans-culotte* ranges the prisoners in a semi-circle and proceeds to harangue them. He tells them that they all deserved to be executed: but where could they have found an executioner prepared to soil his hands in their vile and corrupt blood? Instead, they are to be left to their remorse, or rather to their impotent rage ('Nous vous livrons à vos remords, ou plutôt à votre rage impuissante'). They are depicted as cowardly villains, responsible for the death of millions, the worst of whom was worth more than the pack of them:

> Les voilà, ces bouchers d'hommes en temps de guerre, ces corrupteurs de l'espèce humaine en temps de paix. C'est du sein des cours de ces êtres immondes que s'exhalait dans les villes et sur les campagnes la contagion de tous les vices; exista-t-il jamais une nation ayant en même temps un roi et des mœurs?
>
> (v. 1321)

> There they are, these butchers of men in time of war, these corrupters of humankind in time of peace. It is from the bosom

of the Courts of these foul beings that there issued forth into towns and over the countryside the contagion of all the vices. Did there ever exist a nation which had at one and the same time a king and a sense of morality?

The French *sans-culotte* expresses the hope that Nature, through the volcano, will finish off all the monarchs (and the Pope) quickly:

> Nature, hâte-toi d'achever l'œuvre des sans-culottes; souffle ton haleine sur ce rebut de la société, et fais rentrer pour toujours les rois dans le néant d'où ils n'auraient jamais dû sortir.
>
> Fais-y rentrer aussi le premier d'entre nous qui désormais prononcerait le mot *roi* sans l'accompagner des imprécations que l'idée attachée à ce mot infâme présente naturellement à tout esprit républicain.
>
> (v. 1322)

> Nature, hasten to complete the work of the *sans-culottes*; blow with your breath on these dregs of society, and drive the kings for ever back into the void from which they should never have emerged.
>
> Make the first of us to utter the word *king* without the imprecations which the idea associated with that loathsome word naturally offers to every republican spirit return to that void too.

The *sans-culottes* depart at this point. They do not go far, however, but remain where they can observe the behaviour of their prisoners. In scene vi, however, the European monarchs and the Pope believe that they have been left to their own devices. The monarchs' first act is to ask the Pope for a miracle. He admits that he cannot oblige them in this respect and, significantly enough using the language of witchcraft, remarks,

> Le temps en est passé. . . . Où est-il le bon temps où les saints traversaient les airs à cheval sur un bâton?
>
> (vi. 1322)

> The time of miracles is passed. . . Where are the good old days when the saints flew across the sky astride a stick?

The King of Spain says that the guillotined Louis XVI is better off than any of them. He blames the Emperor and George III for having got them all into their present predicament, and says they should never have meddled with the French Revolution. They begin to quarrel. George III says that if Charles of Spain had supported them at the right time they could have dealt satisfactorily with the French question. At this point Catherine the Great declares that she intends to go and lie down in a nearby cave and asks whether anyone would care to join her. She particularly invites Stanislas of Poland, who ungallantly suggests that she take a look at herself in the waters of the stream. She retorts that he was not always so choosy. In 1793 Catherine (1729-96), played in *Le Jugement dernier des rois* by a man, was no longer young. Stanislas II (1732-98) was a contemporary of hers. This is not comedy of a very subtle or elevated kind.

The exiles next turn their minds to might-have-beens. Charles of Spain says that he should have made an *auto-da-fé* of the *sans-culottes* 'pour servir d'exemple aux autres'. The Pope says that he should have excommunicated them all as early as 1789. The King of Naples remarks that these thoughts are all very well, but they do come rather late in the day. He suggests that they make the best of it:

Nous sommes dans la galère, il faut ramer. Avant tout, il faut manger; occupons-nous, d'abord, de pêche, de chasse ou de labourage.

(vi. 1323)

We are all in the same boat, so it is up to us to row it. First of all, we have to eat. To begin with, let us set about fishing, hunting or digging the soil.

Francis II promptly objects that it would be a fine sight, an Emperor of the House of Austria scratching at the earth in order to live, at which the King of Spain somewhat testily enquires whether the Emperor would prefer to draw lots to decide which of them should serve as food for the others.

Matters are made worse when the Pope, bewailing the fact that he has not even the wherewithal to perform the miracle of the loaves, remarks that, on the other hand, this is not surprising, since there are schismatics amongst them. Catherine the Great sees this as a slighting reference to herself and challenges the Pope to a fight. The flavour of this grotesque comedy, brimming over with republican bile, is conveyed by Maréchal's stage direction at this point:

L'impératrice et le pape se battent, l'une avec son sceptre et l'autre avec sa croix; un coup de sceptre casse la croix; le pape jette sa tiare à la tête de Catherine et lui renverse sa couronne. Ils se battent avec leurs chaînes. Le roi de Pologne veut mettre le holà, en ôtant des mains le sceptre à Catherine.

(vi. 1323)

The Empress and the Pope fight, she with her sceptre, he with his crucifix; a blow from the sceptre breaks the crucifix; the Pope throws his tiara at Catherine's head and knocks her crown off. They fight with their chains. The King of Poland tries to put a stop to the fight, by grabbing Catherine's sceptre.

The fight continues, however, until the Pope begs for mercy, offering Catherine absolution for all her sins. She is not interested in that, but agrees to stop hitting him if he will repeat after her, 'Un prêtre . . . un pape . . . est un charlatan . . . un joueur de gobelets' ('A priest . . . a Pope . . . is a charlatan . . . a conjurer'). This he does. The King of Spain then discovers that he still has about his person a piece of black bread. He is set upon by the rest, and the scene closes with the following stage direction:

Les rois se battent; la terre est jonchée de débris de chaînes, de sceptres, de couronnes; les manteaux sont en haillons.

(vi. 1324)

The kings fight; the ground is strewn with pieces of chains, sceptres and crowns; their robes are torn to shreds.

In scene vii the *sans-culottes* return and roll a barrel of biscuits in amongst the hungry monarchs. One of them, as he breaks open the barrel and tips the biscuits out, offers a final example of *sans-culotte* humanity. He says,

Tenez, faquins, voilà de la pâture. Bouffez. Le proverbe qui dit *Il faut que tout le monde vive* n'a pas été fait pour vous, car il n'y a pas de nécessité que des rois vivent. Mais les sans-culottes sont aussi susceptibles de pitié que de justice. Repaissez-vous donc de ce biscuit de mer, jusqu'à ce que vous soyez acclimatés dans ce pays.

(vii. 1324-5)

Here you wretches, here's some grub. Fill your guts. The proverb which says *Everybody has to live* wasn't dreamed up with you in mind, for there is no need for kings to live. But *sans-culottes* are as susceptible to pity as they are to justice. Feed yourselves on these sea-biscuits, until you become acclimatized to this place.

In the eighth and final scene of the play the monarchs and the Pope throw themselves upon the biscuits and squabble over them. Lava is seen emerging from the volcano. In their terror, the King of Spain promises that, if he is spared, he will become a *sans-culotte*, the Pope promises to take a wife and Catherine the Great promises to join the Jacobins or the Cordeliers. Then there comes the final spectacle, which necessitated the supply of saltpetre and gunpowder to which reference has already been made. We are told,

> *Le volcan commence son éruption: il jette sur le théâtre des pierres, des charbons brûlants . . . etc.*
>
> *L'explosion se fait: le feu assiège les rois de toutes parts; ils tombent, consumés, dans les entrailles de la terre entrouverte.*
>
> (viii. 1325)

> *The volcano starts to erupt: it hurls stones, burning coals, etc. on to the stage.*
>
> *It explodes: fire threatens the kings on all sides; they fall into the gaping bowels of the earth and are consumed.*

Jacques Truchet is at pains to argue that *Le Jugement dernier des rois*, for all its reputation, is no scurrilous, crude play. He points out that the text offers only a couple of familiar terms, 'embêter' (which actually appears in italics) in scene ii and 'bouffer' in scene vii, together with the scabrously offensive expression in scene v where Catherine the Great is called 'Madame de l'Enjambée'.[44] Apart from these examples, the accusation of vulgarity often levelled over the years at Maréchal's play cannot seriously be sustained, if one confines oneself to the linguistic expression of the work. On the other hand, one must not go too far in the opposite direction in one's defence of the play. When Truchet argues that

> S'il faut parler ici d'un langage 'sans-culotte', celui-ci ne peut se définir que comme éloquent, voire fleuri: il vient de la tribune, non de la rue; et si certains personnages manquent de tenue, ce ne sont pas les révolutionnaires, mais – effet très concerté – les rois. En réalité *Le Jugement dernier des rois* apparaît comme une œuvre littéraire, et même comme très élaboré[45]

If one must speak here of a '*sans-culotte*' language, this language can only be defined as eloquent, flowery even: it comes from the political platform and not from the street, and if certain of the characters lack good manners, these are not the revolutionaries, but – a carefully contrived effect – the kings. In reality *Day of Judgement for the Kings* strikes one as a literary work, and even as a very elaborate one,

he is only partly right. Etienne and Martainville exaggerate grossly in describing the play as, if not the most atrocious play, at least the one which most clearly demonstrates the degradation of the dramatic art in the Revolutionary years, just as Gaiffe more recently exaggerates in describing it as reaching the ultimate in terms of comic vulgarity. The crudeness, it is true, does not reside essentially in the language which for the most part is perfectly normal and does possess some of the pompous eloquence of the hustings – the *sans-culottes* can even reasonably be accused of a certain self-righteous sententiousness at times. There can be no denying, however, the violence of the play.

We must be careful not to become too solemn about this little play which is, in many ways, a fairly lightweight piece (although, as Truchet suggests, an attempt is made to present quite precise political criticisms of the principal European monarchs).[46] Maréchal himself concedes, as we have already seen, that parts of his play are a little strong ('un peu chargés'), but this element surely is not the use of language but such spectacles as the Empress of All the Russias brawling with the Pope and breaking his crucifix in the process. It is what Truchet calls the 'masquerade' element in the play which has proved so shocking over the years, the burlesque pantomime elements in the context of the undermining of the political and religious Establishment of the *Ancien Régime*. In this respect Truchet is right to point out that Maréchal's play departs from all customary theatrical norms and therefore it is easy, if one is so inclined, to dismiss it as an aberration, an ugly duckling of a play which need not be taken seriously. And indeed this is a play which is not to be taken seriously, if one is looking for a work which is likely to appeal to modern audiences, to have the quality of universality of appeal through the ages. It is true that a version of the play devised by Jacques Chabannes was performed by a group of amateurs in Paris in 1936 and that extracts from it were broadcast by Radio-Paris on 15 June 1939, the year of the

150th anniversary of the Revolution,[47] but this can not be said to be a play of such quality as to impose itself on successive generations.

It is nonetheless a play to which it is difficult to make a simple response, a play which is interesting as an expression of its own day, combining as it does in its *sans-culotte* characters a certain idealism (which, for all its naïveté, speaks well for the spirit of the Revolution at its best) with the rather self-righteous sententiousness to which reference has already been made. The Rousseauesque respect for old age is touching enough, no doubt, but there is a certain moral ambivalence about the attitudes of these sentimental *sans-culottes* who (having guillotined Louis XVI and Marie-Antoinette) express their humanity by giving food to the exiled monarchs for whom they consider death by judicial execution too easy a way out, in the confident hope that the volcano will soon spare them the necessity of soiling their hands by executing them. Underlying all this – and this is arguably the most alarming and (in a sense) the most violent impression left by the play – is the fact that the *sans-culottes* are presenting an attitude which, in its ideologically pure self-righteousness, is in its own way quite as absolutist as that represented by the monarchs whom they have overthrown. All is black and white: the monarchs and the Pope are described not only as brigands (scene iii), as wicked (scene iii), as not deserving a merciful end (scene iii), as poison (scene iii), as monsters (scenes iii and v). They are depicted as socially useless, mentally, physically and morally inadequate and degenerate. The grotesque, Punch-and-Judy-like fight in scene vi and the squabble over the sea-biscuits as the volcano begins to erupt in scene viii reduces them to the level of animals. The bitterness here is markedly stronger than anything one might find in, say, a Rowlandson caricature. There is no doubt about it, though: France and Europe are offered one way, and one way only, forward. That is the Jacobin way, the way of the Terror. The only good king is a dead one. All organized religion is a confidence trick, with the Pope as principal charlatan, although Mother Nature is to be revered. Federalism and moderantism are merely alternative royalist plots, attempts by the coalition of European monarchs (but not of European peoples) to undermine the French Revolution and to destroy the nucleus of liberty which has been formed in Paris ('. . .pour dissoudre ce noyau de liberté que Paris avait formé') (iii.

186

1314). The violence of the play lies in its fanaticism rather than in the language in which that fanaticism is expressed. The mixture of sentimentality and grotesque parody is a heady one. One can appreciate its propaganda appeal in the torrid days of the Terror (the destruction of all the representatives of monarchy together with the symbols of their (usurped) authority) but one may hope that its appeal today may be simply that of its historical interest.[48]

The next, and final, chapter will examine two plays, one of which, Ducancel's *L'Intérieur des comités révolutionnaires (Inside the Revolutionary Committees)* is a three-act play reacting with scorn (after the event) against the perpetrators of the horrors of the Terror, whilst the other, Lebrun's one-act *Les Rivaux d'eux-mêmes (Their Own Rivals)*, is a play with no political content whatsoever from the period of the Directory. The world has been transformed. Or has it returned to what it was before the Revolution? It almost seems so.

8

TOWARDS A NEW LIGHTHEARTEDNESS

Many indeed were the events which took place between the appearance of *Le Jugement dernier des rois* and Pigault-Lebrun's *Les Rivaux d'eux-mêmes*. On 8 November 1793 Mme Roland was executed, on 10 November the Festival of Reason was celebrated in Notre Dame, on 11 November Bailly, erstwhile mayor of Paris, was executed, on 23 November the Commune ordered the closing of all the churches in the city. In December Toulon was recaptured by the revolutionaries, the Vendéens were defeated and mass executions took place of those captured under arms against the Revolution: almost two thousand were killed in Lyon, by guillotine and by cannon fire; there were many shootings in Toulon, and 2,000 Vendéen prisoners were drowned in barges scuttled in the Loire, while 3,000 more were shot. Hébert and the partisans of extreme violence began, however, to meet with growing opposition from more moderate Deputies, led by Danton. In March 1794 Hébert and nearly twenty others were executed. The Committee of Public Safety began to insist that all its critics were counter-revolutionaries and, after the Hébertists it was the turn of the Dantonists to appear before the Revolutionary Tribunal. On 5 April 1794 Danton, Camille Desmoulins, Fabre d'Eglantine and a number of others went to the guillotine. All power was now with the governing committees and Robespierre and Saint-Just were in total control. On 8 June Robespierre played the leading part, as President of the Convention, in the Festival of the Supreme Being. The law of 22 Prairial (10 June 1794) widened the category of suspects or 'public enemies' and the death penalty became the only penalty for such enemies of the State. Witnesses were more or less dispensed with and there was a dramatic increase in the number of executions.

Gradually, however, opposition began to develop, with internal conflict within the Committee of Public Safety becoming apparent. Carnot and Collot d'Herbois attacked Robespierre and Saint-Just as dictators. On 26 July Robespierre launched an attack on his enemies in the Convention, but the very fact that members of the Committee found it necessary to appeal against each other to the Convention of itself weakened their position. On the following day, 27 July (9 Thermidor) Saint-Just spoke up in support of Robespierre but was given a rowdy reception and, after a good deal of confusion Robespierre, Saint-Just and Couthon were arrested and, in company with a number of others, were guillotined on 28 July. Thereafter the powers of the Committee of Public Safety and of the Revolutionary Tribunal were much curtailed. The Public Prosecutor, Fouquier-Tinville, was arrested. The Terror was coming to an end.

As part of the reaction, the well-to-do *jeunesse dorée* appeared in the streets of Paris. The Jacobin Club was closed on 12 November and on 24 December the law of the *maximum*, which had been introduced to control the highest price at which a merchant could sell his goods (high penalties for infringement of the law were accompanied by the offender's name being placed on the list of suspects), was suppressed in December as being contrary to the spirit of free commerce. Salon life reappeared and the families of the victims of the guillotine flaunted their loss at *bals des victimes*. Fouquier-Tinville was brought to trial on 28 March 1795 and subsequently executed. On 10 April the Convention ordered the disarming, throughout France, of all who had played a significant part in the Terror. Collot d'Herbois and Billaud-Varenne were exiled to Cayenne, in French Guiana.

It was on 27 April 1795 (8 Floréal, Year III of the Republic) that Charles-Pierre Ducancel's three-act play, *L'Intérieur des comités révolutionnaires, ou les Aristides modernes* had its first performance, at the Théâtre de la Cité-Variétés. By 1793 there were more than forty theatres in Paris, but lamentably few of their productions over the next few years were of any great note. This play of Ducancel's, however, to which some reference has already been made,[1] is to some degree an exception for, although by no stretch of the imagination can it be described as a theatrical masterpiece, it did enjoy considerable success[2] and stands as an excellent illustration of the fact that the Jacobins of the Terror were not the only ones by any means to seek, when the time was ripe, to use the stage as a political platform. *L'Intérieur des comités révolutionnaires* is as representative of the Thermidorean Reaction as *Le Jugement dernier des rois* was of the Terror itself. It therefore seems appropriate to attempt, fairly briefly, to give something of the flavour of this play before going on to consider Pigault-Lebrun's play from the period of the Directory.

According to Ducancel himself, the play arose from dinner party conversation in May 1795, when he discovered that every single one of his guests had a tale to tell of trouble involving

> . . . les ridicules bévues, l'ignorance crasse et les brutalités stupides des agents des Comités révolutionnaires. . . . Pendant tout le repas, ce ne fut qu'un feu roulant d'anecdotes plus ou moins atroces ou ridicules contre les révolutionnaires parisiens et provinciaux.

> . . . the ridiculous blunders, the crass ignorance and the stupid acts of brutality of the agents of the Revolutionary Committees. . . .[3] Throughout the entire meal, it was one continual barrage of anecdotes of varying degrees of atrociousness or ridiculousness against the revolutionaries of Paris and the provinces.

He also claims that the play was written, accepted, learned and produced within the space of twenty-seven days.[4]

The action of the play is set in Dijon, the Revolutionary Committee of which town was the only one to distinguish itself by sending a note to the Convention protesting against the fall of Robespierre on 9 Thermidor. The members of the committee are, in the best republican manner of the day, given Roman names. Aristide, the president of the committee, was (until elevated to this powerful office) a professional swindler; Caton was a lackey and confidence trickster; Scévola, a Gascon and therefore a traditional figure of fun, was a barber; Brutus was a doorkeeper; Torquatus was an upholsterer. They have it as their intention to ruin the only man of principle on the committee, Dufour, and his family. They are shown to be continuing along their villainous ways, but now with official blessing and power of life and death. They are totally unscrupulous, illiterate and (apart from their native cunning) stupid, not knowing whether Bourges is in France or not, not understanding the geography of Spain, and so on.

The play gives quite an interesting flavour of Revolutionary values: the use of the word 'Monsieur' rather than 'citoyen' is enough to damn a man as a royalist, as is the use of the second person plural mode of address rather than the second person singular (I. iii). In this play all civilized values are turned upside down: it is characteristic that the character named Vilain is a man of principle, who defines Revolutionary Committees as places where the language of honest folk is not understood ('L'on n'y comprend pas le langage des honnêtes gens' (I. viii)). The same Vilain remarks in a soliloquy, after a conversation with Brutus and Torquatus,

> Et voilà deux membres d'un comité révolutionnaire! Grand Dieu! dans quel siècle sommes-nous? Est-ce croyable que trente mille bons citoyens tremblent devant des misérables de cette espèce!
>
> (I. ix)

> And those two are members of a Revolutionary Committee! God Almighty! What century are we living in? Is it believable that thirty thousand good citizens tremble before scoundrels of that type?

The honest Dufour points out that legality has been thrown out of the window: laws are unnecessary when society is composed solely of victims and executioners ('Des lois! il n'en faut plus . . . quand la société n'est composée que de bourreaux et de victimes'). For him, the scaffold is now a field of honour for people of talent and worth, since they have no role to play in the existing social structure ('L'échafaud . . . est maintenant le champ d'honneur des talents et des vertus' (I. xi)).

Even the servant girl Fanchette is capable of telling irony on the subject of Revolutionary liberty:

> Depuis que nous sommes libres, nous ne pouvons plus sortir des portes de la ville sans un passeport.
>
> (II. ii)

> Now that we are free, we can no longer go out through the town gates without a passport.

Reference is made to the banning of religious signs, symbols and names. Brutus remarks that in the place of all the older mumblers of paternosters the calendar now honours the names of Saint Brutus, Saint Torquatus and Saint Marat (II. iii). There are references to the closing of the churches, and the members of the Revolutionary Committee of Dijon have no greater desire than to turn the town's thirty churches into prisons to house the many conspirators they expect to arrest (I. iii; II. vi). The law of the *maximum* is defended by Aristide on the grounds that its aim is gradually to destroy trade, which is by definition incompatible with republicanism ('Son objet est d'anéantir lentement le commerce, qui par sa nature est incompatible avec une république'). This calls forth from Dufour a panegyric of commerce which is in the same spirit as Voltaire's views in the *Lettres philosophiques* or those of Sedaine's merchant M. Vanderk in *Le Philosophe sans le savoir*:

> Je vous arrête ici, président: quelque soit le sort qui m'attend, je combattrai toujours vos principes, parce qu'ils nous mèneraient de la barbarie à l'esclavage. On ne sert pas la liberté avec les armes qui la détruisent. . . . Le commerce, quand il est sagement combiné avec l'agriculture, est le véhicule de l'industrie et des arts; il est la force tutélaire des républiques; il soutient dehors, par une marine imposante, la dignité nationale; il empêche qu'un peuple libre ne devienne jamais le tributaire de ses voisins; il propage au sein des deux mondes, et jusque dans l'antre des sauvages, les inventions utiles à l'humanité; il apprend aux hommes de tous les climats qu'ils sont frères; il fait de l'univers entier une seule et même famille dont la philosophie est la mère.
>
> (II. v)

> I stop you there, President: whatever the fate which awaits me I shall always oppose your principles, because they would lead us from barbarism to slavery. You cannot serve freedom with the weapons which destroy freedom. . . . Trade, when it is wisely combined with agriculture, is the means by which industry and the arts develop; it is the force which protects republics; externally, through a large fleet, it maintains a nation's dignity; it prevents a free people becoming dependent on its neighbours; it disseminates inventions useful to humanity throughout the Old World and the New, even into the cave of the savage; it teaches men of every clime that they are brothers; it makes the entire universe into one single family whose mother is philosophy.

The word 'philosophie' which closes this speech seems to carry the sense of eighteenth-century liberal enlightenment. Certainly a speech such as this is very much in the spirit of the mercantile internationalism of the great French *philosophes* of the eighteenth century and stands comparison as an expression of idealism with anything to be found in *Le Jugement dernier des rois*. It may be vaguer than much that is to be found in Maréchal's play, but it does attempt to be constructive rather than destructive and is expressed, perhaps, with just a little less sententiousness. It is also a markedly less egalitarian view that is being put forward by Dufour. A little later in the same scene he remarks,

> Tant que l'éducation n'aura point propagé les lumières et la raison dans toutes les classes de la société le peuple aura toujours besoin d'hommes éclairés et purs, pour diriger son énergie, et régler ses mouvements; voilà cependant, citoyens, les hommes qu'on voudrait écarter des administrations.

> So long as education has not disseminated enlightenment and reason throughout all classes of the society the people will always need men of integrity to lead the way, to direct their energy and regulate their movements. Yet, citizens, those are the very men you wish to keep out of government.

He goes on to point out that far from regenerating peoples, terror brutalizes and degrades them ('Loin de régénérer les peuples, la terreur les abrutit et les dégrade' (II. v)). Fortunately for Dufour and his family, the news of the overthrow and execution of Robespierre, Couthon and Saint-Just reaches Dijon in time to save them, together with the news of the suspension of the Revolutionary Tribunals and the intention to investigate the Revolutionary Committees and prosecute the activists of the Terror (III. vi).

No doubt Ducancel is as unfair to the Jacobins as Maréchal had been to the targets of his satire. Certainly the members of the Dijon committee are portrayed as villains and ignoramuses, but highly dangerous ones. No doubt too it is true, as John Paxton suggests, that

> the committees had a great influence on the course of the Revolution and were composed of, in the main, sincere republicans and patriots.

Paxton qualifies this by conceding that, 'in fighting strongly against counterrevolutionaries and Royalists they did, however, commit excesses'.[5] Truth is never as simple, never as black-and-white, as propagandists would have us believe. *Le Jugement dernier des rois* and *L'Intérieur des comités révolutionnaires* are excellent illustrations of that. Ducancel's play may, in terms of its message, have a greater appeal for us, now that we are two centuries away from the passions and the particular sense of injustice of the revolutionary years, but Maréchal's one-acter, for all its violent over-simplification (and indeed perhaps precisely because of it), has more life than the later, more conventional play.

What is more, if we have a tendency to relate more readily to Ducancel, this is surely only a matter of relativities. Maréchal's play does have, as we have seen, an undoubted idealism about it: the methods proposed (even if one does not take the play literally in any simplistic sense) seem distinctly sanguinary, and there can be no doubt that the excesses to which Paxton refers did take place. On the other hand, in the attack on this kind of violence which is to be found in Ducancel's play and in its relative moderation of outlook there is something which smacks of a canting élitism: the Great and the Good are clearly waiting in the wings, convinced of their own superiority and the justice of what they see as their role in society. It is clear in fact that the Committee of Public Safety during the Terror and the new reactionaries of the post-Thermidorean days both firmly envisaged a need for a group of leaders in their different democratic republics. For that matter, this seems to have been true even of Maréchal's colleagues in the Directory days, the Babouvists who, as in George Orwell's satire of twentieth-century communists, felt that it was necessary (at least for a while) for some animals to be more equal than others. This, it has to be said to his credit (or at least to illustrate the consistency of his idealistically egalitarian views) was not the case with Maréchal himself: when he drafted the *Manifeste des Egaux* for the Babouvists in 1796 much of that manifesto was very much in tune with the spirit of *Le Jugement dernier des rois*, as the following passage clearly illustrates:

La révolution française n'est que l'avant-courrière d'une autre révolution bien plus grande, bien plus solennelle, et qui sera la dernière.

Le peuple a marché sur le corps aux rois et aux prêtres coalisés contre lui: il en fera de même aux nouveaux tyrans, aux nouveaux tartuffes politiques assis à la place des anciens.

The French Revolution is merely the forerunner of another, much greater, much more solemn revolution, which will be the final one.

The people have marched over the coalition of kings and priests ranged against them: they will do the same for the new tyrants, the new political hypocrites seated in the place of the old ones.

Maréchal's manifesto insists that the Babouvists will bring about real equality, no matter at what price ('n'importe à quel prix'), an attitude of mind which may well make one shudder and which clearly relates back to the activities of the Reign of Terror. All the more interesting, then, that there were only two passages in the manifesto drafted by Maréchal which proved unacceptable to the *Comité directoire secret* of the conspiracy. One was a clause reading 'Périssent, s'il le faut, tous les arts, pourvu qu'il nous reste l'égalité réelle!' ('Let all the arts perish, if necessary, provided that we are left with real equality!') and the other was one which called for the ending of all class distinctions:

Disparaissez enfin, révoltantes distinctions de riches et de pauvres, de grands et de petits, de maîtres et de valets, de gouvernants et de gouvernés.

Finally disappear, revolting distinctions between rich and poor, between great and small, between master and servant, between governors and governed.

Maurice Dommanget says that one can only infer from this that Babeuf and his followers in the *Comité directoire secret* rejected as dangerous (and conceivably insane) any vision of a society without the structure of the State ('On peut conjecturer néanmoins que le Comité . . . rejetait comme dangereuse, peut-être même insensée, toute vision d'une société sans Etat').[6] It is no doubt right, as Dommanget argues, to stress the anarchist tendencies of Maréchal's text and the extent to which it broke away from the authoritarian traditions of the Jacobins and announced the beginnings of the great conflict which still continues between democratic or libertarian communism on the one hand and authoritarian communism on the other.[7]

On 20 May 1795, three weeks after the first night of Ducancel's play, there was an attempt by radicals from the Faubourg Saint-Antoine to seize power back from the new reactionaries (the *journée du 1er prairial*). It soon collapsed, to be followed by many arrests and some executions. In August 1795 the Constitution of Year III was passed. It was designed to preserve a conservative republic from monarchy on the one hand and radical dictatorship on the other. On 5 October there was an insurrection by royalists (the *journée du 13 vendémiaire*). In November the rule of the Directory began. In May 1796 the Babeuf conspiracy of the Equals was crushed with little difficulty. In 1796 and 1797 Bonaparte was becoming increasingly significant as a military leader. After the April 1797 elections most of the new members of the two *Conseils* were constitutional monarchists and in September the three republican Directors, Reubell, La Reveillière-Lépeaux and Barras decided to take decisive action against the other two Directors and against the royalist majority in the two chambers. The army was the key to the situation and on 4 September (18 Fructidor) Paris was under military occupation. Press censorship was quickly imposed. By the end of the year France had made peace with every European power except Great Britain. Early in 1798 Bonaparte sailed from Toulon on his Egyptian campaign. On 9 August 1798, only some sixteen months before Bonaparte put an end to the Directory and established the Consulate, Pigault-Lebrun's *Les Rivaux d'eux-mêmes* had its first performance at the Théâtre de la Cité-Variétés. It was revived at the Théâtre-Français on 4 October 1799. It was a very different play from the last two which we have examined. The Revolution was over.

Indeed, when one considers Pigault-Lebrun's play one has almost the impression that the Revolution had never even happened. Charles-Antoine-Guillaume Pigault de l'Epinay, to give him his proper name, was born in Calais in 1753 of a family which was proud of its long lineage. A romanticized biography shows him as having lived a very varied and adventurous youth.[8] Before producing *Les Rivaux d'eux-mêmes* he had tried his hand at comedy as well as at the *drame* and in 1794 he came out, in harmony with the times, with an anti-clerical play, *Les Dragons et les bénédictines*. He also published a number of works of prose fiction, sometimes somewhat *risqué* in character.[9] Pigault-Lebrun died in 1835.[10] The source of the one-act play with which we are here concerned is a short story by Marmontel of the same title, *Les Rivaux d'eux-mêmes*, published in the August and September issues of the *Mercure de France* in 1792. Marmontel's story is a sentimental one about a sixteen-year-old boy and a thirteen-year-old girl whose parents wish them to marry. They are made to write to each other for three years without seeing each other and without knowing the identity of their intended partner. An attachment develops and the young people are then brought face to face. They fall in love, but each refuses to give in to this love since it is seen as an act of unfaithfulness to the person to whom he and she have been writing. The truth is revealed and they joyfully discover that they have been their own rivals. Pigault-Lebrun considerably alters the tone of the sentimental, moral story which he uses as his starting-point. As Jacques Truchet says, by the time he has finished Pigault-Lebrun's play and Marmontel's short story have little in common apart from the intrinsic implausibility of both of them.[11]

With Pigault-Lebrun's play we are back in the War of Austrian Succession. It is 1745 and Dupont, the landlord of an inn on the road from Paris to Flanders, is preparing to receive officers wounded at the battle of Fontenoy in which the Maréchal de Saxe has defeated the English and the Dutch in the presence of Louis XV. Mme Derval arrives, on the way to greet her husband, who has captured an enemy banner at Fontenoy. She is now sixteen, but was married at the age of ten to a lad of fourteen. Immediately after being married they were separated and have only communicated with each other by letter since. In scene v we learn that Derval is returning to Paris with all the enthusiasm of a twenty-year-old husband, eager to meet his wife, whose letters have, for the moment at any rate, turned his head ('avec l'empressement d'un mari de vingt ans qui brûle de connaître sa femme, dont les lettres lui ont provisoirement tourné la tête' (v. 1330)). Mme Derval intends to appear before her young husband under the name of Mme d'Alleville (D'Alleville happens to be a general in the French army). She wishes Derval to be given the room next to hers in the inn. The aim is that he should fall in love with her not realizing that she is his young wife.

The parallel between this situation and the kind of plot used by Marivaux in the early part of the eighteenth century is apparent. In particular the plot of Marivaux's best known play, *Le Jeu de l'amour et du hasard* (1730), in which Silvia and Dorante, intended by their parents to marry, disguise themselves so as to observe each other, comes to mind. There are differences, however, as we shall see. In scene x we are to be treated to badinage between Mme Derval and her servant/companion Lise on the subject of husbands. The dialogue does bear some resemblance to that which takes place between Silvia and her servant Lisette in the opening scene of Marivaux's play:

MME DERVAL   Mais je l'aime si bien, ce Derval.
LISE   On assure qu'il est si bien!
MME DERVAL   Je ne tiens pas essentiellement à la figure.
LISE   Heu! un joli homme en vaut bien un autre . . .

(Les Rivaux d'eux-mêmes, x. 1333)

LISETTE   On dit que votre futur est un des plus honnêtes hommes du monde; qu'il est bien fait, aimable, de bonne mine. . . .
SILVIA   . . . Il est bel homme, dit-on, et c'est presque tant pis.
LISETTE   Tant pis! tant pis! mais voilà une pensée bien hétéroclite!
SILVIA   C'est une pensée de très bon sens. Volontiers un bel homme est fat; je l'ai remarqué.
LISETTE   Oh! il a tort d'être fat, mais il a raison d'être beau.
SILVIA   On ajoute qu'il est bien fait; passe!
LISETTE   Oui-dà; cela est pardonnable.
SILVIA   De beauté et de bonne mine, je l'en dispense; ce sont là des agréments superflus.
LISETTE   Vertuchoux! si je me marie jamais, ce superflu-là sera mon nécessaire.

(Le Jeu de l'amour et du hasard, I. i)

MME DERVAL   But I love Derval so.
LISE   They say that he is so good-looking!
MME DERVAL   What he looks like is not particularly important to me.
LISE   Huh! a handsome man is surely as good as another. . .

LISETTE   They say your husband-to-be is one of the finest men in the world, that he has a good figure, that he is nice, that he is handsome. . . .
SILVIA   . . .He is a handsome man, they say, the more's the pity, almost.

LISETTE   The more's the pity! The more's the pity! Well, that's a most peculiar thought.

SILVIA   It's a very sensible thought. A handsome man is often conceited. I have noticed that.

LISETTE   Oh! He is wrong to be conceited, but he is right to be handsome.

SILVIA   They say that he has a good figure. Pass.

LISETTE   Right-ho! That is forgivable.

SILVIA   I do not require him to have a good figure or to be handsome. Those are superfluous charms.

LISETTE   Goodness gracious! If I ever marry, that superfluity will be absolutely necessary for me.

Derval duly arrives, in scene xi, not only a hero but a wounded hero, having been bayonetted in the arm. He has been promoted on the field of battle to the rank of lieutenant-colonel and been rewarded for his heroism with the estate of Ericourt. His friend Forville calls him by this name, thus making it possible for neither Mme Derval nor Lise to realize who he is. Derval flirts with Lise and Forville asks him what his wife would think of such behaviour. Derval replies,

> Ma foi, mon ami, toute fille un peu jolie a droit aux hommages d'un officier français; un baiser pris sans conséquence n'est pas une infidélité, et il n'est pas défendu d'adoucir un peu les tourments de l'absence.
>
> (xiii. 1337)

> Well, my friend, any girl who is at all pretty is entitled to the attentions of a French officer; a kiss which is taken inconsequentially is not an act of infidelity, and it is not forbidden to sweeten the torments of absence a little.

He professes love for his young wife.

Under the name of d'Ericourt, Derval insists on having the room next to Mme Derval's. When he sees Mme Derval he fails to recognize her but finds her remarkably attractive ('Je n'ai jamais vu de femme aussi séduisante' (xvi. 1339)) and it is made quite clear that he has amorous designs upon her. He pays court to her and charms her, so that she feels very attracted to him and is made rather to regret the arranged marriage which she underwent at such an early age:

On m'a imposé des devoirs, je les respecte (*tristement*), je les chéris, et je les trahirais en restant plus longtemps avec vous.

(xvii. 1343)

I have had duties imposed upon me. I respect them, (*sadly*) I cherish them, and I should betray them were I to remain longer with you.

In her lack of enthusiasm for her arranged marriage at this point she sounds remarkably like Mme de Tourvel on the subject of hers in Laclos's novel *Les Liaisons dangereuses* (1782) before she succumbs to the *roué* Valmont, and is no more convincing:

Non, je n'oublie point, je n'oublierai jamais ce que je me dois, ce que je dois à des nœuds que j'ai formés, que je respecte et que je chéris . . .

(*Les Liaisons dangereuses*, Letter LXXVIII)

No, I do not forget, I shall never forget what I owe to myself, what I owe to bonds which I have formed, which I respect and which I cherish . . .

It transpires in scene xviii that Derval is aware that General D'Alleville is not married. Lise is embroidering some writing: Derval recognizes his young wife's hand-writing from the delightful letters which she has sent him and realizes, of course, Mme Derval's true identity. Lise tells Mme Derval about her conversation with 'M. d'Ericourt' and, in particular, that the latter knows that General D'Alleville is a bachelor. Mme Derval now fears that 'M. d'Ericourt' will take her for

. . . une femme sans état, sans caractère, sans délicatesse, une de ces femmes avec qui on peut tout se permettre. Me voilà perdue dans son esprit.

(xix. 1347)

. . . a woman without a position in society, without character, without delicacy, one of those women with whom one is free to behave in any way one wishes. This means that I am ruined in his estimation.

When Lise asks her why that should worry her, since it is highly improbable that she will ever meet 'M. d'Ericourt' again, Mme Derval admits that she hopes that her husband has something of the qualities shown by 'M. d'Ericourt'. This, says Lise, is the predicament in which the institution of the arranged marriage (the *mariage de raison* or *de convenance*) has placed them, and Mme Derval is inclined to agree. The parallel with Marivaux is there again: in *Le Jeu de l'amour et du hasard* the marriage arranged for Silvia and Dorante is transformed into a love match and the two young people rather like to see themselves as characters in a novel as their love develops. The same, in the more genuinely romantic circumstances of the aftermath of the battle of Fontenoy, is clearly going to happen here, but this time in a marriage which has already taken place although without, as yet, having been consummated (xix. 1348-9). Lise expresses to Mme Derval her conviction that 'M. d'Ericourt' too has been the victim of an arranged marriage and says that he does not seem too taken with his wife, adding '. . . et si vous étiez libres l'un et l'autre', to which Mme Derval replies in a tender voice (*d'un ton caressant*), 'Oh, suppose nothing, I beg of you!' (Oh! ne suppose rien, je t'en prie' (xix. 1349)).

In Marivaux's *Le Jeu de l'amour et du hasard* the audience is made to derive pleasure from knowing more than the characters on stage: in particular the audience is privy to the true identities of the young couple who are falling in love with each other, each thinking that the other is a social inferior, and is aware that their feelings for each other over which they agonize are perfectly licit. Something very similar is happening in *Les Rivaux d'eux-mêmes*, except that whereas in Marivaux's comedies love is always pure and leads to matrimony in Pigault-Lebrun's play the frisson induced in the audience, with the thought of the adjacent rooms in the inn, is one which has very much to do with the possibility of the principal characters embarking on what they think to be an adulterous relationship, although they are in fact husband and wife.

In scene xx a further twist in the plot is contrived when 'M. d'Ericourt' pretends that Florville is in fact the true Derval, a stratagem which does not please Mme Derval at all, since the reluctant Florville strikes her as a distinctly cold fish. In scene xxi Lise, none too convincingly, finally tumbles to what is going on and declares to Mme Derval, 'D'Ericourt est votre époux' ('D'Ericourt is your husband'). Mme Derval's reply, 'Ah! que j'ai besoin de te croire' ('Ah, how I need to believe you!') (xx. 1354) is surely a conscious echo of Silvia's words in Act II, scene xii of

Marivaux's play, when she discovers that the apparent servant Bourgignon is in fact Dorante: 'Allons, j'avais grand besoin que ce fût là Dorante' ('You know, I very much needed him to be Dorante').

In Marivaux's play, Silvia reveals a certain cruelty when she refuses in her turn to unmask and tell Dorante that she is not the maid-servant he takes her to be:

> Cela vaut fait, Dorante est vaincu; j'attends mon captif . . . Mais il faut que j'arrache ma victoire, et non pas qu'il me la donne; je veux un combat entre l'amour et la raison.
>
> (Le Jeu de l'amour et du hasard, III. iv)

> It is as good as done. I await my prisoner. . . But it is essential that I wrest my victory by force, not that he give it to me; I want a battle between love and reason.

In *Les Rivaux d'eux-mêmes* it is the servant Lise who shows the hardness of heart when she urges Mme Derval to get her own back on her husband: 'Il vous a fait trembler. Qu'il tremble à son tour. . .' ('He made you tremble. Let him tremble in his turn. . .'). The gentle Mme Derval is too soft-hearted for this and cannot understand Lise's attitude: 'Tu es persuadé que c'est lui, et tu veux l'affliger!' ('You are convinced that he is my husband, and yet you wish to distress him!'). Lise's response to this shows rather more bite than the whole of the rest of the play: 'Point de pitié! Désoler un mari, c'est venger tout un sexe' ('No quarter! To distress a husband is to avenge an entire sex') (xxi. 1354).[12]

Mme Derval and Lise do, however, play a trick on Derval, by pretending in scene xxii to accept that Florville is indeed the real Derval and by seeking to arrange a tête-à-tête between him and Mme Derval in her bedroom. Forville shows some sign of going along with this proposal and Derval announces his true identity, at which Mme Derval prolongs matters by pretending to think that he is joking, and pointing out that it was he, after all, who convinced her that Florville was her husband. Derval goes down on to his knees and confesses.

> J'ai voulu plaisanter et j'ai eu tort, je le sens. Le plus fin de nous n'est qu'un enfant, même avec la plus ingénue. Mon aimable, ma séduisante amie, vous prétendez me punir; n'est-ce pas vous punir aussi vous-même? Le temps perdu ne se retrouve

jamais. . . Grâce, femme charmante, et pour vous et pour moi.
MME DERVAL (*mollement*)   Ah! je suis trop heureuse pour me
défendre plus longtemps. Il est si doux de céder à ce qu'on aime!

(xxii. 1356)

I wanted to play a joke and I was wrong, I feel that. The
cleverest of us men is no more than a child, by comparison with
even the most artless of women. My kind, lovely dear, you seek
to punish me, but isn't that to punish yourself at the same time?
Lost time is never regained. . . Have mercy, charming lady, for
your sake and for mine.
MME DERVAL (*softly*)   Ah! I am too happy to resist any
longer. It is so sweet to give in to the one you love!

Lise reminds us once again of the Silvia of *Le Jeu de l'amour et du
hasard* when she ends the scene with the following aside: 'Je ne me
serais pas rendue ainsi; il eût acheté la victoire' ('I wouldn't have
given in like that: he would have had to pay for his victory') (xxii.
1356).

The play ends with Mme Derval and her husband about to go
and consummate the marriage. The closing words are given to the
perhaps somewhat world-weary Forville:

Vous vous êtes éprouvés tous deux, et vous n'avez pas à vous
plaindre; tenez-vous-en là, je vous le conseille: on ne s'éprouve
pas toujours aussi heureusement.

(xxiii. 1357)

The pair of you have tested each other, and neither of you has
anything to complain about. Leave it at that, that is my advice
to you: people do not always test each other with such pleasing
results.

No doubt the advice is sound enough: it is certainly less cheery
than the way in which Marivaux's comedies habitually end. The
whole tone of the play is markedly more dubious than that of
Marivaux's work.

The justification for dwelling on this sub-Marivaux offering
produced sixty years or more after Marivaux himself had produced
his masterpieces is to demonstrate that, not surprisingly in view of
what had happened over the previous few years, there had
developed a taste for theatrical entertainment devoid of any

political content.[13] The wheel had turned full circle.[14] The absence of political propaganda from public entertainment can itself be a telling social and political point.

CONCLUSION

None of the plays which we have considered could, it has to be conceded, be rated as an incontestably first-rate piece of drama. Certainly, no academic analysis of these plays is going to convince anyone that he is in the presence of a literary masterpiece. It has further to be conceded that it is extremely unlikely that such an analysis of any of the multifarious plays produced during the hectic years of the French Revolution, over and above the few about which it has been possible to say something in this book, would ever be likely to lead to the notion that one had come across such a masterpiece, wrongly neglected for two hundred years. It is improbable that somewhere, blushing unseen, is the script of a *Phèdre* or a *Misanthrope* of the Revolutionary years – certainly Fabre d'Eglantine's *Le Philinte de Molière, ou la Suite du Misanthrope* of 1791, despite its title, is not such. This, however, is scarcely the point.

In the first place, it is still too frequently the case that plays are seen simply as pieces of literature to be read and dissected in the tranquillity and privacy of the study. The fact that the best of Racine's or Molière's plays have survived such dissection over the centuries and can still be performed with justified acclaim in the living theatre where they belong is no doubt the best proof that, in addition to being excellent pieces of theatre they are indeed literary masterpieces. It has been no part of the purpose of this book to seek to suggest that any of the seven plays examined falls into such a category. Most of them are not bad plays, however, and one or two of them are quite good. No doubt most of them could be revived for isolated performances today and give pleasure to an audience. But the pleasure would not be of a literary kind; there might well (depending in large measure on the talents of the

205

players) be genuine theatrical pleasure to be derived from such a performance, the pleasure of watching accomplished performers getting as much as they can out of a script. This is perhaps particularly true of Collin d'Harleville's *Le Vieux Célibataire*, arguably the best, in purely theatrical terms, of the seven plays examined here, but it would also be interesting to see a revival of Laya's *L'Ami des lois*. Produced 'straight', with all temptations to guy it being stoutly resisted, it should work quite well. One can conceive quite readily of Maréchal's lively little one-acter, *Le Jugement dernier des rois*, being received with good humour as part of a Bastille Day celebration, but it is unlikely that any of our plays could hope to draw an audience for more than a couple of performances, and then only as historical curiosities.

Most of the plays which we have considered are pieces of propaganda, politics in action in a very direct way. Their importance lies in what they are saying, in the message they are putting across to the audience of the day. It is true of a number of them that they very rapidly indeed became out-of-date, were overtaken by events and thus lost their appeal even to their contemporaries. They belong very directly to their own day. Now, of course it is true that a play such as *Le Misanthrope* is in many ways very closely attached to the social attitudes and values of its own day, the notion of the *honnête homme* and how to behave in a society of a particular kind, and of course it is equally true that the *Le Misanthrope* has something to say about those social attitudes and values. Molière, however, by means of something which it is not our function to analyse in detail here but which can no doubt be described as genius, succeeds in transcending that which is peculiar to his own society in a particular place and at a particular time and manages to continue to make a strong appeal to successive generations of theatre audiences (and of academics) long after the circumstances in which his plays were written and first performed have ceased in any significant sense to be part of the terms of reference of the majority of those who watch or read them.

The same cannot, in all honesty, be said of Chénier, Sade, Laya, Maréchal, Ducancel, Pigault-Lebrun, or even Collin d'Harleville. It is often true, however, that it is the minor art of a given period which seems to speak most strongly and most clearly of the preoccupations of the people of that time, and never can this have been truer than of the years from 1789 onward. One certainly has a sense, as one reads these plays, of participating almost in the quarrels and rivalries of different political and social groupings. Some of the strands of the Revolutionary years of which one becomes aware as one reads these plays are, inevitably, less than pleasant, but there are other strands which express the idealism (sometimes perhaps, but by no means always, a little ingenuous) which was undoubtedly one of the characteristics of those years. These are some of the plays which people were prepared to pay to go and see in those very troubled times and so they have some claim to our attention, if we are to try to arrive at a fuller understanding of what kind of a thing that complex, changing thing the Revolution was. It is hoped that this book will have given the reader some sense of the flavour of those days. There is, of course, no substitute for familiarizing oneself with the text of the plays themselves. It is further hoped that this book may encourage the reader to set about that process of familiarization.

NOTES

INTRODUCTION

1 Marvin Carlson, *The Theatre of the French Revolution*, (Cornell University Press, Ithaca, New York, 1966), v.

2 Michèle Root-Bernstein, *Boulevard Theater and Revolution in Eighteenth-Century Paris*, (Ann Arbor, Michigan, 1984), 240. (The Republican Calendar, which replaced the Gregorian Calendar in France, was decreed on 24 November 1793 but antedated to begin from 22 September 1792, the day on which the Republic had been proclaimed. Thus, Year II of the Republic began on 22 September 1793. The new calendar consisted of 12 months each of 30 days, with each month being divided into 3 decades (or periods of 10 days) instead of the seven-day weeks of the Gregorian calendar. This gave a year of 360 days. In addition there were 5 supplementary days (6 in a leap year) known by the splendidly revolutionary name of *sans-culottides* and observed as public holidays. The Revolutionary Calendar was discontinued with effect from 1 January 1806.)

3 Louis Moland (ed.), *Théâtre de la Révolution, ou Choix de pièces de théâtre qui ont fait sensation pendant la période révolutionnaire*, (Garnier, Paris, 1877).

4 Jacques Truchet (ed.), *Théâtre du XVIIIe siècle*, (2 vols, Gallimard, Bibliothèque de la Pléiade, 1972-4). All references to the six plays referred to here will be to Truchet's edition. In the case of verse plays line numbers will be given; in the case of plays in prose page numbers will be given.

1 AFTER FIGARO: THE LAST YEARS OF THE MONARCHY

1 More detailed accounts can be found in a number of works listed in the bibliography, in particular M. Carlson, *The Theatre of the French Revolution*, (Cornell University Press, 1966), C.-G. Etienne and A. Martainville, *Histoire du théâtre français depuis le commencement de la Révolution jusqu'à la Réunion générale*, (4 vols, Paris, 1802), A. Pougin, *La*

Comédie-Française et la Révolution, (Paris, 1902) and *L'Opéra-Comique pendant la Révolution de 1788 à 1801*, (Paris, 1891), Michèle Root-Bernstein, *Boulevard Theater and Revolution in Eighteenth-Century Paris*, (Ann Arbor, Michigan, 1984), and H. Welschinger, *Le Théâtre de la Révolution, 1789-1799*, (Paris, 1880).

2 M. Carlson, *The Theatre of the French Revolution*, v.

3 J. Lough, *Paris Theatre Audiences in the Seventeenth and Eighteenth Centuries*, (Oxford University Press, 1957), 3.

4 See M. Root-Bernstein, *Boulevard Theater*, 24-5.

5 J. Lough, *Paris Theatre Audiences*, 166.

6 M. Root-Bernstein, *Boulevard Theater*, 24.

7 L.-P. de Bachaumont, *Mémoires secrets pour servir à l'histoire de la République des lettres en France de 1762 jusqu'à nos jours*, (36 vols, London, 1777-89), XIX, 49-50.

8 J. Lough, *Paris Theatre Audiences*, 166.

9 John McCormick, *Melodrama Theatres of the French Boulevard*, (Chadwyck-Healey, Cambridge and Teaneck, N.J., 1982), 12. One of the slides accompanying this monograph is a view of the Boulevard du Temple in 1775, showing Nicolet's theatre. See Carlson, *The Theatre of the French Revolution*, (226) for plans of the Gaîté (1759) and the Ambigu-Comique (1769), the two oldest boulevard houses.

10 L.-S. Mercier, *Du Théâtre, ou Nouvel Essai sur l'art dramatique*, (Amsterdam, 1773), 213n.

11 L.-S. Mercier, *Du Théâtre*, 216.

12 Guilbert de Pixerécourt, *Rapport. – Observations sur l'état où se trouvaient les théâtres avant la Révolution*, published by Edmond Estève in 'Observations de Guilbert de Pixerécourt sur les théâtres et la Révolution', *Revue d'histoire littéraire de la France*, (1916), 546-61, (549).

13 G. de Pixerécourt, *Rapport*, 551 ('La Révolution arrive; et ce que les philosophes seuls avaient senti jusque-là, la Nation le devine, c'est-à-dire l'influence que les théâtres pouvaient avoir sur l'opinion publique').

14 M. Root-Bernstein, *Boulevard Theater*, 240, and above, Introduction, p.2.

15 Daniel Hamiche, *Le Théâtre et la Révolution. La lutte des classes au théâtre en 1789 et en 1793*, (Paris, 1973), 15.

16 D. Hamiche, *Le Théâtre et la Révolution*, 171.

17 D. Hamiche, *Le Théâtre et la Révolution*, 65.

18 See Chapter 3, 62-3.

19 See M. Root-Bernstein, *Boulevard Theater*, 43.

20 See M. Carlson, *The Theatre of the French Revolution*, 17-18.

21 M. Root-Bernstein, *Boulevard Theater*, 132.

22 Quoted in D. Hamiche, *Le Théâtre et la Révolution*, 40-1.

23 Quoted in D. Hamiche, *Le Théâtre et la Révolution*, 42.

24 See Chapter 3.

25 M. Root-Bernstein, *Boulevard Theater*, 141.

26 See J. Truchet (ed.), *Théâtre du XVIIIe siècle*, (2 vols, Gallimard, Bibliothèque de la Pléiade, Paris, 1972-74), II, 1520, n. 1.

27 See D. Hamiche, *Le Théâtre et la Révolution*, 88.
28 See D. Hamiche, *Le Théâtre et la Révolution*, 96.
29 For the text of this decree, see D. Hamiche, *Le Théâtre et la Révolution*, 141-2.
30 M. Carlson, *The Theatre of the French Revolution*, 50. For an account of another, unsuccessful, petition which was organized by a boulevard director and playwright, Parisau, which argued, like La Harpe's petition, in favour of an author's lifetime property rights but differed from the successful petition in arguing that the established hierarchy of theatres should not be undone, see M. Root-Bernstein, *Boulevard Theater*, 177-8.
31 M. Carlson, *The Theatre of the French Revolution*, 111.
32 See A. Pougin, *La Comédie-Française et la Révolution*, (Paris, 1902), 50.
33 See M. Carlson, *The Theatre of the French Revolution*, 75.
34 See H.C. Lancaster, *French Tragedy in the Reign of Louis XVI and the Early Years of the French Revolution, 1774-1792*, (Baltimore, 1953), 107-10.
35 D.I. Wright (ed.), *The French Revolution: Introductory Documents*, (University of Queensland Press, 1974 [1980]), 91.
36 See M. Carlson, *The Theatre of the French Revolution*, 92, and M. Root-Bernstein, *Boulevard Theater*, 219.
37 M. Carlson, *The Theatre of the French Revolution*, 55.
38 For a modern edition, see M.-J. Chénier, *Jean Calas, tragédie*, édition critique par Malcolm Cook, (University of Exeter, 1987).
39 M. Carlson, *The Theatre of the French Revolution*, 100.
40 See A. Liéby, *Etude sur le théâtre de Marie-Joseph Chénier*, (Paris, 1901), 89; H. C. Lancaster, *French Tragedy in the . . . Early Years of the French Revolution*, 117; M. Carlson, *The Theatre of the French Revolution*, 105.
41 N. Hampson, *A Social History of the French Revolution*, (London, 1963), 148.
42 Quoted in H. Welschinger, *Le Théâtre de la Révolution*, 80.
43 Alexandre Tuetey, *Répertoire général des sources manuscrites de l'histoire de Paris pendant la Révolution française*, (11 vols, Paris, 1890-1914), VI, item 2610.

2 FROM THE DECLARATION OF THE REPUBLIC

1 The text of the Commune's decree can be found in H. Welschinger, *Le Théâtre de la Révolution 1789-1799*, (Paris, 1880), 389-90.
2 The full text of Laya's letter to the Convention, from which this is an extract, is to be found in A. Pougin, *La Comédie-Française et la Révolution*, (Paris, 1902), 80-2.
3 *Chronique de Paris*, 16 June 1793, quoted in A. Pougin, *La Comédie-Française et la Révolution*, 89.
4 The text of this memorandum is given in A. Pougin, *La Comédie-Française et la Révolution*, 91.
5 See A. Pougin, *La Comédie-Française et la Révolution*, 92-4.
6 A. Pougin, *La Comédie-Française et la Révolution*, 98.

7 See A. Liéby, *Etude sur le théâtre de Marie-Joseph Chénier*, (Paris, 1901), 112-113.

8 M. Carlson, *The Theatre of the French Revolution*, 154.

9 See M. Carlson, *The Theatre of the French Revolution*, 157.

10 The murder of Marat by Charlotte Corday took place on 13 July 1793: it was suspected of being a Girondist plot.

11 Quoted in A. Pougin, *La Comédie-Française et la Révolution*, 105-6.

12 See A. Pougin, *La Comédie-Française et la Révolution*, 110-15.

13 See M. Carlson, *The Theatre of the French Revolution*, 161-8.

14 A. Liéby, *Théâtre de Chénier*, 141.

15 See M. Carlson, *The Theatre of the French Revolution*, 178.

16 See Michel-Jean Sedaine, *Le Philosophe sans le savoir*, ed. Graham E. Rodmell, (University of Durham, 1987), 14 and n. 9.

17 Quoted in H. Welschinger, *Le Théâtre de la Révolution*, 148.

18 H. Welschinger, *Le Théâtre de la Révolution*, 375.

19 See H. Welschinger, *Le Théâtre de la Révolution*, 157-8.

20 See M. Carlson, *The Theatre of the French Revolution*, 188.

21 For the text of this report, see H. Welschinger, *Le Théâtre de la Révolution*, 149-50.

22 See P.-A.C. de Beaumarchais, *Théâtre complet. Lettres relatives à théâtre*, ed. Maurice Allem and Paul-Courant, (Bibliothèque de la Pléiade, 1957), 807.

23 See M. Carlson, *The Theatre of the French Revolution*, 195-8.

24 Quoted in H. Welschinger, *Le Théâtre de la Révolution*, 62-3.

25 See M. Carlson, *The Theatre of the French Revolution*, 200-6, and A. Pougin, *La Comédie-Française et la Révolution*, 134-183.

26 N. Hampson, *A Social History of the French Revolution*, 233.

27 Quoted in H. Welschinger, *Le Théâtre de la Révolution*, 160.

28 For the text of this decree, see A. Pougin, *L'Opéra-Comique pendant la Révolution de 1788 à 1801*, (Paris, 1891), 158.

29 See H. Welschinger, *Le Théâtre de la Révolution*, 495.

30 N. Hampson, *A Social History*, 245.

31 See H. Welschinger, *Le Théâtre de la Révolution*, 161-2.

32 See L. Moland (ed.), *Théâtre de la Révolution, ou Choix de pièces de théâtre qui ont fait sensation pendant la période révolutionnaire*, (Paris, 1877), xxv.

33 L. Moland, *Théâtre de la Révolution*, xxvi-xxvii.

34 A. Cobban, *A History of Modern France*, (2 vols, London, 1957-61), I, 251.

35 For the text of a number of police reports of this period, see H. Welschinger, *Le Théâtre de la Révolution*, 162-7.

36 See M. Carlson, *The Theatre of the French Revolution*, 249-50.

37 For these reports, see H. Welschinger, *Le Théâtre de la Révolution*, 122.

38 See M. Carlson, *The Theatre of the French Revolution*, 253-4.

39 A. Pougin, *L'Opéra-Comique pendant la Révolution*, 200-2.

40 M. Carlson, *The Theatre of the French Revolution*, 256.

41 A. Pougin, *L'Opéra-Comique pendant la Révolution*, 207.

42 For an account of this affair, with the text of the police report and the theatre's reply, see A. Pougin, *L'Opéra-Comique et la Révolution*, 233-5.

43 See H. Welschinger, *Le Théâtre de la Révolution*, 124.
44 Quoted in A. Pougin, *L'Opéra-Comique et la Révolution*, 238-9.
45 See M. Carlson, *The Theatre of the French Revolution*, 279.
46 See H. Welschinger, *Le Théâtre de la Révolution*, 137-8.
47 For the full text of this letter, see A. Pougin, *L'Opéra-Comique et la Révolution*, 245.
48 See M. Carlson, *The Theatre of the French Revolution*, 285-7.

3 A SCHOOL FOR KINGS

1 M.-J. Chénier, *Discours préliminaire to Charles IX*, in L. Moland (ed.), *Le Théâtre de la Révolution, ou Choix de pièces de théâtre qui ont fait sensation pendant la période révolutionnaire*, (Paris, 1877), 16. J. Truchet (ed.), *Théâtre du XVIIIe siècle*, (2 vols. Paris, 1972–4), does not include this *Discours*.
2 In M.-J. Chénier's notes to an *Epître aux mânes de Voltaire*, which was one of several accompaniments to the first published text of the play in 1790. Quoted in J. Truchet, *Théâtre du XVIIIe siècle*, II, 1524.
3 *Epître dédicatoire à la Nation française*, dated 15 December 1789 and published with the first (1790) edition of the play. In J. Truchet, *Théâtre du XVIIIe siècle*, II, 1522.
4 Jean Gaulmier, 'De la Saint-Barthélemy au *Chant du départ*', *Revue d'histoire littéraire de la France*, September-October 1973, 840.
5 *Discours préliminaire*, in L. Moland, *Le Théâtre de la Révolution*, 14-15.
6 Marie-Joseph Chénier was born in Constantinople, where his father was Consul-general, in 1764, two years after his brother André, and just before his parents returned to France. His mother was Greek. He studied at the Collège de Navarre (which Napoleon was later to make into the Ecole polytechnique) and served for two years in the dragoons at Niort. From September 1792 until March 1802 he was a member of all the legislative assemblies. He was criticized, almost certainly unfairly, for not saving his brother André from the guillotine under the Terror. He was *inspecteur général de l'Université* from 1803 until 1806 and had the courage in 1805 to demonstrate his continuing republicanism in an elegy entitled *La Promenade*. He wrote a number of tragedies under the Empire, but none of them was either performed or published. He became a member of the Institut and died, out of favour, on 10 January 1811. Jean Gaulmier remarks, 'Pas de symbole plus éloquent de la défaite de la République que l'élection de Chateaubriand, à la Seconde Classe de l'Institut en 1811, au fauteuil de Chénier, mort à quarante-six ans.' ('There is no more eloquent symbol of the defeat of the Republic than the election of Chateaubriand to the Second Class of the Institut in 1811, to the seat left vacant by the death, at the age of 46, of Chénier.') ('De la Saint-Barthélemy au *Chant du départ*', 844).
7 For a detailed account of the 'bataille de *Charles IX*' waged by Chénier prior to the performance of his play, see Daniel Hamiche, *Le Théâtre et*

la Révolution, La Lutte des classes au théâtre en 1789 et en 1793, (Paris, 1973), 26-147.

8 H.C. Ault, '*Charles IX, ou l'Ecole des rois*: tragédie nationale', *The Modern Language Review*, October 1953, 398.

9 A.-V. Arnault, *Souvenirs d'un sexagénaire*, (4 vols., Paris, 1833), I, 188-93.

10 An allusion to the lynching of a baker by the name of Denis on 20 October 1789.

11 J. Truchet, *Théâtre du XVIIIe siècle*, II, 1521. Truchet's anthology offers the most accessible text of *Charles IX*, and it is the revised version that he gives. He does, however, indicate the principal changes in his notes.

12 See A. Liéby, *Etude sur le théâtre de M.-J. Chénier*, 54-5; H.C. Lancaster, *French Tragedy in the Reign of Louis XVI and the Early Years of the French Revolution*, 107; M. Carlson, *The Theatre of the French Revolution*, 75.

13 H. C. Ault, '*Charles IX*', 398, 400.

14 *Discours préliminaire*, in L. Moland, *Le Théâtre de la Révolution*, 16: 'M. de Voltaire a plus approfondi dans ses tragédies la morale proprement dite, que la politique. Il a combattu, durant soixante ans, le fléau de la superstition. Sa plume a sans cesse retracé les usurpations du sacerdoce, rarement les prétentions arbitraires des rois et des grands' ('In his tragedies M. de Voltaire went more deeply into morality proper than into politics. He attacked, over a period of sixty years, the plague of superstition. His pen ceaselessly recalled the usurpations committed by the priesthood, only rarely the arbitrary claims of kings and grandees').

15 *Discours préliminaire*, in L. Moland, *Le Théâtre de la Révolution*, 19-20.

16 *Discours préliminaire*, in L. Moland, *Le Théâtre de le Révolution*, 17.

17 J. Truchet, *Théâtre du XVIIIe siècle*, II, 1520-1.

18 *Discours préliminaire*, in L. Moland, *Le Théâtre de la Révolution*, 10.

19 *Discours préliminaire*, in L. Moland, *Le Théâtre de la Révolution*, 11-12, 21.

20 *Discours préliminaire*, in L. Moland, *Le Théâtre de la Révolution*, 21, 22.

21 H. C. Ault, '*Charles IX*', 401.

22 Denis Diderot, *De la Poésie dramatique*, in *Œuvres esthétiques* (ed. P. Vernière), (Paris, Garnier, n.d. [1959]), 259.

23 Epître dédicatoire, in J. Truchet, *Théâtre du XVIIIe siècle*, II, 1521.

24 *Epître dédicatoire*, in J. Truchet, *Théâtre du XVIIIe siècle*, II, 1523.

25 *Discours préliminaire*, in L.Moland, *Le Théâtre de la Révolution*, 14.

26 The verse epistle *Au Roi*, in L. Moland, *Le Théâtre de la Révolution*, 25-7, ll. 1-2, 7-8, 15-16.

27 J. Truchet, *Théâtre du XVIIIe siècle*, II, 1519.

28 C. Collé, *La Partie de chasse de Henri IV*, in J. Truchet, *Théâtre du XVIIIe siècle*, II, 599.

29 De Belloy (whose real name was Pierre-Laurent Buirette) opens his preface to *Le Siège de Calais* with the following words: 'Voici peut-être la première tragédie française où l'on ait procuré à la nation le plaisir de s'intéresser pour elle-même . . .' ('This is perhaps the first French tragedy in which the nation has been accorded the pleasure of feeling an interest on its own account. . .') (in J. Truchet, *Théâtre du XVIIIe siècle*, II, 448).

30 De Belloy, preface to *Le Siège de Calais*, in J. Truchet, *Théâtre du XVIIIe siècle*, II, 449.

31 J. Truchet, *Théâtre du XVIIIe siècle*, II, 1519.

32 *Discours préliminaire*, in L. Moland, *Le Théâtre de la Révolution*, 18.

33 See J. Truchet, *Théâtre du XVIIIe siècle*, II, 1045n; and J.-A. Rivoire, *Le Patriotisme dans le théâtre sérieux de la Révolution (1789-1799)*, (Paris, 1950), 45.

34 John R. Alden, *A History of the American Revolution*, (London, 1969), 512-13.

35 D.I. Wright (ed.), *The French Revolution: Introductory Documents*, (University of Queensland Press, 1980), 51.

36 J.-A.-N. Caritat, marquis de Condorcet, *Esquisse d'un tableau historique des progrès de l'esprit humain* (ed. M. and F. Hincker), (Paris, Editions Sociales, 1966), 77.

37 See J. Truchet, *Théâtre du XVIIIe siècle*, II, 1045n.

38 J. Gaulmier, 'De la Saint-Barthélemy au *Chant du départ*', 841-2.

39 *Epître dédicatoire*, in J. Truchet, *Théâtre du XVIIIe siècle*, II, 1522.

40 M.-J. Chénier, *De la liberté du théâtre en France*, in A. Liéby, *Théâtre de M.-J. Chénier*, (Paris, Baudouin, 1818), III, xliv.

41 H. C. Ault, '*Charles IX*', 405.

42 *Epître dédicatoire*, in J. Truchet, *Théâtre du XVIIIe siècle*, II, 1522-3.

43 M. Carlson, *The Theatre of the French Revolution*, 104-5.

44 C.-G. Etienne and A. Martainville, *Histoire du théâtre français depuis le commencement de la Révolution jusqu'à la Réunion générale*, (4 vols, Paris, 1802), III, 150-1. Quoted in J.-A. Rivoire, *Le Patriotisme dans le théâtre sérieux*, 111-12.

45 J.-A. Rivoire, *Le Patriotisme dans le théâtre sérieux (1789–1799)*.

4   THE DANGERS OF LIBERTINAGE

1 For further particulars of this episode in Sade's life see Gilbert Lély, *Vie du Marquis de Sade*, in Sade, *Œuvres complètes*, (16 vols., Cercle du livre précieux, Paris, 1966-7), II, 190-3 (henceforth, this edition will be referred to simply as *Œuvres complètes*). Sade, who was born on 2 June 1740, inherited the title of Comte (which he rarely used) on the death of his father in 1767. He died in the hospital for the insane at Charenton on 2 December 1814. For a useful chronological outline of his life, see Ronald Hayman, *De Sade. A Critical Biography*, (London, 1978), xiii-xxiii.

2 Archives nationales F^7 4954^3, pièce 9. Quoted by Lély in *Œuvres complètes*, II, 190.

3 Sade, *Correspondance*, in *Œuvres complètes*, XII, 476.

4 Quoted by Jean-Jacques Brochier in Sade, *Œuvres complètes*, (35 vols., Pauvert, Paris), 33 (1970), 13.

5 Paris, 1792, pp. 250-64. Quoted in *Œuvres complètes*, XI, 320, n. 3.

6 *Œuvres complètes*, II, 229.

7 *Œuvres complètes*, XII, 509.

8 *Œuvres complètes*, XI, 85, n. Eleutherian refers to the attribute of Zeus as protector of political freedom.

9 *Œuvres complètes*, XI, 69-74.

10 *Œuvres complètes*, XI, 85.

11 *Œuvres complètes*, XII, 505.

12 See Chapter 3, 71.

13 *Œuvres complètes*, XII, 497.

14 *Le Moniteur*, 6 novembre 1791, quoted in *Œuvres complètes*, II, 321-2.

15 J. Truchet (ed.), *Théatre du XVIIIe siècle*, II, 1532.

16 R.-C. Guilbert de Pixerécourt, *Cœlina ou l'Enfant du mystère*, ed. Norma Perry (University of Exeter, 1972), xiii.

17 De Miramond to Sade, 15 juillet 1791. Quoted by J.-J. Brochier in Sade, *Œuvres complètes*, 33, 11-12.

18 J.-J. Brochier, in Sade, *Œuvres complètes*, 32 (1970), 29-33.

19 J.-J. Brochier, in Sade, *Œuvres complètes*, 32, 25.

20 See J. Truchet, II, 1532, n. 2.

21 J.-J. Brochier, in Sade, *Œuvres complètes*, 32, 26-7.

22 J.-J. Brochier, in Sade, *Œuvres complètes*, 32, 31.

23 See J. Truchet, II, 1532.

24 Sade, *Oxtiern*, in J. Truchet, II, 1082.

25 Diderot, *Le Neveu de Rameau* (ed. Jean Fabre), (Geneva, 1950), 44.

26 Diderot, *Le Neveu de Rameau*, 72.

27 Diderot, *De la Poésie dramatique*, in *Œuvres esthétiques* (ed. P. Vernière), (Paris, Garnier, n.d. [1959]), 269.

28 See Chapter 3, 94.

29 See Chapter 3, 98.

30 J. Truchet, II, 1534.

31 The text of *Ernestine, nouvelle suédoise*, is to be found in *Œuvres complètes*, X, 317-75.

32 *Œuvres complètes*, X, 320, n.

33 *Œuvres complètes*, X, 341.

34 *Œuvres complètes*, X, 325.

35 *Œuvres complètes*, II, 268-9.

36 *Œuvres complètes*, X, 371-4.

37 J. Truchet, II, 1533 and n. 1.

38 Letter from Boursault-Malherbe to Sade, 23 October 1791, quoted by J.-J. Brochier, in *Œuvres complètes*, 33, 15.

5 A BACHELOR'S LIFE

1 François-René Molé played the part of M. Dubriage, and Louise Contat played that of Mme Evrard. Fleury played Armand and Mme Petit-Vanhove (Mme Talma) played Laure. For full details of the cast list on the opening night of *Le Vieux Célibataire*, see André Tissier's excellent and indispensable doctoral thesis, *Collin d'Harleville, chantre de la vertu souriante (1755-1806)*, (2 vols, Nizet, Paris, 1963-65), II, 390.

2 Tissier, I, 126.

3 It has, with regret, to be accepted that (as this sample shows) Collin was far from being a great poet. One loses relatively little by translating him into English prose. As will be suggested later, if he succeeds (when at his best) in producing lively colloquial dialogue, this is often in direct relationship to the extent to which he fractures the classical alexandrine couplet which he inherited from the seventeenth century.

4 Tissier, I, 170-1. See Chapter 1, 16-22.

5 For an outline of this dispute, see Tissier, I, 115-23, and Philippe Fabre d'Eglantine, *Lettre de M. Fabre d'Eglantine à Monsieur de ***, relativement à la contestation survenue au sujet du 'Présomptueux ou l'Heureux Imaginaire' et 'les Châteaux en Espagne'* (n.p., n.d.), (the letter is dated 12 January 1789).

6 *Mes Souvenirs* appeared in the *Almanach des Muses* for 1789.

7 Philippe Fabre d'Eglantine, *Le Philinte de Molière, ou la suite du Misanthrope*, (Prault, Paris, 1791).

8 Fabre d'Eglantine, *Le Philinte de Molière*, xi.

9 Tissier, I, 199.

10 See Chapter 2, 33.

11 Truchet, *Théâtre du XVIIIe siècle*, (2 vols, Paris, 1972-4), II, 1111.

12 See Tissier, I, 209-11.

13 Tissier, II, 335.

14 Truchet, II, 1110.

15 Words spoken by Frontin, in Lesage's *Turcaret*, Act I, scene xi.

16 Tissier, II, 306.

17 Tissier, II, 312.

18 J.-J. Rousseau, *La Nouvelle Héloïse*, Part II, Letter xvii.

19 In the third *Entretien sur le Fils naturel*, Diderot makes it quite clear that by the word 'condition' he understands not only professions but human relationships:

> MOI   Ainsi, vous voudriez qu'on jouât l'homme de lettres, le philosophe, le commerçant, le juge, l'avocat, le citoyen, le magistrat, le financier, le grand seigneur, l'intendant.

> DORVAL   Ajoutez à cela, toutes les relations: le père de famille, l'époux, la sœur, les frères. . .

> (Diderot, *Œuvres esthétiques*, ed. P. Vernière, (Garnier, Paris, n.d.), 154)

> I   Thus, you would like there to be played on stage the man of letters, the philosopher, the merchant, the judge, the advocate, the citizen, the magistrate, the financier, the great lord, the steward.

> DORVAL   Add to that all the relationships: the father of a family, the spouse, the sister, the brothers. . .

The old bachelor could properly be added to the list.

20 Diderot, *Pensées philosophiques*, no. 5.

21 See Wright, *The French Revolution. Introductory Documents*, (University of

Queensland Press, 1980), 68.
22 See Tissier, II, 343, n. 23.
23 Grimod de la Reynière (attrib.), *Réflexions philosophiques sur le plaisir; par un célibataire*, (2e édition, Neufchâtel and Paris, 1783).
24 Tissier, II, 342.
25 S.-R.-N. Chamfort, *Maximes et pensées, caractères et anecdotes*, ed. Claude Roy, (10/18, Paris, 1963), 99. It should, however, be noted that on the subject of marriage and celibacy Chamfort remarks that both states have disadvantages and that the one to be preferred is the state the disadvantages of which are not without remedy . . . (103).
26 La Rochefoucauld, *Maximes*, ed. J. Truchet, (Garnier, Paris, 1967), no. 203, 51.
27 Molière, *Le Misanthrope*, I, i, 63.
28 Rousseau, *Lettre à M. d'Alembert sur les spectacles*, ed. M. Fuchs, (Droz, Geneva, 1948), 48.
29 Truchet, II, 1542.
30 Tissier, II, 336.
31 Tissier, II, 337-8.
32 See Tissier, II, 337-41.
33 L.H. Skinner, *Collin d'Harleville, dramatist*, (Columbia University, New York, 1933), 125.
34 C. Lenient, *La Comédie au XVIIIe siècle*, (2 vols, Paris, 1888), II, 341.
35 See Tissier, II, 360 and Appendix III, 392.
36 P.-D. Lemazurier, *Galerie historique des acteurs du Théâtre Français, depuis 1600 jusqu'à nos jours*, (2 vols, Paris, 1810), I, 373.
37 See Tissier, II, 360, n. 18.
38 See Tissier, I, 276-320.

6 LIBERTY AND LICENCE

1 See Chapter 1, 23-4.
2 See Chapter 2, 27-30.
3 C.-G. Etienne and A. Martainville, *Histoire du Théâtre français depuis le commencement de la Révolution jusqu'à la Réunion générale*, (4 vols, Paris, 1802), III, 47, n.
4 J. Truchet, *Théâtre du XVIIIe siècle*, (2 vols, Paris, 1972-4), II, 1545, n. 3.
5 Laya's submission to the Convention, quoted in H. Welschinger, *Le Théatre de la Révolution 1789-1799*, (Paris, 1880), 397.
6 H. Welschinger's attitude in *Le Théâtre de la Révolution 1789-1799*, (Paris, 1880), is a good example of this:

   L'Ami des lois était le dernier effort des vrais défenseurs de la liberté. De pluviôse à thermidor, c'est-à-dire pendant six mois, la Commune et les Jacobins sont les maîtres absolus. Ils exercent la censure la plus redoutable, ils suppriment et les pièces et les auteurs qui les gênent. La Terreur règne. On ne joue que des pièces patriotiques et

Dieu sait à quelles pièces on prostitue cette superbe épithète!

(Welschinger, 409)

L'Ami des lois was the last effort of the true defenders of freedom. From the month of pluviôse to the month of thermidor, that is to say for six months, the Commune and the Jacobins were absolute masters. They imposed the most fearsome censorship, they suppressed not only plays which bothered them but authors too. It was the reign of Terror. Only patriotic plays were performed, and God knows to what plays that proud epithet was prostituted.

7 See J. Truchet, II, 1544-5.

8 As Truchet points out, in the play the *particule* 'de' is sometimes used for Forlis and Versac and for the latter's wife and sometimes not: it suggests that the suppression of this aristocratic part of speech was not yet absolute in 1793, but it is not known whether Laya himself was responsible for this inconsistency, or his printers (Truchet, II, 1234, n. 3).

9 Palissot had used the same basic situation as the setting for his attack on the great liberal thinkers of the Enlightenment in his satirical comedy *Les Philosophes* (1760).

10 H. Welschinger, 406.

11 In J. Truchet, II, 1231.

12 In J. Truchet, II, 1233.

13 See J. Truchet, II, 1545, n. 3. Prieur de la Marne is reported as having said in the debate on *L'Ami des lois* in the Convention on 10 January 1793 that although he had not seen the play [a common weakness of would-be censors] he had seen a quotation from it containing the words, 'Aristocrate, mais honnête homme'. He is reported to have added, 'Je demande comment on peut être honnête homme et aristocrate?' ('I wish to know how one can be both an honest man and an aristocrat') (in H. Welschinger, 386). The lines referred to are spoken by Versac:

Je suis, puisqu'aujourd'hui tout noble ainsi se nomme,
Aristocrate, soit; mais avant, honnête homme

(I. i. 97-8)

I am, since these days every nobleman is so called, an aristocrat. So be it. But first I am an honest man.

14 See Chapter 5, 128-31.

15 M.-J. Sedaine, *Le Philosophe sans le savoir*, II, iv.

16 Diderot, *De la Poésie dramatique*, in *Œuvres esthétiques*, ed. P. Vernière, (Garnier, Paris, n.d.), 269.

17 Truchet, II, 1545.

18 Diderot, *Le Neveu de Rameau*. Edition critique avec notes et lexique par Jean Fabre, (Droz, Geneva, 1950), 72. It is important to recall that although Diderot probably began this work as early as 1761 and

worked on it at various times (1765, 1772, 1774), it had a very
complicated history and was not published in a satisfactory French text
until 1823.

19 Diderot, *Le Rêve de d'Alembert*, in *Œuvres philosophiques*, ed. P. Vernière,
(Garnier, Paris, n.d.), 310-11.

20 Diderot, *Le Rêve de d'Alembert*, 313.

21 Diderot, *Le Rêve de d'Alembert*, 364.

22 Diderot, *Jacques le fataliste et son maître*, in *Œuvres romanesques*, ed. H.
Bénac (Garnier, Paris, n.d.), 498-9.

23 J.-J. Rousseau, *Du Contrat social*, book I, chapter vii. See also book II,
chapter vi.

24 J.-A. Rivoire, *Le Patriotisme dans le théâtre sérieux de la Révolution (1789-
1799)*, (Paris, 1950), 94: 'Il est piquant de voir Laya accuser les
Montagnards de vouloir démembrer la France, quand ceux-ci se posent
en champions de la République "une et indivisible" et accusent les
Girondins de "fédéralisme"'.

25 J.-J. Rousseau, *Discours sur l'origine et les fondements de l'inégalité parmi les
hommes*, part II.

26 J.-A. Rivoire, *Le Patriotisme dans le théâtre sérieux de la Révolution*, 93.

27 See notes 6 and 7.

7 A *SANS-CULOTTE* VERDICT ON MONARCHY

1 M. Dommanget, *Sylvain Maréchal l'Egalitaire. 'L'Homme sans Dieu'. Sa
Vie. Son Œuvre*, (Paris, 1950), 258.

2 C.-G. Etienne and A. Martainville, *Histoire du théâtre français depuis le
commencement de la Révolution jusqu'à la Réunion générale*, (4 vols, Paris,
1802), III, 117.

3 C.-G. Etienne and A. Martainville, III, 122, n.

4 H. Welschinger, *Le Théâtre de la Révolution 1789-1799*, (Paris, 1880), 203.

5 Hipolyte Lucas, *Histoire philosophique et littéraire du théâtre français depuis
son origine*, (3 vols, Paris, 1896), II, 99. For further examples of adverse
reaction to Maréchal's play in the nineteenth century, see
M. Dommanget, 271-3 and Daniel Hamiche, *Le Théâtre et la Révolution.
La lutte des classes au théâtre en 1789 et en 1793*, (Paris, 1973), 177-9.

6 F. Gaiffe, *Le Rire et la scène française*, quoted in J. Truchet, *Théâtre du
XVIIIe siècle*, (2 vols, Paris, 1972-4), II, 1557.

7 D. Hamiche, 189-91.

8 M. Dommanget, 269.

9 D. Hamiche, 162.

10 See Chapter 2, 33.

11 D. Hamiche, 182.

12 *Fragments d'un poème moral sur Dieu*, fragment XXXVIII, quoted in
M. Dommanget, 141.

13 '*Livre échappé au Déluge*. L'éditeur bien intentionné au lecteur bénévole'.
Quoted in M. Dommanget, 105.

14 *Premières Leçons du fils aîné d'un roi*, 25. Quoted in M. Dommanget, 142.

15 *Premières Leçons. . .*, Lesson XXVIIII, 30-31.

16 *Dame Nature à la barre de l'Assemblée nationale*, 13. Quoted in
    M. Dommanget, 184-5.

17 *Dame Nature. . .*, 32. Quoted in M. Dommanget, 185.

18 M. Dommanget, 188.

19 Beatrice F. Hyslop, 'Le Théâtre parisien pendant la Terreur', in *Actes
    du 77e Congrès des Sociétés savantes, Grenoble, 1952* (Paris, 1952). (Beatrice
    F. Hyslop, like Marvin Carlson, is anathematized by Daniel Hamiche
    for apparently not having bothered to read Maréchal's play
    (D. Hamiche, p. 190, n.)); J. Truchet, II, 1558, n. 2.

20 See M. Dommanget, 263-4 and D. Hamiche, 306, n. 1.

21 See M. Dommanget, 169-83.

22 *Révolutions de Paris*, no. 212.

23 For the early press coverage of *Le Jugement dernier des rois*, see
    M. Dommanget, 267-71 and D. Hamiche, 171-3.

24 See Victor Hallaÿs-Dabot, *Histoire de la censure théâtrale en France*, (Paris,
    1862), 184, and Augustin Challamel and Wilhelm Tenint, *Les Français
    sous la Révolution* (Paris, 1843), 271.

25 See F.-A. Aulard, *Recueil des Actes du Comité de Salut public*, (28 vols,
    Paris, 1895) VIII, 413; *Annales révolutionnaires* (10e année, no. 1, 1918),
    113; M. Dommanget, 262; D. Hamiche, 174.

26 F.-A. Aulard, *Recueil des Actes du Comité de Salut public*, VIII, 555.

27 See D. Hamiche, 175.

28 F.-A. Aulard, *La Société des Jacobins. Recueil de documents pour l'histoire du
    Club des Jacobins de Paris*, (6 vols, Paris, 1889-97), V, 616.

29 By C.-F. Patris, Paris, 1793.

30 The line in Act II, scene i of Gresset's comedy reads, 'Les sots sont ici-
    bas pour nos menus plaisirs'. Laclos uses it in his novel *Les Liaisons
    dangereuses*, published in 1782 (Letter LXIII).

31 J. Truchet, II, 1307-8.

32 This line in Act II, scene i of Gresset's comedy reads, 'Fools are here
    on earth for our amusement'. See note 30.

33 Antoine Michot (1765-1826). The old Frenchman was played by
    Monvel (1745-1812), the French *sans-culotte* by Desrosières (b. *circa*
    1748), the Pope by Dugazon (1746-1809), along with Talma one of the
    radicals within the Comédie at the time of the *Charles IX* affair. The
    King of Spain was played by Baptiste-Cadet (1765-1839) and the King
    of Poland by Grandménil (1737-1816).

34 J. Truchet, II, 1310, n. 1.

35 See J. Truchet, II, 1322, n. 1.

36 See John Paxton, *Companion to the French Revolution*, (New York and
    Oxford, 1988), 1-2.

37 The passage about the Queen was not used in the version of the play
    which was performed the day after the execution of Marie-Antoinette.
    A moment of delicacy?

38 It is interesting to see the word 'section', normally used of the divisions
    of Revolutionary Paris, being used here. 14 July 1789 refers, of course,

to the storming of the Bastille; 5 October 1789 is the date of the march
on Versailles by a Paris mob, mainly female, which obliged Louis XVI
to move to Paris with the royal family; 10 August 1792 is the date on
which the mob invaded the Tuileries, attacked the Swiss Guard and
brought about the incarceration of the royal family in the Temple; 21
September 1792 saw the first session of the Convention, which
proclaimed the abolition of the monarchy and the establishment of the
republic; 31 May 1793 marked the beginning of the insurrection in
Paris which led on 2 June to the arrest of 29 leading Girondins,
including Brissot: the beginning of the Reign of Terror.

39 S.T. Coleridge, *France: An Ode*, (February 1798).
40 W. Wordsworth, *The French Revolution, as it appeared to enthusiasts at its commencement*, (1804; published 1809).
41 This passage, which continues for some time, was omitted from the staged version.
42 J. Truchet (II, 1320, n. 1) draws attention to the echo here of the line from Act V, scene i of Corneille's *Cinna*:

> Le reste ne vaut pas l'honneur d'être nommé.

43 See John Paxton, *Companion to the French Revolution*, 158-9.
44 J. Truchet, II, 1559-60.
45 J. Truchet, II, 1559.
46 J. Truchet, II, 1560.
47 M. Dommanget, 273, n. 63.
48 J. Truchet (II, 1560 and n. 2) suggests a foreshadowing of the 'théâtre de contestation' of writers such as Adamov, whose *Printemps 71* he cites as displaying a similar opposition between two styles, the dignified, humane and often eloquent style of the revolutionaries (in this case the Communards) and the puppet-show style of the Establishment characters (Thiers, Bismarck).

7 TOWARDS A NEW LIGHTHEARTEDNESS

1 See Chapter 2, 44.
2 Louis Moland, *Théâtre de la Révolution, ou Choix de pièces de théâtre qui ont fait sensation pendant la période révoluntionnaire*, (Paris, 1877), (xxvi-xxvii) refers to a hundred consecutive performances of Ducancel's play at the Cité-Variétés and at the Montansier, as well as to many performances in the provinces. The text of *L'Intérieur des comités révolutionnaires* can be found in L. Moland, 329-404.
3 The Revoluntionary Committees (*Comités révolutionnaires de Comités de surveillance*) were popular clubs established throughout France in 1790 and required by the Convention in September 1793 to arrest suspects and pursue conspirators and foreigners without reference to any other authorities (see John Paxton, *Companion to the French Revolution*, (New York and Oxford, 1988) 52-3).

4 C.-P. Ducancel, in *Esquisses dramatiques*, quoted by L. Moland, xxiv-xxv.

5 John Paxton, *Companion to the French Revolution*, 53.

6 M. Dommanget, *Sylvian Maréchal l'Egalitaire. 'L'homme sans Dieu'. Sa vie. Son Œuvre.* (Paris, 1950), 322. The text of the *Manifeste des Egaux* can be found in M. Dommanget, 310-13.

7 See M. Dommanget, 315.

8 Jean-Nicolas Barba, *Vie et aventures de Pigault-Lebrun*, (Paris, 1836).

9 See Angus Martin, Vivienne G. Mylne and Richard Frautschi, *Bibliographie du genre romanesque français, 1751-1800*, (London and Paris, 1977).

10 As J. Truchet points out, *Théâtre du XVIIIe siècle*, (2 vols, Paris, 1972-4) (II, 1564, n. 2) no significant study of Pigault-Lebrun exists.

11 J. Truchet, II, 1565.

12 One is half-reminded of *Les Liaisons dangereuses* once again here, and more particularly of the Marquise de Merteuil's description of herself in a letter to the Vicomte de Valmont as 'née pour venger mon sexe et maîtriser le vôtre' ('born to avenge my sex and to master yours') (Letter LXXXI).

13 No one can have been less of an *homme engagé* than Marivaux. As André Tissier puts it, 'Il n'a rien d'un "politique" préoccupé de réformer la société: il vit et écrit en marge des réalités politiques' ('There was in him nothing of the politician concerned with reforming society: he lived and wrote cut off from political realities' (A. Tissier, '*Les Fausses Confidences' de Marivaux: analyse d'un 'jeu' de l'amour*, (Paris, 1976), 23).

14 See Chapter 2, 46ff.

BIBLIOGRAPHY

Aghion, M. (1926) *Le Théâtre à Paris au XVIIIe siècle*, Paris.

Alasseur, C. (1967) *La Comédie Française au XVIIIe siècle, étude économique*, Paris.

Albert, M. (1900) *Les Théâtres de la foire (1660-1789)*, Paris.

Albert, M. (1902) *Les Théâtres des boulevards (1789-1848)*, Paris.

Alden, J.R. (1969) *A History of the American Revolution*, London.

Arnault, A.-V. (1833) *Souvenirs d'un sexagénaire*, Paris, 4 vols.

Attinger, G. (1950) *L'Esprit de la commedia dell'arte dans le théâtre français*, Paris.

Aulard, F.-A. (1889-97) *La Société des Jacobins, recueil de documents pour l'histoire du Club des Jacobins de Paris*, Paris, 6 vols.

Aulard, F.-A. (1895) *Recueil des Actes du Comité de Salut public*, Paris, 28 vols, VIII.

Ault, H.C. (1953) '*Charles IX ou l'Ecole des rois*, tragédie nationale', in *Modern Languages Review*, October number.

Bachaumont, L.-P. de (1777-89) *Mémoires secrets pour servir à l'histoire de la République des lettres en France de 1762 jusqu'à nos jours*, London, 36 vols.

Bapst, G. (1893) *Essai sur l'histoire du théâtre*, Paris.

Barba, J.-N. (1836) *Vie et aventures de Pigault-Lebrun*, Paris.

Beaulieu, H. (1905) *Les Théâtres du boulevard du crime de Nicolet à Déjazet, 1752-1862*, Paris.

Beaumarchais, P.-A. C. de (1957) *Théâtre complet. Lettres relatives à son théâtre* (ed. Maurice Allem and Paul-Courant), Bibliothèque de la Pléiade, Paris.

Bingham, A.J. (1939) *Marie-Joseph Chénier, Early Political Life and Ideas (1789-1794)*, privately printed, New York.

Bonassiès, J. (1874) *Les Auteurs dramatiques et la Comédie française à Paris aux XVIIe et XVIIIe siècles*, Paris.

Bonassiès, J. (1875) *Les Spectacles forains et la Comédie française*, Paris.

Brazier, N. (1838) *Histoire des petits théâtres de Paris*, Paris, 2 vols.

Brenner, C.D. (1947) *A Bibliographical List of Plays in the French Language, 1700-1815*, Berkeley.

Brenner, C.D. (1961) *The Théâtre Italien: its Repertory, 1716-1793*, Berkeley and Los Angeles.

Cailhava, J.-F. de (1789) *Causes de la décadence du théâtre et les moyens de le faire refleurir*, Paris.

Campardon, E. (1877) *Les Spectacles de la foire*, Paris, 2 vols.

Campardon, E. (1880) *Les Comédiens du roi de la troupe italienne pendant les deux derniers siècles*, Paris, 2 vols.

Carlson, M. (1966) *The Theatre of the French Revolution*, Cornell University Press, Ithaca, New York.

Challamel, A. and Tenint, W. (1843) *Les Français sous la Révolution*, Paris.

Chamfort, S.-R.-N. (1963) *Maximes et pensées, caractères et anecdotes* (ed. Claude Roy), 10/18, Paris.

Chénier, M.-J. (1826) *Œuvres*, Paris, 5 vols.

Chénier, M.-J. (1987) *Jean Calas, tragédie* (édition critique par Malcolm Cook), University of Exeter.

Cobban, A. (1957-61) *A History of Modern France*, Penguin, London, 2 vols.

Condorcet, J.-A.-N. Caritat, marquis de (1966) *Esquisse d'un tableau historique des progrès de l'esprit humain* (ed. M. and F. Hincker), Paris.

Copin, A. (1888) *Talma et la Révolution*, Paris.

Desnoiresterres, G. (1885) *La Comédie satirique au XVIIIe siècle*, Paris.

Diderot, D. (1950) *Le Neveu de Rameau* (ed. Jean Fabre), Droz, Geneva.

Diderot, D. (n.d.) *Œuvres esthétiques* (ed. Paul Vernière), Garnier, Paris.

Diderot, D. (n.d.) *Œuvres philosophiques* (ed. Paul Vernière), Garnier, Paris.

Diderot, D. (n.d.) *Œuvres romanesques* (ed. Henri Bénac), Garnier, Paris.

Dommanget, M. (1950) *Sylvain Maréchal l'Egalitaire. 'L'Homme sans Dieu'. Sa Vie. Son Œuvre*, Spartacus, Paris.

Estrée, P. d' [Henri Quentin] (1913) *Le Théâtre sous la Terreur*, Paris.

Etienne, C.-G. and Martainville, A. (1802) *Histoire du théâtre français depuis le commencement de la Révolution jusqu'à la Réunion générale*, Paris, 4 vols.

Fabre, J. (1958) *Le Théâtre au XVIIIe siècle*, in *Histoire des littératures*, Gallimard, Bibliothèque de la Pléiade, III.

Fabre d'Eglantine, P. (n.d. [1789]) *Lettre de M. Fabre d'Eglantine à Monsieur de ***, relativement à la contestation survenue au sujet du Présomptueux ou l'Heureux Imaginaire' et 'les Châteaux en Espagne'*, n.p. [Paris].

Fabre d'Eglantine, P. (1791) *Le Philinte de Molière, ou la Suite du Misanthrope*, Prault, Paris.

Gaiffe, F. (1910) *Le Drame en France au XVIIIe*, Paris.

Gaulmier, J. (1973) 'De la Saint-Barthélemy au *Chant du départ*', in *Revue d'histoire littéraire de la France*, September-October number.

Géruzez, E. (1869) *Histoire de la littérature française pendant la Révolution*, Paris.

Goncourt, E. and J. de (1864) *Histoire de la société française pendant le Directoire*, Paris.

Goncourt, E. and J. de (1869) *Histoire de la société française pendant la Révolution*, Paris.

Guilbert de Pixérécourt, R.-C. (1916) *Rapport. Observations sur l'état où se trouvaient les théâtres avant la Révolution*, published by Edmond Estève in 'Observations de Guilbert de Pixerécourt sur le théâtre et la Révolution', in *Revue d'histoire littéraire de la France*, 1916, 546-61).

Guilbert de Pixérécourt, R.-C. (1972) *Cœlina, ou l'Enfant du mystère* (ed.

Norma Perry), University of Exeter.

Hallaÿs-Dabot, V. (1862) *Histoire de la censure théâtrale en France*, Paris.

Hamiche, D. (1973) *Le Théâtre et la Révolution. La Lutte des classes au théâtre en 1789 et en 1793*, Paris.

Hampson, N. (1963) *A Social History of the French Revolution*, University of London.

Hawkins, F. (1888) *The French Stage in the Eighteenth Century*, London, 2 vols.

Hayman, R. (1978) *De Sade. A Critical Biography*, London.

Hérissay, J. (1922) *Le Monde des théâtres pendant la Révolution*, Paris.

Howe, A. and Waller, R. (eds.) (1987) *En Marge du classicisme. Essays on the French Theatre from the Renaissance to the Enlightenment*, Liverpool University Press.

Hyslop, Beatrice F. (1952) 'Le Théâtre parisien pendant la Terreur', in *Actes du 77e Congrès des Sociétés savantes, Grenoble, 1952*, Paris.

Isherwood, R. (1981) 'Entertainment in the Parisian Fairs in the Eighteenth Century', in *Journal of Modern History*, 53.

Jauffret, E. (1869) *Le Théâtre révolutionnaire*, Paris.

Joannidès, A. (1901) *La Comédie française de 1680 à 1900. Dictionnaire général des pièces et des auteurs*, Paris.

Jourdain, Eleanor F. (1921) *Dramatic Theory and Practice in France (1690-1808)*, New York.

Lancaster, H.C. (1953) *French Tragedy in the Reign of Louis XVI and the Early Years of the French Revolution, 1774-1792*, Baltimore.

La Place, Roselyne (1980) 'Des théâtres d'enfants au XVIIIe siècle', in *Revue d'histoire du théâtre*, 32.

La Reynière, Grimod de (attrib.) (1783) *Réflexions philosophiques sur le plaisir; par un célibataire*, 2nd edition, Neufchâtel and Paris.

La Rochefoucauld, François VI, Duc de (1967) *Maximes* (ed. J. Truchet), Garnier, Paris.

Lecomte, L.-H. (1900) *Napoléon et l'Empire racontés par le théâtre*, Paris.

Lecomte, L.-H. (1905) *Histoire des théâtres de Paris, 1402-1904*, Paris.

Lecomte, L.-H. (1908) *Histoire des théâtres de Paris. Les Variétés Amusantes*, Paris.

Lecomte, L.-H. (1912) *Napoléon et le monde dramatique*, Paris.

Lemazurier, P.-D. (1810) *Galerie historique des acteurs du Théâtre Français, depuis 1600 jusqu'à nos jours*, Paris, 2 vols.

Lenient, C. (1888) *La Comédie en France au XVIIIe siècle*, Paris.

Liéby, A. (1901) *Etude sur le théâtre de M.-J. Chénier*, Paris.

Lioure, M. (1963) *Le Drame*, Paris.

Lough, J. (1957) *Paris Theatre Audiences in the Seventeenth and Eighteenth Centuries*, Oxford University Press.

Lough, J. (1978) *Writer and Public in France from the Middle Ages to the Present Day*, Oxford, Clarendon Press.

Lucas, H. (1896) *Histoire philosophique et littéraire du théâtre français depuis son origine*, Paris, 3 vols.

Lunel, E. (1911) *Le Théâtre et la Révolution*, Paris.

McCormick, J. (1982) *Melodrama Theatres of the French Boulevard*, Cambridge and Teaneck, N.J.

225

Martin, A., Mylne, V.G., and Frautschi, R. (1977) *Bibliographie du genre romanesque français, 1751-1800*, London and Paris.

Mercier, L.-S. (1773) *Du Théâtre; ou Nouvel Essai sur l'art dramatique*, Amsterdam.

Michaud, J.-F. (ed.) (1811-62) *Biographie universelle, ancienne et moderne*, Paris, 55 vols.

Moland, L. (ed.) (1877) *Le Théâtre de la Révolution, ou Choix de pièces de théâtre qui ont fait sensation pendant la période révolutionnaire*, Paris.

Morel, J. (1964) *La Tragédie*, Paris.

Nicoll, A. (1963) *The World of Harlequin: a critical study of the commedia dell'arte*, Cambridge University Press.

Niklaus, R. (1970) *A Literary History of France: the Eighteenth Century (1715-1789)*, London and New York.

Paxton, J. (1988) *Companion to the French Revolution*, New York and Oxford.

Péricaud, L. (1908) *Le Théâtre de Monsieur*, Paris.

Péricaud, L. (1909) *Le Théâtre des Petits Comédiens de S.A.S. Monseigneur le Comte de Beaujolais*, Paris.

Pougin, A. (1891) *L'Opéra-Comique pendant la Revolution de 1788 à 1801*, Paris.

Pougin, A. (1902) *La Comédie-Française et la Révolution*, Paris.

Rivoire, J.-A. (1950) *Le Patriotisme dans le théâtre sérieux de la Révolution, (1789-1799)*, Paris.

Root-Bernstein, Michèle (1984) *Boulevard Theater and Revolution in Eighteenth-Century Paris*, UMI Research Press, Ann Arbor, Michigan.

Rougemont, Martine de (1988) *La Vie théâtrale en France au XVIIIe siècle*, H. Champion, Paris.

Rousseau, J.-J. (1948) *Lettre à M. d'Alembert sur les spectacles* (ed. M. Fuchs), Droz, Geneva.

Sade, D.-A.-F., Marquis de (1966-67) *Œuvres complètes* (ed. Gilbert Lély), Cercle du livre précieux, Paris, 16 vols.

Sade, D.-A.-F., Marquis de (1970) *Œuvres complètes* (ed. J.-J. Brochier), Pauvert, Paris, vol. 33.

Sedaine, M.-J. (1987) *Le Philosophe sans le savoir* (ed. Graham E. Rodmell), University of Durham.

Skinner, L.H. (1933) *Collin D'Harleville, Dramatist*, New York.

Tissier, A. (1963-65) *Collin d'Harleville, chantre de la vertu souriante, 1755-1806*, Paris, 2 vols.

Tissier, A. (1976) *'Les Fausses Confidences' de Marivaux: analyse d'un 'jeu' de l'amour*, Paris.

Truchet, J. (ed.) (1972-74) *Théâtre du XVIIIe siècle*, Gallimard, Bibliothèque de la Pléiade, Paris, 2 vols.

Tuetey, A. (1890-1914) *Répertoire général des sources manuscrites de l'histoire de Paris pendant la Révolution française*, Paris, 11 vols.

Vibert, L. (1942-45) *Au Temps de la Carmagnole*, Paris, 3 vols.

Voltz, P. (1964) *La Comédie*, Paris.

Welschinger, H. (1880) *Le Théâtre de la Révolution 1789-1799*, Paris.

Wright, D.I. (ed.) (1974 [reprinted 1980]) *The French Revolution: Introductory Documents*, University of Queensland Press.

INDEX

227

233